CW00419022

Tangible
press

DDLRJLpNRRMA

Item Descriptions	Quantity
Skipping Reels of Rhyme: A Guide to Rare and Unreleased Bob Dylan Recordings	1

Skipping Reels of Rhyme

A Guide to Rare and Unreleased Bob Dylan Recordings

John Howells

Skipping Reels of Rhyme © 2018 by John Howells

All rights reserved. No part of this publication may be reproduced, distributed, stored in a retrieval system, or transmitted in any form or by any means, electronic, mechanical, photocopying, recording, or otherwise, without prior written permission of the publisher, except in the case of brief quotations embodied in a book review. For information regarding permission requests, write to the publisher, Tangible Press, addressed "Attention: Permissions Coordinator," at www.tangiblepress.net

Printed in the United States of America

First Printing, 2018

ISBN-13: 978-1-7323892-3-6

Dedicated to the memories of Paul Williams and John Bauldie.

Table of Contents

Introduction

The purpose of this book is twofold. First, this book is intended to document some of the contents of the first comprehensive Bob Dylan website on the Internet: *Bringing It All Back Homepage*[1], which was started in 1994 at the birth of the World Wide Web, and continues to this day (as of this writing). See the Appendix for some of the articles from that website. The second, and larger purpose is to document, in book format, the unreleased recordings of Bob Dylan, which at the time of publication on the website consisted primarily of cassette tapes as well as bootleg vinyl and CD.

Since the original content was written, two things have occurred. First, tape trading became largely a thing of the past and Bob Dylan collectors around the world found a new and more convenient way of circulating the rarities that fans have longed to hear, not to mention the tons of newly recorded live shows which continue to this day (as of this writing). Now it's all about downloading from bit torrent sites and various other file sharing platforms. The world is now digital instead of analog, for the most part, and the availability of Dylan recordings is much more widespread. This leads to the second occurrence: Sony (Dylan's recording company) has been releasing most of the recordings discussed in this book in various editions designed to prevent material older than fifty years from entering the public domain and allowing bootleggers to release legal product containing previously hard-to-find gems, thus depriving the record company of substantial revenue. This is being done not only through the Bootleg Series of releases, available to the general public, but also through a series of 50th Anniversary copyright protection releases available in extremely limited quantities in the European market, where the fifty year rule is most important. In most cases, these releases are limited to 100 copies in either CD-R or vinyl format, although in one case made available strictly through MP3 download aimed at customers who purchased a specific Sony

---

[1] See http://dobbylan.com

product. These releases will be discussed in more detail later in this book.

While going through the various articles I intended to include in this book, it became obvious that much updating needed to be done, especially now that so many of the recordings mentioned have become more readily available to the general public, but at the same time the original articles present a sort of time capsule of what it was like to be a tape collector in the '80s and '90s. In some cases I have updated the articles in question, but in many other cases I decided to leave them the way they were and include postscripts to bring us up to date on what has happened with the recordings as far as official release is concerned. In a great many cases there are new recordings that were entirely unknown (or merely rumored) when these articles were written, such as the entire studio sessions for *Bringing It All Back Home, Highway 61 Revisited*, and *Blonde on Blonde* which are all available in the massive *Bootleg Series Volume 12: The Cutting Edge.* Where it is relevant, I have noted where previously unavailable recordings are now part of the new Bootleg Series and Copyright protection releases.

Skipping Reels of Rhyme

Bob Dylan's Unreleased Tapes

This is an attempt to document all of the circulating tapes known to be in existence. I believe I have heard every one of these tapes, but there may be a reference to an occasional item here and there that I have yet to hear. The views expressed here are my own subjective opinions on the quality of these tapes and performances, and the work herein is intended to be an overview of all the material that's currently available and is certainly not definitive.

In addition to comments about sound and performance quality, I also try to indicate on which CDs and LPs this material is available. More and more of this material is becoming available on CD, and when I originally started this project some years ago, there were relatively few CDs of this nature in existence and most of the unreleased material was available on vinyl, a sadly disappearing medium. Therefore, my information about CD releases is no doubt incomplete. This is an ongoing project. Many of the items listed below have not been completed yet. Those that are completed may have missing or incorrect information. In particular, I would like to know of any CDs or LPs that I haven't mentioned. If you have more information on any of these items, please drop me a line.

Please note that at this time I have only listed tapes up to 1975. There are two reasons for doing this. First, Dylan's life after 1975 became very hectic and he began to tour frequently, thus providing an overwhelming number of tapes. It is not my intention to discuss each and every concert tape individually, so I will just talk about each tour separately and describe in greater detail what I consider to be the highlights. Secondly, although I will continue to describe all studio and other non-tour tapes individually, I would like to wait until I've finished with the pre-1975 years first. So, for now, if you see items missing from the end of the list it's not because I don't know about them, it's just that I haven't gotten around to listing them yet!

Before we get to the tape discussions, the next two sections will discuss what Sony has been doing to release most of the rarities that up until now were very hard to find.

The Bootleg Series

In 1991 Columbia launched the first in a series of official releases featuring previously unreleased recordings from various sources, mostly from their own vaults but also including some famous circulating recordings that had heretofore been unavailable to the general public. The first in this ongoing series was a 3-CD and 5-LP edition titled *The Bootleg Series Volumes 1-3 (Rare & Unreleased) 1961-1991*. The recordings were somewhat chronologically random – giving a great overview of the gems that had been hidden from the public but available to the most fanatical collectors. Most of the recordings were already fairly well known, but there were some surprises as well. The success of the first Bootleg Series release led to further editions, which in the future dispensed with the multi-volume designation in favor of a single volume title regardless of how many discs were involved. Thus, the second Bootleg Series release was the 2-CD live album *The Bootleg Series Volume 4: "The Royal Albert Hall Concert"* – the quotes acknowledging the mistaken belief that what was actually a concert taking place in Manchester was long presumed to be from the Royal Albert Hall.

As the series continued, the releases became more elaborate, often with deluxe collector's editions containing additional discs or other materials, along with a more affordable standard 2-CD version. For example, *Volume 8: Tell Tale Signs* featured a deluxe edition with a bonus disc and a hardcover book, along with a standard 2-CD version. *Volume 10: Another Self Portrait (1969-1971)* contained the entire 1969 Isle of Wight concert as a bonus disc, along with a remastered *Self Portrait* and other materials. The most elaborate of these to date is *Volume 12:The Cutting Edge* which came in three different editions: the standard 2-CD set; a 6-CD Deluxe edition; and best of all, the 18-CD Collector's Edition which contained everything recorded in the studio in 1965 and 1966. This means the entire *Bringing It All Back Home*, *Highway 61 Revisited*, and *Blonde on Blonde* sessions – every note recorded in the studio during those years.

There are many reasons for the release of these deluxe editions, not the least of which is that with the sales of physical CDs declining in the 1990s, deluxe box sets are seen as the best way to ensure robust sales of new product by important recording artists. Many collectors assume that corporate greed is behind the release of these gems, but that is only if you consider it greedy to protect your investments. The release of the 18-CD Collector's Edition of *The Cutting Edge* was strongly criticized by Dylan fans as being a rip-off because of the shockingly high price asked for the elaborate box set (somewhere in the range of $600 USD). However, when you consider that it contains the ***entire*** *Blonde on Blonde* studio sessions, not to mention the previous two albums, in fantastic audio quality – remixed, remastered, and unedited – it doesn't seem so outrageous to me. I'm sure there are collectors who would have paid thousands of dollars just to hear the complete studio sessions of *Blonde on Blonde* alone. $600 seems like a bargain to me. But the real reason for releasing everything from those years was not to make a lot of money, per se, but rather to ensure that the recordings do not fall into the public domain, thus depriving Sony of any future profits from the music that they have invested in all these years. Under European copyright law, copyright lasts between 50 and 70 years, but only to recordings that have been released within 50 years of them being made. For this reason, we might expect to see new 50th anniversary releases of currently bootlegged material each and every year that milestone is reached. More on this in the next section.

The 50th Anniversary Collections

As previously mentioned, recordings that are older than 50 years enter the public domain in Europe. The rules vary from territory to territory, but in order to prevent bootleggers from legally releasing recordings currently owned by Sony, they have been producing a series of limited edition releases intended to copyright-protect the recordings they currently own, and in many cases recordings that they do not actually own but can be obtained on the collector's market, such as audience recordings, radio and TV broadcasts, private party tapes, etc.

The first of these releases was in 2012 to protect all of the important 1962 recordings in circulation among collectors, as well as previously unknown recordings that may be intended for future Bootleg Series editions and so forth. The second release was in 2013, protecting 1963 recordings, and subsequently a 1964 50th anniversary release appeared in 2014. The 2015 release of *The Cutting Edge* (see previous section) took a different approach to solve this copyright problem. Both 1965 and 1966 were protected in one fell swoop in a set of releases that spanned the entire world, and not just limited editions in the European market (although the Collector's Edition was produced in a limited edition of 5000 copies). Since 1967 has already been taken care of with *The Bootleg Series Volume 11: The Complete Basement Tapes*, there was no 50th Anniversary release in 2017. As of this writing there has been no 2018 release to protect any *John Wesley Harding* outtakes, and The *Bootleg Series Volume 10: Another Self Portrait (1969-1971)* already protects most, if not all of recordings between those years, so we may have seen the last of the 50th Anniversary editions for the near future.

Subsequent notes on the individual tapes will address which recordings appear on both Bootleg Series and 50th Anniversary releases. Here they are one by one:

The 50th Anniversary Collection: The Copyright Extension Collection, Volume 1. Sony reportedly released only 100 copies each of the four-CD-R 1962 set. This set was released only in Europe.

The 50th Anniversary Collection 1963. Released only on vinyl in November 2013. Only 100 copies of the six-LP set were produced.

The 50th Anniversary Collection 1964. Released only on vinyl in November 2014. Only 100 copies of the nine-LP set were produced.

Bob Dylan's 50th Anniversary Collection: 1965. Limited edition download of live recordings from 1965. In December 2015, and in advance of the forthcoming holiday, this set was offered as a gift to those who purchased the *Bob Dylan - The Cutting Edge 1965 – 1966: The Bootleg Series Vol.12: Collector's Edition* box-set released the previous month.

Since these releases were limited to 100 copies, and only in the European market, they are extremely rare and unlikely (at this time) to be obtainable by the majority of Dylan collectors who do not already own them. However, as with tape trading in the days prior to digital file sharing, they are considered to be "in circulation" and obtainable through other collectors who may own the real thing, or copies thereof. The best we can assume is that they are "semi-official". Often the quality of the recordings in these releases is roughly the same as the original tapes used to source them, and in some cases far better. It's still possible that collectors may own better quality tapes than what appears on these limited releases, so it's still worth checking with other collectors as to best quality.

The Unreleased Recordings

Even though most of these tapes have now seen either official or semi-official release, I am still referring to them as "unreleased", only because they were never expected to see the light of day. The following descriptions originally appeared on my website *Bringing It All Back Homepage* in 1994, and since that time much has changed. For many people, tracking down these recordings may prove to be quite a chore, but finding them on The Dark Web (that's a joke) could prove to be both fun and enlightening.

It may be helpful to refer to Michael Krogsgaard's *Bob Dylan: The Recording Sessions,* which was originally serialized in *The Telegraph* and then, after it had ceased publication, continued in *The Bridge*. For my own purposes, I added them to my website with the kind permission of the late John Bauldie, who was the editor and publisher of *The Telegraph*. You may find the session notes at:

http://www.punkhart.com/dylan/sessions.html

John Bucklen Tape
1958

Hey Little Richard
Buzz, Buzz, Buzz
Jenny Take A Ride
Blue Moon

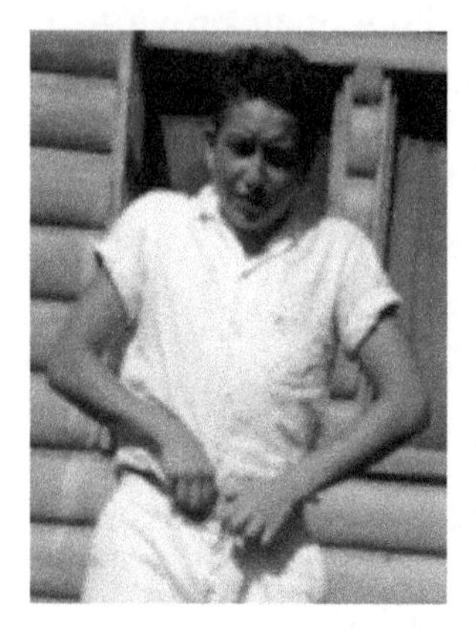

So far, the earliest tape known of the young Bob Dylan. This tape appeared scattered throughout the soundtrack of the BBC TV show *Tales of Rock and Roll* broadcast on the BBC 2 ARENA TV show on May 8, 1993. Portions of this tape, or perhaps all of it, were originally scheduled to appear on the *Highway 61 Interactive* CD-ROM but those plans were scrapped at the last minute due to legal restrictions.

What appears on this tape is extremely fragmentary and features the young Dylan and boyhood pal John Bucklen fooling around with a tape recorder and trying out a few songs. There's some lively conversation, including Dylan's comments about Ricky Nelson and Little Richard, as well as Johnny Cash (not too complementary, as I recall). There doesn't seem to be any evidence of an interest in folk or traditional blues and instead the emphasis is on "hard silly rock and roll", as Bob would later come to call it. Bob plays some piano and guitar and John Bucklen only vocalizes.

Sound quality is not too bad, and it only lasts about 5 minutes, so it would make a good filler or a nice intro to an early 60's Dylan compilation tape. Otherwise, casual fans can avoid it altogether.

CDs:

- **I Was So Much Younger Then** [Dandelion]

The St. Paul Tape
May 1960

Gotta Travel On
Doney Gal
I'm A Rovin' Gambler
Go Down You Murderers
Bay Of Mexico
The Two Sisters
Go Way From My Window
This Land Is Your Land
Go Tell It To The Mountain
Fare Thee Well
Pastures Of Plenty
Saro Jane
Take This Hammer
Nobody Knows You When You're Down And Out
The Great Historical Bum
Mary Ann
Every Night When The Sun Goes In
Sinner Man
Delia's Gone
Wope de Alano
Who's Gonna Shoe Your Pretty Little Feet?
Abner Young
500 Miles
Blues Yodel No 8 (Muleskinner Blues)
One Eyed Jacks
Columbus Stockade Blues
Payday At Coal Creek

This tape was recorded in the apartment of Karen Wallace in St. Paul, Minnesota in May of 1960. It used to be a matter of controversy over whether or not this tape was truly a young Bob Dylan, but I believe the matter has finally been settled and the tape has been authenticated. It's easy to see why there was doubt, though, because the singer sounds very little like the Dylan we're familiar with. The singing sounds very affected and (dare I say it?) phony.

Chalk it up to youth and the struggle to find a style, I guess. Still, this tape, or what can be heard of it that is, leaves much to be desired. Most of the songs are just fragments and the sound quality is so abysmal that it's nearly impossible to tell what songs are actually being sung. The number of songs listed above would indicate a much longer tape than its 36 minutes, but that's because, as I say, it's so fragmentary.

A small portion of this tape appears in excellent sound quality on a separately circulating "sampler" tape that Karen Wallace was using as a sales device. According to Clinton Heylin's book, *The Recording Sessions*, Wallace wanted $10,000 for the original reel tape. There were no buyers and Karen Wallace has since disappeared, along with the tape. It looks like all we have for now is the "armpit" tape. For historical reasons, this is a shame, but for artistic considerations it's no big loss. This tape is only for completists.

CDs:

- **I Was So Much Younger Then** [Dandelion]

Minnesota University Tape
September 1960

Red Rosey Bush
Johnny I Hardly Knew You
Jesus Christ
Streets Of Glory
K.C. Moan
Blues Yodel No 8 (Muleskinner Blues)
I'm A Gambler
Talking Columbia
Talking Merchant Marine
Talking Hugh Brown
Talking Lobbyist

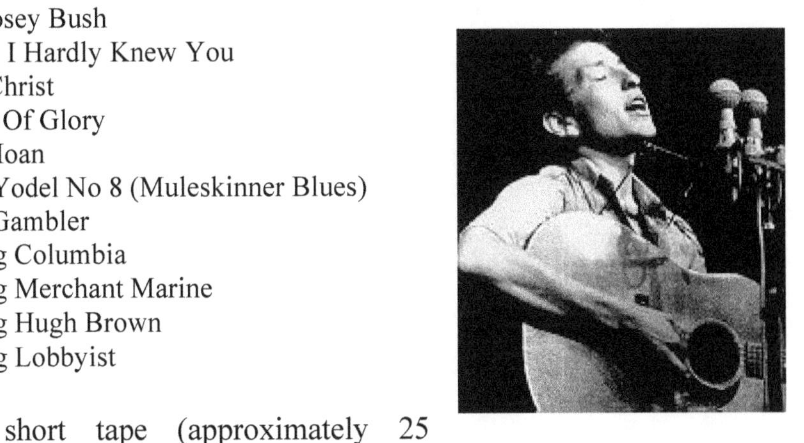

This short tape (approximately 25 minutes) was most likely recorded in Dylan's apartment in Minneapolis. It's the first "true" Dylan tape we have, by that I mean that the voice is recognizably Dylan and the style and selection of songs closer to what we normally think of when we talk about the early years. There's still a little bit of the sweetness in Dylan's voice when he sings "Red Rosey Bush", and the guitar playing is gentler than usual, but by the time he's finished the four talking blues songs at the end of the tape, there's no doubt that it's the young Bobby Dylan singing in the style of his idol Woody Guthrie. This tape is a far cry from the St. Paul Tape of a few months prior to this recording. It would only be a short time before his true individual style would emerge, but we would have to wait until the Minnesota Hotel Tape for that to happen.

The material on this tape leaves a lot to be desired, and Dylan hasn't yet figured out how to break out of his shell. At one point he gets so rattled at a woman singing along with one of the talking blues songs, that he breaks out in mock anger and swears at her. It's hard to tell if he's serious or not.
The sound quality is what you might expect for a tape of this time period: poor. Nevertheless, it's listenable - far more listenable than

the St. Paul Tape - and well worth adding to your collection if you're interested in a peek at the early Bob Dylan struggling to emerge.

CDs:

- **I Was So Much Younger Then** [Dandelion]

LPs:

- **Number One**

East Orange Tape
February-March 1961

San Francisco Bay Blues
Jesus Met The Woman At The Well
Gypsy Davey
Pastures Of Plenty
Trail Of The Buffalo
Jesse James
Car, Car
Southern Cannonball
Bring Me Back, My Blue-Eyed Boy
Remember Me

Another short home-style recording featuring the early Bob Dylan struggling to break out of his Woody Guthrie mold. This approximately 25 minute tape was recorded in the home of the Gleason's and features mostly Woody Guthrie songs. There are still no original compositions being recorded at this point, but it wouldn't be too long before that would change. Meanwhile, this is a very satisfying tape and clearly shows a huge advance over the previous Minnesota University Tape, both in performance and spirit. There is a certain roughness to this performance that predicts what will come on the first album, although there is a distinct lack of polish at this point.

Highlights for me are "Gypsy Davey", "Pastures of Plenty", and "Remember Me". Some songs are fragments and at one point Dylan seems to be very frustrated and has a hard time coming up with something he really wants to play, but when he finally does the result is the beautiful "Remember Me", which closes out the tape. Sound quality is not too bad, but still a long way from excellent.

CDs:

- **The Dylan's Root**

LPs:

- **Let Me Die In My Footsteps** (incomplete)
- **The Demo Tapes** (the rest of the missing songs)

Minneapolis Party Tape
May 1961

Ramblin' Round
Death Don't Have No Mercy
It's Hard To Be Blind
This Train Is Bound For Glory
Harp Blues
Talking Fish Blues
Pastures Of Plenty
Railroad Bill
Will The Circle Be Unbroken
Man Of Constant Sorrow
Pretty Polly
Railroad Boy
James Alley Blues
Why'd You Cut My Hair?
This Land Is Your Land
Still A Fool
Wild Mountain Thyme
Howdido, Car Car
Don't You Push Me Down
Come See
I Want It Now
San Francisco Bay Blues
A Long Time A Growin'
Devilish Mary

As the title may suggest, this is another in the category of Party Tapes. This is much longer than the East Orange Tape and presents much more of a variety. Most of the songs are traditional folk and blues songs and the obligatory smattering of Guthrie and Fuller songs. There are no original songs yet at this point and Dylan is still concentrating on his catalog of folk standards.

The session is pretty loose and informal. The designation "party tape" seems particularly appropriate here because Dylan is obviously performing for the amusement of himself and his friends. Some interesting songs here: “Railroad Boy”, “Pretty Polly”, “Pastures of Plenty”, “He's Young But Daily Growin'” (aka “Long Time A-Growin'”). Performances range from ragged to excellent. Most common circulating tapes were poor in sound, but the *Minnesota Tapes* 3-CD set presents this material in excellent sound, marred somewhat by a very loud ground hum running throughout.

CDs:

- **The Minnesota Tapes** [Wanted Man]

Indian Neck Folk Festival

May 6, 1961

Talkin' Columbia
Hangknot, Slipknot
Talkin' Fish Blues

This is the earliest live Dylan performance available on tape. The festival took place at the Montowesi Hotel in Branford, Connecticut. It was at this occasion that Dylan first met Bobby Neuwirth. Dylan's entire set is presented here and it comprises three songs only. The tape starts with Dylan being introduced by someone and ends with the same announcer requesting a banjo and some other instruments for the next act. Dylan is shown to be in the midst of his Woody Guthrie period because all three songs are Guthrie tunes. It's hard to hear whether or not he did justice to the songs because you can barely hear the vocal even though the guitar comes through loud and clear. The audience is very appreciative, though. Mono audience recording. There are worse sounding live tapes around and for historical purposes this is a must. Not for the casual Dylan listener.

CDs:

- **I Was So Much Younger Then** [Dandelion]

WRVR Riverside Church broadcast

July 29, 1961

Handsome Molly
Omie Wise
Poor Lazarus
Mean Old Railroad
Acne

Another early live recording, this time a live broadcast over radio station WRVR and featuring Jack Elliot and Danny Kalb as well as a young Bob Dylan. I believe Dylan's entire contribution to this radio show is presented on this relatively high quality tape. The first three songs are solo numbers and the last two are duets with Danny Kalb and Jack Elliot respectively.

Dylan is still in his traditional folk period here, although the signs are starting to show that he has a unique voice and delivery, as witnessed by the excellent “Handsome Molly” and “Poor Lazarus”, both fine songs worthy of our attention. “Omie Wise” has never really been one of my favorites, but it's still interesting to hear as an example of the kind of songs Dylan was singing in those days. The last two songs are the most dispensable, and in fact “Acne” is pretty painful to listen to even though you realize it's supposed to be a joke.

As an example of early folk Dylan, in reasonably good sound, this could be of interest to casual Dylan listeners. To the committed collector it's indispensible.

CDs:

- “Mean Old Railroad” and “Acne” appear on **Alias : The Sideman Story Vol. 1.**

LPs:

- **Early Sixties Revisited** [said to contain the entire performance]
- “Handsome Molly” and “Acne” appear on the terrible **Help** bootleg.

First Gaslight Tape
September 6, 1961

Man On The Street
He Was A Friend Of Mine
Talking Bear Mountain Picnic Massacre Blues
Song To Woody
Pretty Polly
Car, Car

In 1961 Dylan began playing a series of gigs at the Gaslight Cafe in New York City. This is the earliest known recording of his appearances at that club and the sound is quite good. Early versions of this tape were poor, but it seems that a better quality tape has been in circulation for some time now and this material appears in very good quality on at least one vinyl boot that I've heard. At any rate, I would say this short tape (approximately 25 minutes) is absolutely essential. Of special interest is the appearance of four original songs. The first three have only recently been officially released on *The Bootleg Series* in their original studio versions, but these live performances are far better. Dylan seems to take his time singing them and really seems to connect with what he's singing. "Song To Woody" is especially riveting. It seems somehow sad in spite of the uplifting nature of the lyrics. There is a weariness to this performance that gives the impression of a singer much older than his years. I guess he really was so much older then!

The other two songs, "Pretty Polly" and "Car Car", fare less successfully, but "Pretty Polly" has the distinction of having the same melody as "Hollis Brown".

CDs:

- **Bob Dylan Rare Live Performances of the Sixties (Volume II)** [Magic Music]

LPs:

- **Gaslight Tapes** (3 LP - also contains Gaslight II)

Gerde's Folk City 1961

September 29, 1961

San Francisco Bay Blues
The Great Divide

Only two songs of this much longer PA tape are in circulation. Where is the rest? For now we have to content ourselves with this very good sounding sample. On this tape, Dylan and Jim Kweskin duet on "San Francisco Bay Blues" and "The Great Divide", and the results are raucous and informal.

This short tape (approximately 10 minutes), like the first Gaslight Tape from earlier in the same month, is a good example of the type of live performances Dylan was giving in late 1961. Still finding his voice, still finding his style, but still deeply immersed in the Woody Guthrie songbook.

This tape is not essential, but would certainly make a nice companion piece or filler for the Gaslight or Riverside Church tapes.

CDs:

- **Hard Times in New York City 1961 -1962**
- **I Was So Much Younger Then** [Dandelion]

Oscar Brand's Folk Song Festival
WBAI-FM, New York City October 29, 1961

Sally Gal
The Girl I Left Behind

This previously unknown radio broadcast from 1961, if it was actually broadcast at all, came to light as part of a Dylan special retrospective on WBAI-FM in 1994. When first broadcast in 1994, only "Sally Gal" and a short interview were heard, but sometime later an additional song from the same show appeared, the previously unheard of "The Girl I Left Behind", which is no doubt a traditional. Bob mentions his upcoming Carnegie Chapter Hall concert during his pleasant brief chat with Oscar Brand, and his performance of both songs is excellent.

Although brief (a mere 10 minutes), this is a highly worthwhile tape of a rare early performance. The sound is as good as it gets. For a later Oscar Brand radio appearance, see **Oscar Brand Show 4/63**.

CDs:

- **I Was So Much Younger Then** [Dandelion]
- **Genuine Bootleg Series 3**

Carnegie Chapter Hall 1961

November 4, 1961

Pretty Peggy-O
In the Pines
Gospel Plow
1913 Massacre
Backwater Blues
Long Time A-Growin'
Fixin' to Die
Talking Bear Mountain Picnic Massacre
Man on the Street
Talking Merchant Marine
Black Cross
Freight Train Blues
Song to Woody
Talking New York

This concert took place in the "small" Carnegie Hall in November 1961. This hall is really nothing more than an annex to the bigger, more prestigious Carnegie Hall. The crowd was supposed to have been pretty small for this early concert, but they seem very enthusiastic. Dylan himself seems very friendly and talkative, if a little nervous, and seems to be attempting to hone his stagecraft a little bit. His stage patter is amusing and self-effacing. For instance he talks about the set list taped on his guitar and says he looked at other set lists on other singers' guitars and copied down some of those songs, and so some of them he doesn't know too well. In fact he does all of these songs very well and it's easy to see why he attracted so much attention in his early years.

THE FOLKLORE CENTER
Presents
BOB DYLAN
IN HIS FIRST NEW YORK CONCERT
SAT. NOV. 4, 1961 8:40pm
CARNEGIE CHAPTER HALL
154 WEST 57th STREET • NEW YORK CITY
All seats $2.00
Tickets available at: The Folklore Center
110 MacDougal Street
New York City 12, New York
or at door
GR 7-5987

No original songs here[2]. Three of these songs appeared on the first album and the others are among those rarely heard on any Dylan tape. “In the Pines” is an old song that seems to have had its origins in post-slavery days. I've heard this song under the alternate title “Black Girl”, but Dylan sings it as "little girl". “Backwater Blues” is a Leadbelly song and Dylan gets to sing some down-home blues. His guitar playing is pretty impressive. “1913 Massacre” is note for note “Song To Woody”! So this is where he got the tune. The story in this song is a tragic tale of death and destruction during a miner's strike. By far the most shocking thing on this tape is “Long Time A-Growin'”, because Dylan sings this in none other than his Nashville Skyline voice - eight years before he shocked the world with his transformed voice on that album.

Obviously, Dylan was capable of modifying his vocal style when the song demanded it as far back as 1961. Apparently what he's trying to do here is sing in an Irish style. The results are not at all bad and the song has long been one of my favorites. The songs that appeared on the first album sound pretty much the same. “Fixin' To Die” stands out in particular and is a pretty powerful performance overall. The sound is pretty good too - Definitely a PA tape.

CDs:

- **Acoustic Troubadour** [Vigotone]
- **Hard Times in New York City 1961 -1962**
- **Live NYC 1961**
- **Carnegie Chapter Hall 1961**

---

[2] On the original circulating tape. A more complete one now exists.

First MacKenzie Tape
November 23 and December 4, 1961

Hard Times In New York Town
Wayfaring Stranger
A Long Time Man Feel Bad
Lonesome Whistle Blues
Worried Blues
Baby Of Mine
Instrumental
Baby Let Me Follow You Down
Fixin' To Die
San Francisco Bay Blues
You're No Good
House Of The Risin' Sun
Instrumental
This Land Is Your Land
Roll In My Sweet Baby's Arms
Bells Of Rhymney
Come All You Fair And Tender Ladies
Instrumental
Instrumental
Highway 51
This Land Is Your Land

This tape was recorded in the home of Eve and Mac MacKenzie, friends of Dylan during his early years in New York City. The tape is fragmentary and often muddled. I believe the story goes that Anthony Scaduto managed to surreptitiously record as much of the tape as he could while visiting with the MacKenzie's during research for his authorized biography of Bob Dylan. As the story goes, he had to hide his portable tape recorder every time someone entered the room.

The performances, what can be heard of them, seem to be about average for Dylan circa 1961. Some of the songs wound up being recorded for the first album, but overall the material here isn't too interesting. The Second MacKenzie tape of 1963 is much more interesting.

For completists only.

CDs:

- **I Was So Much Younger Then** [Dandelion]

POSTSCRIPT:

As previously mentioned, in 2012 Sony released *The 50th Anniversary Collection: The Copyright Extension Collection, Volume 1.* Among the recordings released on this album were songs from the two MacKenzie tapes. Since the MacKenzie tapes never had a year of 1962 attached to their circulation, the dates are somewhat in dispute. Nevertheless, the songs that appear are:

Hard Times in New York Town
The Death of Emmett Till
I Rode Out One Morning
House of the Rising Sun
See That My Grave Is Kept Clean
Ballad of Donald White

The latter four songs are from the second MacKenzie tape, which is covered later in this book.

Minnesota Hotel Tape

December 22, 1961

Candy Man
Baby Please Don't Go
Hard Times in New York
Stealin'
Poor Lazarus
I Ain't Got No Home
It's Hard to Be Blind
Dink's Song
Man of Constant Sorrow
East Orange
Omie Wise
Wade in the Water
I Was Young When I Left Home
In the Evening When the Sun Goes Down
Baby Let Me Follow You Down
Sally Gal
Gospel Plow
Long John
Cocaine
VD Waltz
VD Blues
VD City
VD Gunner's Blues
See That My Grave is Kept Clean
Ramblin' Round
Black Cross

This is the classic party tape that made up the bulk of the famous *Great White Wonder* bootleg, widely regarded as the first of its kind. Originally assumed to have been recorded in a hotel room in Minnesota, it turns out to have been recorded in Bonnie Beecher's apartment in Dinkytown, a small 'student-centric' shopping and entertainment area just off of the campus of the University of Minnesota. This is the area of town where Bob played his earliest shows in the city, at a coffee house called the 10 O'clock Scholar, in front of people like 'Spider' John Koerner and Tony 'Little Sun'

Glover. Tony is the person who recorded this tape. Bonnie Beecher's apartment was called "The Minnesota Hotel" because it was a revolving door for 'musician types' and a well-known 'place to crash'. Thus the title: "The Minnesota Hotel Tape".

It has an informal air about it that finds Dylan in a very relaxed mood among friends. At the same time the tape acts as a sort of demo tape and represents the entire spectrum of Dylan's song catalog at the time. Hardly any original songs here, and those that do appear are very derivative, but he hadn't yet approached his true writing years yet. At this point he is a performer of folk, blues, and country standards and the influence of Woody Guthrie and others is especially strong.

Highlights are "Poor Lazarus", "Dink's Song", "Black Cross", "Ramblin' Round", "It's Hard To Be Blind", "I Was Young When I Left Home", etc. Many people will quibble with the quality of some of his blues numbers such as "Long John" and "In the Evening", but I find them entertaining. There can be no doubt that this is one of his most historic tapes, though, and is a must for anyone interested in Dylan's formative years. The sound is very good, but on some vinyl bootlegs the quality is less than stellar. The best vinyl boot I've heard yet is *Blind Boy Grunt* where the sound is second only to official album quality. The worst I've heard is actually on that famous *Great White Wonder* bootleg where the sound is muddy. All of this material is available, with the exception of one song for some odd reason, on the *Ten of Swords* 10-record bootleg set. Most recently, all of this material appears in excellent sound quality on the 3-CD set *The Minnesota Tapes*, along with the entire Minneapolis Party Tape.

CDs:

- **The Minnesota Tapes** [Wanted Man]
- **Love and Theft** [Columbia] (official album bonus disc)
  "I Was Young When I Left Home"

LPs:

- **Ten of Swords** (nearly complete)
- **Great White Wonder** (about half complete)

- **GWW Talkin' John Birch Society** (a few songs - does not duplicate material on **GWW**)
- **Blind Boy Grunt** (about half complete - does not duplicate material on **GWW**)
- **The Kindest Cut** (same as above)
- **Bob Dylan volume 1-3** (Joker label - duplicates material on **GWW**)
- **Little White Wonder volume 1-3** (essentially the same as above)
- **VD Waltz** (contains the *VD Medley* only - no duplication with **GWW** but does duplicate **BBG**)
- **Stealin'** (just a few songs - does not duplicate material on **GWW** but does duplicate **BBG**)

First Album Sessions
November 1961

You're No Good
Fixin' To Die
He Was a Friend of Mine
House of the Risin' Sun
Talking New York
Song To Woody
Baby, Let Me Follow You Down
Man of Constant Sorrow
In My Time of Dyin'
Man on the Street
(As I Go) Ramblin' Round
Pretty Peggy-O
See That My Grave Is Kept Clean
Gospel Plow
Highway 51
Freight Train Blues
House Carpenter

Sessions for the first Bob Dylan album took place over a span of two days in late November 1961. Most of the material recorded at the sessions were the traditional folk tunes that he had been performing at various places before being discovered by John Hammond and signed to Columbia. Three songs did not make the album, but in 1991 Columbia released them on the first edition of the Bootleg Series.

The performances were very good and faithfully represented his repertoire. Only two originals made the final album ("Talking New York" and "Song To Woody") with a third ("Man on the Street") not being officially released until 1991. As far as I know, "Ramblin' Round" has never appeared anywhere.

CDs:

- **Bob Dylan** [Columbia] (official release)
- **The Bootleg Series Volumes 1-3**
  He Was a Friend of Mine
  Man On The Street
  House Carpenter

Billy James Interview
Late 1961

This is just a short fragment of what must have been a longer interview with Columbia Records publicist Billy James. The 5 minutes we have is not very illuminating, but it appears to be the earliest known official interview. Not much to say here. Poor sound.

A complete transcript can be found at
http://www.punkhart.com/dylan/interviews/61-fall.txt

CDs:

- **I Was So Much Younger Then** [Dandelion]

Leeds Demos

Jan or Feb 1962

He Was a Friend of Mine
Man in the Street (1)
Hard Times in New York
Poor Boy Blues
Ballad for a Friend
Ramblin' Gamblin' Willie
Man in the Street (2)
Talking Bear Mountain Picnic Massacre Disaster Blues
Standing on the Highway

These early demos for Leeds Publishing were made in order to present some Dylan songs for other artists to use. The only one of these officially released by Dylan was "Ramblin' Gamblin' Willie" and that was quickly withdrawn soon after release on the *Freewheelin'* album. The others have rarely been heard. "He Was a Friend of Mine", "Man in the Street", and "Talking Bear Mountain" have all been performed at the Gaslight Cafe in late 1961. "Hard Times in New York" appeared on the Minnesota Hotel Tape. The others are very rare indeed. It's easy to see why these songs were never recorded by other artists (as far as I know). They're pretty much just quickly dashed-off run-throughs of songs never completely worked out. The first "Man in the Street" is a false start and the second the full version. Both of these were actually from the sessions for the first album. These songs are very interesting for early Dylan but hardly indispensible. Sound quality is decent but I imagine the originals sound much better.

CDs:

- **In the Pines**

LPs:

- **Poems in Naked Wonder**
- **Early Sixties Revisited**
- **Ten of Swords**

Cynthia Gooding Tape

February 1962

Ballad of Donald White
Wichita
Acne
Rocks and Gravel
Long Time Man
Ranger's Command

This is one of the more interesting party tapes around. The sound is good, the performances relaxed and uninhibited, and everyone involved sounds like they're having a good time. "Acne" is pretty unbearable overall and just shows Dylan to be having a great time fooling around with his friends. "Rocks and Gravel" is much more basic than the version that eventually appeared on early pressings of the *Freewheelin'* album. "Ballad of Donald White" isn't too good, but then this is true of most early Dylan originals. The tune was adapted from another old tune. "Wichita" is, of course, an old blues tune and not too badly done, although I much prefer the studio version recorded during the *Freewheelin'* sessions. Overall, a rather dispensable tape for the casual collector. For completists only.

CDs:

- **Hard Times in New York City 1961 -1962**
  - Wichita
  - Rocks and Gravel
  - Ranger's Command
- **I Was So Much Younger Then** [Dandelion]

Folksinger's Choice
March 11, 1962

Lonesome Whistle Blues
Fixin' To Die
Smokestack Lightning
Hard Travelin'
Death Of Emmett Till
Standing On The Highway
Roll On, John
Stealin', Stealin'
Long Time Man
Baby Please Don't Go
Hard Times In New York Town

When this tape surfaced, it took the world completely by surprise because hardly anyone knew of its existence. This is a complete one-hour radio show in excellent quality. I'm not sure if this show was ever actually broadcast, but it seems unlikely that it was, otherwise we would have known about this tape years before. The quality is so good, it has to come from the master tape rather than an over-the-air broadcast.

There are a number of firsts here, such as the earliest known recording of "Emmett Till" and the rare performances of "Smokestack Lightning" and "Roll On, John". Material wise, there are better tapes around (such as the excellent Minnesota Hotel Tape), and the few originals here don't show much promise, but Dylan is very relaxed and in excellent voice throughout.

The show is hosted by Cynthia Gooding and features an interview interspersed with songs. The tape was apparently recorded not long after the tape that was recorded at her apartment (known as the *Cynthia Gooding Tape*). She is obviously taken with the young Bob and he seems to feel at ease in her presence. One particularly funny exchange occurs when Dylan finishes a song with lots of harmonica and Gooding asks if he's just recently started playing harmonica. She's surprised to hear him say that he's played for a long time. His harp style was so crude at the time, and has never improved (thankfully!) over the years, that it sounded like a first time player. Dylan doesn't seem in the least embarrassed by the exchange.

CDs:

- **Folksinger's Choice**
- **You Don't Know Me**

Gerde's Folk City 1962

May 1962

Honey Just Allow Me One More Chance
Talking New York Blues
Corrina, Corrina
Deep Elem Blues
Blowin' in the Wind

This is an excellent recording of one of Dylan's appearances at Gerde's Folk City, a club that afforded him excellent opportunities for much needed exposure in his early years. We find him here at his most confident. He's really starting to hit his stride here. The most unusual part of this tape is the song "Deep Elem Blues" that finds Dylan singing a fast upbeat blues in a different singing style for him. He really swoops up on the word "deep" in this song and manages to sound a thousand years old. Very convincing blues performance. "Corrina, Corrina" is very beautiful - much different from the *Freewheelin'* version. "Blowin' In the Wind" is missing a verse, so it must be a very early run-through. All in all, excellent sound and a very dynamic performance. Very highly recommended for anyone interested in Dylan.

CDs:

- **Paranoid Blues** [Diamonds in Your Ear] (complete)
- **Bob Dylan's Dream** [Living Legend] (missing one song)
- **Hard Times in New York City 1961 -1962**

LPs:

- **The Australian Connection** [Toasted] 10 Record Set

Also appears on *The 50th Anniversary Collection: The Copyright Extension Collection, Volume 1.*

WBAI broadcast

May 1962

Ballad of Donald White
The Death of Emmett Till
Blowin' In the Wind

This FM radio show was recorded but for some reason never actually broadcast. It's sort of an informal chat and hootenanny involving Dylan and Pete Seeger, who allows Dylan to come up with some famous and amusing answers to his fawning questions. Seeger asks how he comes up with his songs, asking if he spreads newspapers out and picks out stories to sing about, and Dylan comes up with the famous line about how he doesn't really write the songs, they were always there waiting for him to put them down with pen and paper. Two of the three songs on this tape are not among Dylan's best, but he performs them well enough considering their lack of sophistication. “The Ballad of Donald White” appears officially on the album *Broadside Reunion*, and is about a man released from prison who finds he can't cope with the outside world and longs to go back to prison where he fits in. He commits murder (which seems a little extreme) in order to go back to jail, but finds himself marked for execution instead (well, what did he expect?). The point seems labored and completely out of focus, or else I'm missing something here. Anyway, a very forgettable song. “The Death of Emmett Till” is even worse. This has to be one of his all-time worst songs, and it should have been much better considering the subject matter: Emmett Till's death was one of the catalytic events of the early civil rights movement and deserves much better than the treatment given here. The lyrics are lurid and always leave me with a feeling of disgust, which I suppose is the intention. The final verse, which tries to bring some hope to the despairing mood of the song, is totally contrived. Interestingly, Dylan admits that he stole the tunes for both of these songs from other songs. At least he wasn't trying to pass off traditional song structures as something brand new. Not recommended to anyone but diehard fans.

CDs:

- **Broadside**

LPs:

- "Ballad of Donald White" appears on **Blind Boy Grunt** and **The Kindest Cut** (both the same albums under different names)
- "The Death of Emmett Till" appears on **Great White Wonder**

Finjan Club in Montreal 1962
July 2, 1962

The Death of Emmett Till
Stealin'
Hiram Hubbard
Blowin' in the Wind
Rocks and Gravel
Quit Your Lowdown Ways
He Was a Friend of Mine
Let Me Die in My Footsteps
Two Trains a Runnin'
Ramblin' on My Mind
Blues Yodel No 8 (Muleskinner Blues)

This is wonderful stuff. For years this tape was thought to be part of the Gaslight Tapes, but recently the consensus has been that this is from the Finjan Club in Montreal. The sound is certainly excellent and the performances all classic early Dylan. "Emmett Till" appears again, unfortunately, but the others are much better: "Let Me Die in My Footsteps", rarely heard; "Rocks and Gravel", an excellent live version; "Quit Your Lowdown Ways", another rarity; Robert Johnson's "Ramblin' On My Mind", which sounds a lot like "Corrina, Corrina"; and my favorite song on the tape – "Hiram Hubbard". I'm not sure why I like this song so much (which I'm sure isn't an original composition), but I think it's just the genre that appeals to me so much. It seems to fit in with that group of songs about falsely condemned men destroyed not so much for any specific crime but for the general crime of rebelling against authority, songs such as "Poor Lazarus" and "Midnight Special" among others. Also, the structure is simple and compelling, with each chorus seeming to reaffirm the belief that a horrible wrong has been done and there's nothing anyone can do about it except to repeat over and over "Hiram Hubbard wasn't guilty". This would have been a great song for Roger McGuinn and The Byrds.

Entire tape very highly recommended to anyone interested in Dylan. Some of the very best live early material available.

CDs:

- **Finjan Club** [Yellow Dog]
- **Bob Dylan Rare Live Performances of the Sixties (Volume II & III)** [Magic Music]
- **Hard Times in New York City 1961 -1962** (Muleskinner Blues)

LPs:

- **The Gaslight Tapes** (incorrectly identified)
- **The Australian Connection** (10-record set)

Also appears on *The 50th Anniversary Collection: The Copyright Extension Collection, Volume 1.*

Carnegie Hall Hootenanny 1962
September 22, 1962

Sally Gal
Highway 51
Talking John Birch Society Blues
Ballad of Hollis Brown
A Hard Rain's A-Gonna Fall

This is a fair sounding audience tape but a good one musically. Three excellent early original compositions are featured here: "Talking John Birch", "Hollis Brown", and "Hard Rain" - all among Dylan's best early "protest" songs. The first one is light and satirical, the other two grim and despairing. To balance it all out, we have two rousing traditional songs. "Sally Gal" is the type of song that Bob would use to open his 1963 shows and get things off to a comfortable start. "Highway 51" is an upbeat blues number that gives Bob a chance to show off a little bottleneck guitar. Overall a very worthwhile tape, but not indispensible. Bob sounds pretty far away at times.

Appears on *The 50th Anniversary Collection: The Copyright Extension Collection, Volume 1.*

Second Gaslight Tape

Late 1962

Barbara Allen
A Hard Rain's A-Gonna Fall
Don't Think Twice
Black Cross
No More Auction Block
Rocks and Gravel
Moonshine Blues
John Brown
Ballad of Hollis Brown
See That My Grave is Kept Clean
Cocaine
Cuckoo is a Pretty Bird
Ain't No More Cane
Motherless Children
Handsome Molly
Kind Hearted Woman
West Texas

This is, without a doubt, the best early Dylan (pre-1964) live material I've ever heard. This is a must for any Dylan fan, and fortunately this material is widely available on CD (Italian import -- check your local CD store for availability) and in very decent sound.

The performances are all at the Gaslight Cafe, but the audience is barely in evidence. It could have been recorded on a slow night or possibly during a time when the club was closed to the public. The recording sounds very professional, so maybe this was an informal recording session. The audience can be heard during "Hard Rain" singing along, so maybe this was a private session of sorts (party tape?). Dylan seems to have left his harmonica holder at home because none of the songs on this tape feature his trademark harmonica at all. This actually adds to the greatness of the performances, I think, because it forced Dylan to attempt something interesting on the guitar during the spots where the harmonica breaks should fall. This is most evident on "Don't Think Twice" and "Cocaine", two songs where harmonica had been the dominant instrument. All the songs on this tape sound very unusual for this reason.

Dylan is in exceptionally good voice throughout. Of special note is his vocal on "Barbara Allen", where (as has been noted by others) his voice sounds strangely like his Nashville Skyline voice of many years later. On "No More Auction Block" he manages to sound 100 years old and his singing from the viewpoint of an ex-slave is very convincing. The other blues and spirituals are equally impressive, my favorite being "West Texas", which features a very compelling guitar figure and an excellent blues vocal. But I think my very favorite song on the tape has to be "Handsome Molly". This is just an incredible song (not written by Dylan, btw) that never fails to move me. I also like "Barbara Allen", "Motherless Children", and "Moonshine Blues". Actually, there isn't one dead spot in this entire set. The original songs, many being heard possibly for the first time, are: "Hard Rain", "Don't Think Twice", "John Brown", "Hollis Brown" (hmmm, wonder if they're related :-), and if you insist "Rocks and Gravel", but I'm pretty sure that this song doesn't belong in the list of original Dylan songs.

CDs:

- **Live at the Gaslight 1962** [Columbia] (official release)
- **The Gaslight Tapes** [Laser]
- **The Gaslight Tapes** [Rattle Snake] (upgrade)
- **Bob Dylan Rare Live Performances of the Sixties (Volume I & II)** [Magic Music]

LPs:

- **The Gaslight Tapes**

The *Laser* disc is reported to be the world's first bootleg CD

POSTSCRIPT:

Ten tracks from this tape are now officially available from Columbia through special arrangement with Starbucks. The additional missing tracks that did not appear on the Starbucks special edition of this show have now been released on the *50th Anniversary Collection: The Copyright Extension Collection, Volume 1.* In addition, it is rumored as of this writing that the complete Gaslight tapes may be released as part of Sony's *Bootleg Series*, reportedly in much improved sound quality.

Billy Faier Show

October 1962

Baby, Let Me Follow You Down
Talkin' John Birch Society Blues
The Death of Emmett Till
Make Me a Pallet on Your Floor

This radio broadcast (on WBAI-FM in New York City) is one of the more interesting ones due mainly to the appearance of the song "Make Me a Pallet on Your Floor", which is the only known performance of this song by Dylan. I don't know the origin of this song, but I doubt very much that it's an original. The others are nice too, although "Emmett Till" is just as tiresome here as it is on other tapes. After singing "John Birch Society", someone calls in and suggests that Dylan give equal time and sing an anti-communist song. Dylan responds that he doesn't know any anti-communist songs. Moments such as this make this tape very enjoyable. Length is about 20 minutes or so and the sound quality is very good, as you would expect from a tape taken from a radio broadcast. This makes a very nice addition to the early Dylan catalog.

CDs:

- **Songs That Made Him Famous**

Broadside Sessions
October 1962 thru February 1963

I'd Hate to Be You on That Dreadful Day
Oxford Town
Paths of Victory
Walking Down the Line
Cuban Blockade
I Shall Be Free
Train a-Travellin'
Ye Playboys and Playgirls
Masters of War
John Brown
Let Me Die in My Footsteps
Only a Hobo
Talking Devil
Farewell

These songs were recorded in the office of Broadside, a magazine devoted to the folk movement of the early 1960s and to which Dylan contributed early in his career. Many of his most famous early songs appeared in lyric form in this magazine, and some of the songs recorded in these sessions remain obscure even to this day. Of the released songs, none of these sound as good as the official versions, and the unreleased songs sound pretty good but there is an overall rushed and offhand feeling to these renditions. Still, it's nice to hear songs like “Cuban Blockade” and “Talkin' Devil”, both pretty rare songs. My personal favorites are “Walking Down the Line”, which he performed in rehearsals with the Grateful Dead in 1987, and “Ye Playboys and Playgirls”, which he performed live at Newport in 1963 and has been officially released on the Vanguard album *Newport Broadside*. Some of the songs on this tape have actually been officially released and were still easily available as recently as the late '70s. These songs include: “Only a Hobo”, “Talking Devil”, “John Brown”, “Let Me Die In My Footsteps”, and “I'd Hate To Be You” - all on albums released by Broadside. “Only a Hobo” is rushed and vastly inferior to the more familiar version recorded at the "Times" sessions. It immediately goes into “Talking Devil”, which is really only a snippet and ends with Dylan explaining that he only had two verses. Certainly these songs were just run-throughs for the purpose of getting the lyrics down on tape for publishing purposes. Sound is very good, considering the amateurishness of the whole affair. Performance is loose and informal but interesting and indispensible for Dylan collectors.

CDs:

- **Broadside**

LPs:

- Some songs appear on **Broadside Reunion** and **Broadside Ballads**, both legitimate releases.
- **Blind Boy Grunt**
- **The Kindest Cut**
- **Ten of Swords**
- **Let Me Die In My Footsteps**
- **The Demo Tapes** (misnamed, obviously)

Madhouse On Castle Street

December 30, 1962 - January 4, 1963
Broadcast January 12, 1963 on the BBC

Blowin' in the Wind
Ballad of the Gliding Swan

The cast of *Madhouse on Castle Street: left to right,* David Warner, Bob Dylan, Maureen Pryor, James Mellor, Ursula Howells and Reg Lye. The play was screened by BBC TV on 13 January 1963 *(National Film Archive)*

In late 1962, Dylan went to England to act and sing in a BBC play called *Madhouse On Castle Street*. Only a tiny fragment of this broadcast exists in audio form, with Dylan singing two songs. As I understand it, Dylan's role was to act as a sort of Greek chorus and wander about from time to time singing songs to punctuate the action. What we have on this tape is a tiny fragment of "Blowin' In the Wind" and a much longer fragment of a very strange song called "Ballad of the Gliding Swan". This last song seems as if it might be a traditional folk song, judging from the lyrics. The entire tape is somewhere around five minutes and the quality is extremely poor. Makes appropriate filler for an early sixties tape, but otherwise there is no compelling reason to actively seek this one out.

A complete tape with more songs is rumored to exist.

CDs:

- **I Was So Much Younger Then** [Dandelion]

The Freewheelin' Sessions
April 1962 through April 63

(Promotional edition released April 1963; standard edition released May 1963)

[April]
Baby Please Don't Go
Let Me Die in My Footsteps (released on promotional edition and *The Bootleg Series*)
Milk Cow Blues (1)
Milk Cow Blues (2)
Rocks and Gravel (1)
Talking Bear Mountain Picnic Massacre Disaster Blues (*The Bootleg Series*)
Talking Hava Nagilah Blues (*The Bootleg Series*)
Wichita (1)
Wichita (2)
Worried Blues (*The Bootleg Series*)

[July]
Babe I'm in the Mood (1;*Biograph* October, 1985)
Babe I'm in the Mood (2)
Blowin' in the Wind (released)
Corrina, Corrina (1)
The Death of Emmett Till
Down the Highway (released)
Honey Just Allow Me One More Chance (released)
Quit Your Lowdown Ways (*The Bootleg Series*)
Ramblin' Gamblin' Willie (released on promotional edition and *The Bootleg Series*)

[October]
Ballad of Hollis Brown
Corrina, Corrina (2; released)
Going to New Orleans
I Hear That Lonesome Whistle
Kingsport Town (*The Bootleg Series*)

Sally Gal
Watcha Gonna Do

[November]
Corrina, Corrina (3; single released Dec. 1962)
Don't Think Twice (released)
Mixed Up Confusion (1; single released Dec. 1962)
Mixed Up Confusion (2)
Mixed Up Confusion (3; *Biograph*)
Mixed Up Confusion (4)
Mixed Up Confusion (5)
Rocks and Gravel (2; released only on promotional edition)
Talking John Birch Society Blues (released only on promotional edition)
That's Alright Mama (1)
That's Alright Mama (2)

[December]
A Hard Rain's A-Gonna Fall (released)
Bob Dylan's Blues (released)
I Shall Be Free (released)
Oxford Town (released)

[April 1963]
Bob Dylan's Dream (released only on standard edition)
Girl of the North Country (released only on standard edition)
Masters of War (released only on standard edition)
Talking World War III Blues (released only on standard edition)

Lots and lots of really great songs were recorded at these sessions. For the very first time Dylan's true songwriting genius was becoming clearly evident. Up to this point he could only be thought of as an interesting performer who also wrote a few of his own songs that were mostly reworkings of traditional folk songs. Even though his songs were still basically transformed folk songs, it was obvious that he had an incredible talent for lyrics unlike anyone else on the music scene at the time.

It may seem incredible nowadays, when every singer/songwriter is perceived to be a sensitive "poet", that Dylan was unique in this regard, but he was. While the idea of protest songs was hardly new at the time, the way in which Dylan went about writing them certainly was. Most protest songs at the time, usually referred to as "topical songs", were union songs or civil rights anthems with a narrow viewpoint (us against them) told in black and white terms. True, some of Dylan's protest songs from this period do not stray too far from that rigid mold (he wouldn't reach the apex of his protest period until the next album *The Times They Are A-Changin'* where he turned protest music into an art form), but some of the ones that appear here are very unusual and show great potential.

You may have noticed that relatively few of the songs on the list above are of the protest variety. That's because originally the *Freewheelin'* album wasn't intended to be a "protest" album at all. Initial sessions were done with session musicians and the sound being strived for in those early sessions was a sort of rockabilly style popularized by the early Elvis Presley with a touch of Hank Williams thrown in for good measure. Furthermore, the songs performed at the early sessions were more traditional than original. The intention seems to have been to take the concept of the first album one step further and turn Dylan full-blown into a great country/folk/blues/rock performer and not the serious folk purist he was later perceived to be. Somewhere along the line this approach was scrapped and the folk/protest angle was played up. Only one of the full band songs appeared on the final album ("Corrina Corrina", although "Rocks and Gravel", which appeared on the rare first edition of this album, was also from the full-band sessions) and one single, "Mixed Up Confusion" b/w "Corrina Corrina" (different take from the album version) was also released from the sessions as well.

By the time the final album appeared, with new tracks produced by Tom Wilson despite the credit given to John Hammond, there was hardly any trace at all of Dylan the country/folk/blues interpreter and more of Dylan the protest songwriter. To me the final album is a mess and it has never been one of my favorites. Had Columbia stuck to their original concept things would be much different. However, it's also possible that if they had stuck to that first concept we may never have heard of Dylan because it was his songs, and his protest image, which gave him his initial fame in the first place.

All songs are available in excellent sound on various records, most importantly on the official album itself.

CDs:

- **The Freewheelin' Bob Dylan** (official album)
- **Biograph** (official album)
- **The Bootleg Series** (official album)
- **The Freewheelin' Outtakes**

LPs:

- **In the Mood** (all *Freewheelin'* outtakes)
- **GWW - Talking' John Birch Society** (two of the deleted songs)
- **GWW - Talkin' Bear Mountain** (all *Freewheelin'* outtakes)
- **Ten of Swords** (contains some *Freewheelin'* outtakes)

All songs now appear on the *50th Anniversary Collection: The Copyright Extension Collection, Volume 1.*

Unknown Folk Club, NYC

Late 1962 or early 1963

Ramblin' Through This World
Freight Train Blues
Walls of Redwing

Nothing is known about this tape other than that it appears to have been recorded in a folk music club sometime in late 1962 or early 1963, judging from the songs performed. Both "Ramblin' Through This World" and "Walls of Redwing" are known to have been performed in 1963, but it's possible that they were performed earlier. "Freight Train Blues" is a holdover from his early performances, thus bringing up the possibility that this performance comes from late 1962. It seems reasonable.

The sound quality is only fair, being an audience recording, and "Walls of Redwing" cuts off just as it gets started. A perfectly acceptable recording that would make good filler for another early '60s tape.

CDs and LPs: Unknown.

Skip Weshner radio show
February 1963

Tomorrow is a Long Time
Masters of War
Bob Dylan's Blues

This is a very disappointing tape compared to other radio broadcasts. Skip Weshner isn't content to just patronize Dylan, but finds it necessary to actually carry on a monologue the entire time Dylan is sitting in front of him. At least Studs Terkel and Billy Faier tried to get Dylan to open up once in a while, even though those attempts were usually doomed to failure. For his part, Dylan manages to get in a few decent uhms and yeahs here and there, and we actually get to hear Dylan sing three songs in the course of the 30-minute broadcast. Of course those three songs are what we're all interested in here, and they're great of course. Fortunately, the songs chosen are pretty rare - a live version of "Bob Dylan's Blues" and the little heard "Tomorrow Is a Long Time", at least little heard until recently that is. So your best bet is to edit out the non-interview and just group the three songs together on another tape. You'll be glad you did.

CDs:
- **Songs That Made Him Famous**

Gerde's Folk City 1963

("The Banjo Tape")

February 8, 1963

Lonesome River's Edge
Backdoor Blues
Bob Dylan's Dream
You Can Get Her
Farewell
All Over You
Masters of War
Keep Your Hands Off Her
Honey Babe
Goin' Back to Rome
Stealin'

This "party" tape, variably attributed to the home of the Gleasons, or the Gibsons, or any number of other locations, is now known to have taken place at Gerde's Folk City. The reason it's called "the banjo tape" is due to the presence of someone playing banjo and singing along with Bob who plays a 12-string for this occasion. Most of the songs are just fragments and none of the complete songs are really worth much. "All Over You", "Bob Dylan's Dream", "Farewell" and others have all been done better elsewhere. There is some excellent coughing during "Farewell" and Bob has trouble remembering the words for "All Over You", but then it's all in the spirit of fun. Sound quality is excellent throughout.

LPs:

- **GWW - Burn Some More**

All songs now appear on the *50th Anniversary Collection 1963.*

Oscar Brand Show
March 1963

Girl From the North Country
Only a Hobo

This 15-minute radio broadcast is from the Oscar Brand Show, which has been broadcast every Saturday night on WNYC-AM since 1945.

The format of the show is as follows: musical introduction sung by Oscar Brand while a voice-over announces "The World of Folk Music", etc., followed by a spoken introduction by Brand and then another song; then Dylan is introduced. The chat is extremely brief and then Dylan sings "Girl From the North Country" (nice version); then comes a "commercial" (which is pretty funny actually - a "dramatization" from the files of the Social Security Administration) and another song from Dylan, "Only a Hobo" which is apparently supposed to tie-in with the theme of the Social Security sponsorship. Nice version anyway. Finally another song from Brand and the show is over.

Overall not too bad as these radio things go, and at least we get to hear Dylan without excessive hype or the pretense of an in-depth interview. Sound quality is excellent.

CDs:

- **I Was So Much Younger Then** [Dandelion]

This tape now appears on *The 50th Anniversary Collection 1963.*

Town Hall 1963

April 12, 1963

Ramblin' Down Through the World
Bob Dylan's Dream
Talkin' New York
Ballad of Hollis Brown
Walls of Redwing
All Over You
Talkin' John Birch
Boots of Spanish Leather
Hero Blues
Blowin' in the Wind
John Brown
Tomorrow is a Long Time
A Hard Rain's A-Gonna Fall
Dusty Old Fairgrounds
Who Killed Davey Moore
Seven Curses
Highway 51
Pretty Peggy-O
New Orleans Rag
Don't Think Twice
Hiding Too Long
With God on Our Side
Masters of War
Last Thoughts on Woody Guthrie

This concert is one of the best representations of the classic "protest" Dylan in concert at the peak of his form. The sound on most tapes is excellent because this concert was recorded by Columbia for a possible live album. In fact, several of the songs on this tape were selected for inclusion on the official (but unreleased) *Bob Dylan In Concert*. Still another song, "Tomorrow Is a Long Time", was really and truly released on *Greatest Hits Volume II* in 1971.

Individually the songs have their ups and downs, but my absolute favorite has to be, get ready, "Walls of Redwing"! This song is much maligned or dismissed as bland and uninvolving, but I have to disagree. The song lives for me and never fails to leave me with a feeling of remorse, pity, and anger. This chilling song, about a boy's reformatory, has a very disturbing final verse that suggests that we will all pay dearly for the cruelty of a few over-zealous disciplinarians. And he says this with an offhand non-preachy tone that is remarkable in its maturity. Dylan's introduction to this song is very humorous - "Redwing is a reform school. They don't have no high-school cheerleaders, though...", or something to that effect.

The other rare songs are a treat too: "Dusty Old Fairgrounds" has excellent flowing lyrics and strong vivid imagery. "New Orleans Rag" and "Hero Blues" are both pretty funny. The weaker songs are "Last Thoughts On Woody Guthrie" (not really a song at all, but a recitation of a labored poem), "John Brown" (uses a sledgehammer instead of a scalpel), "Who Killed Davey Moore" (one of Dylan's worst songs), and "Ramblin' Down Through the World" (really just a throwaway introductory song to show off Bob's harmonica).

This tape is strongly recommended and readily available on a number of bootlegs. For years it was in circulation only in incomplete form, but with the release of *The 50th Anniversary Collection 1963*, the entire concert came to light.

CDs:

- **Bob Dylan In Concert**
- **Oldies But Goldies...Live**

LPs:

- **While the Establishment Burns** (incomplete)
- **Zimmerman - Looking Back** (really the same as the above)
- **Are You Now Or Have You Ever Been** (bootleg of the official **Bob Dylan In Concert** album)
- **Ten Of Swords** (contains a couple of songs)

Second MacKenzie Tape

April 12, 1963

Instrumental
See That My Grave Is Kept Clean
Ballad Of Donald White
A Hard Rain's A-Gonna Fall
Instrumental
James Alley Blues (Times Ain't What They Used To Be)
I Rode Out One Morning
Instrumental
Don't Think Twice, It's All Right
Instrumental
Long Time Gone
Only A Hobo
House Of The Risin' Sun
Instrumental
Cocaine (instrumental)

The second MacKenzie tape is more interesting than the first because by the time of this recording Dylan was already an established star. In fact, this tape (or most of it anyway) was made the very afternoon of the famous Town Hall concert.

Like the first MacKenzie tape, the sound quality is dismal, but since it contains a few rarities like "I Rode Out One Morning" and "Long Time Gone", it's worth seeking out. The setting is informal and the performances offhand and relaxed. Some of the material at the beginning of the tape could possibly be from an earlier session.

CDs:

- **I Was So Much Younger Then** [Dandelion]

Five songs from this tape appear on the Sony semi-official collection *The 50th Anniversary Collection 1963* released in November 2013.

The Bear Club

April 25, 1963

Honey Just Allow Me One More Chance
Talkin' John Birch Society Blues
Bob Dylan's Dream
Ballad Of Hollis Brown
Talkin' World War III Blues
A Hard Rain's A-Gonna Fall
With God On Our Side (incomplete)

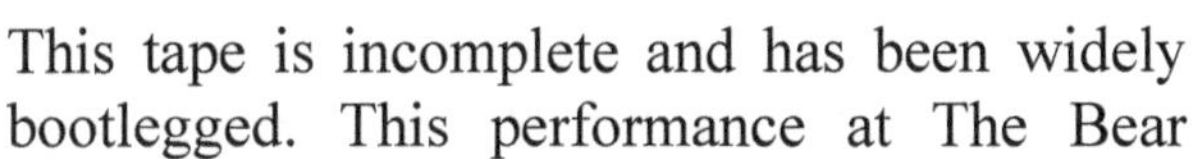

This tape is incomplete and has been widely bootlegged. This performance at The Bear Club in Chicago is a good example of Dylan's live appearances during his so-called "protest" period. The sound is decent and the performances good natured and full of humor. His fame was starting to grow as a result of his topical songs and the song list here pretty much reflects that: "Talkin' John Birch" and "Talkin' World War III" reflecting the comical aspects of the protest style, and "Hard Rain" and "With God On Our Side" taking on a more serious tone. Dylan also gets in one of his more personal songs – "Bob Dylan's Dream". It's a shame the rest of this show isn't available.

CDs:

- **The Bear**

This tape now appears on *The 50th Anniversary Collection 1963.*

Studs Terkel's Wax Museum

WFMT-Radio, Chicago. April 26, 1963

Farewell
A Hard Rain's A-Gonna Fall
Bob Dylan's Dream
Boots Of Spanish Leather
John Brown
Who Killed Davey Moore?
Blowin' In The Wind

The date of this radio broadcast is in question. Krogsgaard says April 25, the same date as The Bear concert, and Dundas says May 3. There is a reference in this broadcast tape to the show Dylan is to give that night at The Bear, which is why Dundas also attributes that tape to May 3 as well. Either way, this is an excellent quality tape from an hour-long FM broadcast, featuring a lengthy (and somewhat fawning) interview by the Pulitzer Prize winning journalist Studs Terkel. Terkel has little idea who Dylan is and is somewhat kindly patronizing. He is clearly impressed with the seven songs he hears Bob perform, and these performances are typically faultless.

CDs:

- **Studs Terkel's Wax Museum** [Yellow Dog]
- **Before the Flood and After the Fire** [Luna Records]

This tape now appears on *The 50th Anniversary Collection 1963* and the date given is April 26, 1963, so that is what I am going with.

Greenwood Mississippi Rally
July 6, 1963

Only A Pawn In Their Game

This is just a fragment. Dylan plays "Only a Pawn in Their Game" at Silas Magee's Farm in Greenwood, Mississippi, as part of a civil rights rally in the Deep South. A filmed excerpt shows up in the film *Don't Look Back*. Not much to say. Dylan looks and sounds earnest and looks both younger and older than his years. In fact, he looks very much as he does on the cover of *The Times They Are A-Changin'*, with his short hair and work shirt. The performance is okay, if a little plain and plodding. About two-minutes long.

CDs and LPs: none that I know of.

Appears in the film *Don't Look Back*, which is available on VHS and DVD.

Newport Folk Festival 1963

July 26-28, 1963

Blowin' In the Wind (July 26)
We Shall Overcome (July 26)
Ye Playboys and Playgirls (July 27)
With God On Our Side (July 28)

The first two songs appear on the official Vanguard album *Evening Concerts At Newport, Vol 1*, and the last two songs appear on the official Vanguard album *Newport Broadside*. Other artists are featured on the same albums and all come from the Newport Folk Festival 1963. The theme of the second album was "topical songs", another term for protest songs. Some of the other people on this album include Phil Ochs and Jack Elliot.

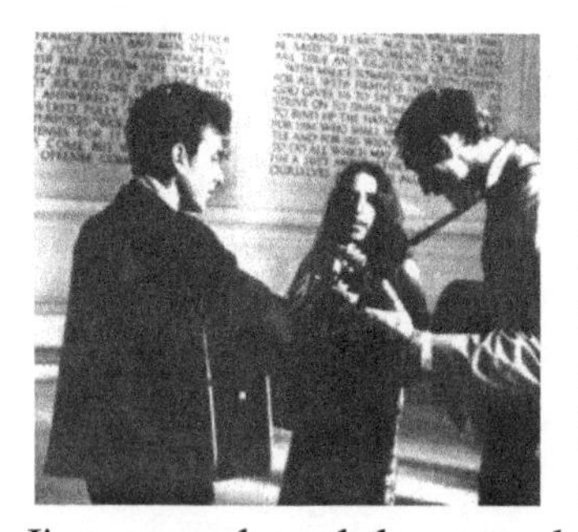

The first two songs are sung along with Peter, Paul & Mary, Joan Baez, The Freedom Singers, Pete Seeger and Theo Bikel. There's not much to say about them, other than they're just what you'd expect and not much in the way of interesting Dylan content. The second album is the more interesting of the two. I've never heard the complete Dylan set (or sets) from this festival, so I have no idea what the rest of it sounded like, but these two songs are unusual for an official Dylan release because they are both duets with giants of the folk world. “Ye Playboys and Playgirls” is sung with Pete Seeger, who tries to lead the audience in a sing-along ("You can all sing along with this song because only one line in each verse changes"), but really this song is much more clever than that and is very compelling in its simplicity. The artist is telling us that he won't be a slave to fashion, bigotry, or decadence. The song form is no doubt based on something much older, but I'm not sure where it came from. The form is simply this: "Ye Playboys and Playgirls ain't gonna run my world...not now or no other time". The same is said for fallout shelter sellers, Jim Crow laws, lynch mobs, etc. The usual anti-racist stuff, but given here a grimness that's hard to put my finger on. The feeling I get is that for all his defiance, it will all come to nothing. There is no joy in opposing oppression, only weariness. The other song is "With God On Our Side" with Joan Baez. This version is pretty unbearable in my opinion - too plodding and monotonous. Plus Joan's voice starts to irritate after a while. It would have been better if Dylan had sung it alone.

So, really one worthwhile performance – "Ye Playboys and Playgirls", a pretty rare song in itself and never officially released except for this live duet.

LPs:

- **Evening Concerts At Newport, Vol 1** (Vanguard Records - official release)
- **Newport Broadside** (Vanguard Records - official release)

Songs of Freedom
July 30,1963

Blowin' In The Wind
Only A Pawn In Their Game

Dylan sings two songs on this TV show broadcast August 26, 1963 on WNEW-TV, New York City. Quality and performance okay, nothing more. Not essential, but a must for collectors of early Dylan.

Appears on *The 50th Anniversary Collection 1963.*

Forest Hills 1963

August 17, 1963

Troubled and I Don't Know Why
Blowin' in the Wind

Only two songs show up on this excellent sounding tape, and unfortunately one of them ("Blowin' in the Wind") is cut off. Joan Baez sings on both, so it could be that these songs come from Joan's set rather than Bob's. Anybody know for sure? Anyway, "Troubled and I Don't Know Why" shows up here in the only version that I know of. It's not a bad song, although a little light as Dylan protest circa 1963 goes. The song is full of humor and shares some of the same feeling of alienation as on "Ye Playboys and Playgirls", except that the mood here is joyous rather than somber. Well worth hearing.

CDs:

- "Troubled and I Don't Know Why" shows up on the Joan Baez boxed set

March on Washington
August 28, 1963

When The Ship Comes In
Only A Pawn In Their Game
Keep Your Eyes On The Prize

On August 28, 1963, Dylan participated in one of the seminal civil rights events of the 1960s: the March on Washington, culminating in a huge gathering at the Lincoln Memorial in Washington DC, the highlight of which was the famous "I have a dream" speech by Martin Luther King. Dylan's performance is captured in part on the album *We Shall Overcome* on the Folkways label, released in 1964. Dylan's contribution to the album consists of two verses of "Only a Pawn In Their Game" and backup vocal (along with Joan Baez) on "Keep Your Eyes on the Prize", performed by Len Chandler. Quality is excellent, since it's an official PA recording, but the speeches that are faded in and out of the music are distracting, but then the purpose of the album is not to present music but to present an historical document.

LPs:

- **We Shall Overcome** (official release - out of print)

The first two songs appear on *The 50th Anniversary Collection 1963.*

Carnegie Hall 1963

October 26, 1963

The Times They Are A-Changin'
The Ballad Of Hollis Brown
Who Killed Davey Moore
Boots Of Spanish Leather
Talkin' John Birch Society Blues
Lay Down Your Weary Tune
Blowin' In The Wind
Percy's Song
Seven Curses
Walls Of Red Wing
North Country Blues
A Hard Rain's A-Gonna Fall
Talkin' World War III Blues
Don't Think Twice
With God On Our Side
Only A Pawn In Their Game
Masters Of War
The Lonesome Death Of Hattie Carroll
When the Ship Comes In

Five of these songs, along with some selections from the April 12 Town Hall concert of the same year, were part of the soon-to-be officially released live album *Bob Dylan In Concert*. The album was never released but a test pressing apparently made the rounds and is now heavily bootlegged. With the exception of "When the Ship Comes In", all of the songs on the projected album were unreleased and these songs, except for "Who Killed Davey Moore" were the best of the lot. Some songs from this concert are now available on *The 50th Anniversary Collection 1963*, but the songs that were slated for the unreleased live album are:

Lay Down Your Weary Tune
When the Ship Comes In
Who Killed Davey Moore
Percy's Song
Seven Curses

“Lay Down Your Weary Tune” is one of the best songs Dylan ever wrote. It's a shame this live album didn't come out so that more people could have had the opportunity to appreciate this song. Same with “Percy's Song”. Instead, the public had to wait until 1985 to hear these songs, although in studio form rather than the live versions heard here. The studio version of “Seven Curses” was only recently released on *The Bootleg Series*, but I think this live version is the best I've heard.

Sound quality is excellent.

Note: Columbia issued a special promo 6-song sampler from what could likely be a future Bootleg Series release of the entire concert. That release did not occur, but, as previously stated, some songs showed up on the 50th Anniversary semi-official release in 2013. Perhaps as a result of the possible official *Bootleg Series* release of the entire concert it came into circulation in full and now appears on the boot *Unraveled Tales*.

CDs:

- **Live at Carnegie Hall 1963** [Columbia] (promo release)
- **Bob Dylan In Concert** (also includes **Town Hall 4/12/63**)
- **Talking Too Much** (the **Bob Dylan In Concert** unreleased album)
- **Unraveled Tales**

LPs:

- **Are You Now Or Have You Ever Been? (His Gotham Ingres)** - live bootleg of the test pressing for **Bob Dylan In Concert**. Contains the five songs mentioned above plus the **Town Hall** songs that complete the live album.
- **Ten Of Swords**

The 50th Anniversary Collection 1963 contains the following songs from this concert:

Blowin' in the Wind
Percy's Song
Seven Curses
Walls of Red Wing
Talkin' World War III Blues
Don't Think Twice, It's All Right
Only a Pawn in Their Game
Masters of War
The Lonesome Death of Hattie Carroll

Witmark Demos

Late 1962 thru mid 1964

[June 62]
Blowin' in the Wind

[November 62]
Long Ago Far Away

[December 62]
A Hard Rain's A-Gonna Fall
Baby I'm in the Mood
Ballad of Hollis Brown
The Death of Emmett Till
Let Me Die in My Footsteps
Quit Your Lowdown Ways
Tomorrow is a Long Time

[late winter 63]
All Over You
Bound to Lose, Bound to Win
I'd Hate to Be You On That Dreadful Day
Talkin' John Birch Society Blues

[March 63]
Don't Think Twice
Long Time Gone
Masters of War
Oxford Town
Walking Down the Line

[April 63]
Bob Dylan's Blues
Bob Dylan's Dream
Boots of Spanish Leather
I Shall be Free

[May 63]
Girl from the North Country

Hero Blues
Seven Curses

[August 63]
Ain't Gonna Grieve
Gypsy Lou
John Brown
Only a Hobo
Watcha Gonna Do

[September 63]
Times They Are A-Changin'
When the Ship Comes In

[December 63]
Farewell
Paths of Victory

[January 64]
Baby Let Me Follow You Down
Guess I'm Doing Fine

[June 64]
I'll Keep it With Mine
Mama You Been on My Mind (guitar)
Mama You Been on My Mind (piano)
Mr. Tambourine Man

This is a large and impressive body of studio work that took place over the course of a couple of years. The purpose of these sessions was to record demos for Witmark Publishing of songs that other artists might be interested in performing. Some of these songs were later released by Dylan, but not the versions here. The most famous of these include "Blowin' In the Wind", "Mr. Tambourine Man", "Hard Rain", etc. Others were recorded at later CBS album sessions but not released, such as "Tomorrow Is a Long Time", "Farewell", "Seven Curses", etc. Then there are the more obscure songs: "Long Ago, Far Away", "Guess I'm Doing Fine", "Bound To Lose", "Ain't Gonna Grieve". It's easy to see why these more obscure songs remain obscure. They just weren't that good. Of the more familiar songs that appear here, I'm convinced that these sound every bit as good, if not better, than the officially released versions. Plus there are some real unusual things here, such as piano demos of "Mr. Tambourine Man", "When the Ship Comes In", "Mama You Been On My Mind", and "The Times They Are A-Changin'", among others.

This tape, along with the Minnesota Hotel tape and the second Gaslight tape, form most of the core of the consistently great body of work that Dylan gave us early in his career. Some of this material has already appeared on *The Bootleg Series*, and the complete collection has been released on *The Bootleg Series Volume 9: The Witmark Demos 1962-1964*.

CDs:

- **The Bootleg Series** (official album)
- **The Witmark Years** [Capricorn]
- **Witmark Demos** [Off Beat]
- **The Bootleg Series Volume 9: The Witmark Demos 1962-1964** (official album)

LPs:

- **Ten of Swords**
- **The Demo Tapes**
- **Poems In Naked Wonder**
- **Ceremonies of the Horsemen**

The entire Witmark Demos now appear officially on *The Bootleg Series Volume 9: The Witmark Demos 1962-1964*.

Times They Are A-Changin' Sessions

August and October 1963
Released January 1964

[August]

Ballad of Hollis Brown (released)
Boots of Spanish Leather (released)
Suze (*The Bootleg Series*)
North Country Blues (released)
One Too Many Mornings (released)
Only a Hobo (*The Bootleg Series*)
Only a Pawn in Their Game (released)
Paths of Victory (*The Bootleg Series*)
Percy's Song (*Biograph*)
Seven Curses (*The Bootleg Series*)
Walls of Redwing (*The Bootleg Series*)
With God on Our Side (released)
Farewell

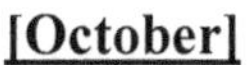
[October]

Eternal Circle (1)
Eternal Circle (2; *The Bootleg Series*)
Lay Down Your Weary Tune (*Biograph*)
Lonesome Death of Hattie Carroll (released)
Restless Farewell (released)
The Times They Are A-Changin' (released)
When the Ship Comes In (released)
Moonshiner (*The Bootleg Series*)
East Laredo Blues
Bob Dylan's New Orleans Rag (1)
Bob Dylan's New Orleans Rag (2; *The Bootleg Series*)
That's Alright Mama
Sally Free And Easy
Hero Blues

Classic classic stuff. *The Times They Are A-Changin'* album is, for my money, the best of the first four acoustic albums. Dylan sounds the surest, the songs are topical without being too heavy-handed, and the production is consistent and top notch throughout.

People may have noticed how serious the album sounds, and this is probably the reason many people consider it to be one of his lesser albums. From the session listing above, it's pretty obvious that this was intended all along because hardly any of the songs performed at the sessions are of a humorous nature, and those that are are still rendered in a somber manner. Check out “The Eternal Circle” for an example of how this is done. Even though the lyrics are funny (singer trying to rush to the end of his long long song so he can go talk to a female admirer in the audience), the delivery is sad in a way ("the song it was long and it was far from the end", etc.). Then there's a couple of joyful anthems (“Paths of Victory” and “When the Ship Comes In”) that are serious enough lyrically but done in a happy style. The effect is still somber nonetheless. Finally, there's the famous “Cough Song” (which we now know by its true title “Suze”) that doesn't fit in at all with anything else done at the session. I think it was just Dylan fooling around between takes. No apparent attempt was made to actually finish the song.

I really love this album, but just as good as the songs on the released version are all the tracks that never made it to the final release. The best of these are “Only a Hobo”, “Walls of Redwing”, “Seven Curses”, and the two that did eventually see official release: “Percy's Song” and “Lay Down Your Weary Tune”. None of these songs would have felt out of place on the album. It's interesting to note that with the release of *The Bootleg Series*, most of the material recorded at these sessions is now available.

Sound quality for the official album is of course excellent. The outtakes have been heavily bootlegged and often show up in sound equal to that of the official album. The best I've heard yet are on the *Ten of Swords* boot.

CDs:

- **The Times They Are A-Changin'** (official release)
- **Biograph**
- **The Bootleg Series Volume 1**

LPs:

- **The Times They Are A-Changin'** (official release)
- **Ten of Swords**
- **VD Waltz**
- **Talkin' John Birch Society**
- **Stealin'**
- **Seems Like a Freeze-Out**
- **Great White Wonder**

The following songs appear on *The 50th Anniversary Collection 1963:*

Eternal Circle
Percy's Song
That's Alright Mama
Hero Blues
East Laredo Blues
Bob Dylan's New Orleans Rag

Quest TV Show

February 1, 1964 (broadcast March, 1964)

The Times They Are A-Changin'
Talkin' World War III Blues
Lonesome Death of Hattie Carroll
Girl From the North Country
A Hard Rain's A-Gonna Fall
Restless Farewell

This soundtrack from the Canadian TV show sounds pretty good to me musically. Others disagree and feel the performance is sterile and lackluster. The video portion of the show is hilarious - Dylan standing stiffly in the foreground singing while hayseed types lounge around in the background. Maybe not seeing the visuals is a great advantage to enjoying this tape. Anyway, I find the renditions of these songs to be very satisfactory.

Nothing very unusual here except for a rare live version of "Restless Farewell". The rest are fine but I think the casual Dylan fan could live without this tape. The sound is decent enough but the tape I've heard is nowhere near as good as the Carnegie Hall '63 or the Town Hall '63, for instance. The complete video is not commercially available.

P.S. A brief portion of this show was seen during the John Hammond *American Masters* profile on PBS.

Included on *The 50th Anniversary Collection 1964.*

Steve Allen Show
February 25, 1964

The Lonesome Death of Hattie Carroll

This is another of Dylan's rare television appearances, this time on the Steve Allen show, which was also the showcase for such offbeat talents as Lenny Bruce, Jack Kerouac, and Elvis Presley (!). In the 1950s Steve Allen had a reputation for hip that attracted such unusual folks as those above (although we all know what happened to Presley) and an appearance on Allen's show was considered to be a real coup.

This tape consists of Allen introducing Dylan by reading a little from the back of the Times album while piano mood music plays in the background. Allen proceeds to gush a little about Dylan before he comes on to sing “Hattie Carroll”. Afterwards there is a short chat and Allen tries to get the reluctant Dylan to open up a little, but Bob remains distant throughout. Dylan's rendition of “Hattie Carroll” is merely okay.

Robert Shelton's Dylan bio *No Direction Home* quotes Steve Allen as confessing that he wasn't very impressed with Dylan and failed to see how he could ever have a future in show business because of his unprofessional attitude.

CDs:

- **I Was So Much Younger Then** [Dandelion]

This performance appears on *The 50th Anniversary Collection 1964.*

Eric Von Schmidt's Home -- Sarasota, Florida
May 1964

Bob And Eric Blues #1
Black Betty
Come All You Fair And Tender Ladies
Florida Woman
Johnny Cuckoo
Money Honey
More And More
Mr. Tambourine Man
Suzie Q
Harmonica Duet
Glory Glory
Dr. Strangelove Blues
Stoned On The Mountain
Stoned On The Mountain
Walkin' Down The Line
Joshua Gone Barbados

I understand that John Bauldie knew of the existence of this tape and reportedly was able to listen to it, but it was not in circulation until it showed up on the *50th Anniversary Collection 1964*. The sound is excellent, as are the performances. Some of them are sung only by Eric Von Schmidt and others only by Dylan. Some are duets, but all feature Bob on guitar or harmonica. I'm not sure of the circumstances behind this tape, but it sounds like they were having a lot of fun.

There are a lot more rock & roll type numbers than you would expect from 1964, indicating the direction that Dylan would be taking in the next couple of years. Of special interest is the earliest known appearance of "Mr. Tambourine Man" with Eric Von Schmidt on harmonica. Other highlights include Bob singing "More and More" by Web Pierce and Merle Kilgore while Eric Plays harmonica. "Dr. Strangelove Blues" is an Eric Von Schmidt original, performed as a duet, and seems to be improvised for the most part. “Stoned on the Mountain” is another improvisation with two attempts.

Of special interest is “Joshua Gone Barbados“ -- the same song that Dylan covered on the Basement Tapes. This version is sung by Von Schmidt with Dylan mostly on harmonica.

All in all, a fun party tape that is well worth seeking out. It appears on *The 50th Anniversary Collection 1964.*

Didsbury Tape, ATV Manchester, England
May 14, 1964

Don't Think Twice

This recently discovered tape is one of two songs performed by Dylan for a TV show in England called *Hallelujah*, broadcast on the ATV network. The other song, which unfortunately didn't survive, was a live debut of “Chimes of Freedom”. For some reason, the person who managed to preserve Dylan's performance on tape wound up erasing “Chimes of Freedom”, which is a tragedy. Still, we're left with an energetic and amazing version of “Don't Think Twice”.

According to firsthand reports, Dylan and manager Albert Grossman showed up at the television studio and refused to do any rehearsal. A very stoned Bob then went out before the cameras soon afterward and proceeded to rip off the version of “Don't Think Twice” and followed it up with the lost version of “Chimes of Freedom” that we may never get to hear. For years the tape went unheard, and in fact the performance itself was little known, until recently the tape surfaced.

Appears on *The 50th Anniversary Collection 1964*

Another Side Sessions

June 9, 1964
Released August 1964

Denise
It Ain't Me, Babe
To Ramona
Spanish Harlem Incident
Last Thoughts On Woody Guthrie
I Don't Believe You
Chimes of Freedom
Motorpsycho Nitemare
Mr. Tambourine Man
All I Really Want To Do
Black Crow Blues
I Shall Be Free No. 10
Mama, You Been On My Mind
My Back Pages

The songs for this album were supposed to have been recorded during one long session on June 9, 1964. Legend has it that Dylan was fortified with a bottle or two of wine during the sessions. The looseness of many of the tracks seems to testify to this story. Whatever the reason, I find this session to be extremely enjoyable and the resulting album one of his best.

At one point it was believed that the song "California" was recorded at these sessions, since the piano seems to match "Black Crow Blues", and it was also assumed that "I'll Keep It With Mine" was recorded at these sessions as well, but it turns out that both were recorded for the *Bringing It All Back Home* album instead.

The recent discovery of the Emmett Grogan acetates has also uncovered a previously unheard alternate version of "I Shall Be Free No. 10", although fragmentary and eventually edited together with other incomplete takes of the same song to produce the final released version. The *Highway 61 Interactive* CD presents yet another previously unheard version of the same song. The real jewel of the Grogan acetates, however, is the appearance of "Mr. Tambourine Man" with Jack Elliott singing harmony on the chorus. This was the version used as a demo by the Byrds. The reason why it doesn't appear on the album was because it was felt that Elliott's vocal wasn't strong enough. It did eventually appear on the first *Bootleg Series* and a different take appears on *The 50th Anniversary Collection 1964.*

Sound is excellent - studio quality.

CDs:

- **Another Side of Bob Dylan** (official album)
- **The Emmett Grogan Acetates**
- **The Bootleg Series** ("Mama You Been On My Mind")

LPs:

- **Ten Of Swords**
- **GWW - Talkin' John Birch**
- **GWW - Seems Like a Freeze-Out**
- **Stealin'**
- **Let Me Die In My Footsteps**

The following songs are now available as part of *The 50th Anniversary Collection 1964:*

Denise
It Ain't Me Babe (take 1)
Spanish Harlem Incident (take 3)
Ballad In Plain D (take 2)
I Don't Believe You (takes 1 & 2)
Chimes Of Freedom (takes 1 & 3)
Mr. Tambourine Man (take 2)
Black Crow Blues (takes 1 & 2)
I Shall Be Free #10 (takes 1, 2, 3, & 4)

Newport Folk Festival 1964
July 26, 1964

All I Really Want To Do
To Ramona
Mr. Tambourine Man
Chimes of Freedom

This is a newly circulating tape, some of which has been available for some time. "All I Really Want To Do" has been available as part of the *Emmett Grogan Acetates*. "Mr. Tambourine Man" recently showed up on the *Genuine Bootleg Series Take Two* set. But "To Ramona" and "Chimes of Freedom" are new. This is one of the very few live versions of "Chimes of Freedom" available from the 1960s, and it's a great version. Dylan sings this song, and the others, with great confidence. He introduces "To Ramona" by saying "This song is called To Ramona. It's just a name". He announces "Mr. Tambourine Man" as being "by request".

CDs:

- **@ Newport 1965** (contains both Newport '64 and '65)

Some songs appear on *The 50th Anniversary Collection 1964.*

Forest Hills 1964
August 8, 1964

Mama, You've Been On My Mind
It Ain't Me Babe
With God On Our Side

This tape comes from a Joan Baez concert in which she introduces Dylan by saying something to the effect "here's something for all the girls in the audience - Bobby Dylan". These duets are well received and typical of the Dylan/Baez team-ups that were common at the time. The sound quality is decent for a 1964 audience tape.

Appears on *The 50th Anniversary Collection 1964.*

Philadelphia Town Hall 1964

October 10, 1964

The Times They Are A-Changin'
Girl From The North Country
Who Killed Davey Moore?
Talkin' John Birch Paranoid Blues
To Ramona
Ballad Of Hollis Brown
Chimes Of Freedom
I Don't Believe You
It's Alright, Ma (I'm Only Bleeding)
Mr. Tambourine Man
Talking World War III Blues
A Hard Rain's A-Gonna Fall
Don't Think Twice, It's All Right
Only A Pawn In Their Game
With God On Our Side
It Ain't Me Babe
The Lonesome Death Of Hattie Carroll
All I Really Want To Do

A complete late 1964 concert in fair audience quality. The echo of the hall is evident and the sound is often shrill and harsh, but entirely listenable. The performances are adequate and may even be brilliant, but with the mediocre sound quality it's very hard to tell. A much better representation of this period of live Dylan is the famous Halloween Concert in October of the same year.

CDs:

- **The Session**

This concert appears on *The 50th Anniversary Collection 1964.*

New York Philharmonic Hall 1964

October 31, 1964

The Times They Are A-Changin'
Spanish Harlem Incident
Talkin' John Birch Society Blues
To Ramona
Who Killed Davey Moore
Gates of Eden
If You Gotta Go, Go Now
It's Alright Ma (I'm Only Bleeding)
I Don't Believe You
Mr. Tambourine Man
A Hard Rain's A-Gonna Fall
Talkin' World War III Blues
Don't Think Twice
The Lonesome Death of Hattie Carroll
Mama You Been on My Mind (w/Baez)
Silver Dagger (Baez w/Dylan harmonica)
With God on Our Side (w/Baez)
It Ain't Me Babe (w/Baez)
All I Really Want to Do

This is the famous Halloween concert that has been heavily bootlegged and is one of the four or five best Dylan concerts of all time. Finally, Columbia has seen the light and officially released this concert as part of *The Bootleg Series*.

A note about some of the CD releases: The 2 separately released Australian semi-legal CDs called *Mr. Tambourine Man* are the only bootleg versions available in the correct speed. The others, while sounding fine, are too fast. Try to find the Australian releases if you can.

CDs:

- **Live 1964 - The Bootleg Series Vol. 6** [Columbia] (official release)
- **All Hallow's Eve**
- **Halloween Masque**
- **Mr. Tambourine Man Volume 1** [Applehouse, Australia]
- **Mr. Tambourine Man Volume 2** [Applehouse, Australia]

LPs:

- **Halloween Masque** (by Blind Boy Grunt)

San Jose Civic Auditorium 1964

November 25, 1964

The Times They Are A-Changin'
Talkin' John Birch Paranoid Blues
To Ramona
Gates of Eden
If You Gotta Go, Go Now
It's Alright, Ma (I'm Only Bleeding)
Mr. Tambourine Man
A Hard Rain's A-Gonna Fall
Talking World War III Blues
Don't Think Twice, It's All Right

I grew up in San Jose, California, and I was twelve years old when this concert occurred, so I was too young to have appreciated it. In fact, I'm pretty sure I didn't know who Dylan was at the time, having only really heard of him in association with the hit single "Mr. Tambourine Man" by The Byrds in 1965. I have fond memories of the San Jose Civic Auditorium, having been to numerous concerts and sporting events there in the 1960s and 1970s. In fact, it still stands to this day and continues to present concerts featuring the San Jose Symphony and the occasional rock concert.

This is a fairly decent sounding audience tape marred somewhat by some talking over the performances here and there, but for the most part respectful and attentive, unlike many of the latter day audience tapes where the talkers couldn't seem to shut the fuck up. The talking here is really only concerned with the operation of the primitive tape player, so it can be excused.

This is a typically great concert from 1964 and well worth listening to. It appears on *The 50th Anniversary Collection 1964.*

Masonic Hall Memorial Auditorium, San Francisco 1964

November 27, 1964

Mama, You've Been On My Mind
It's Alright, Ma (I'm Only Bleeding)
Talking World War III Blues
Don't Think Twice, It's All Right
Gates Of Eden
If You Gotta Go, Go Now

An incomplete audience recording of what seems to have been a relaxed yet highly controlled Dylan concert. It's amazing how effortlessly he went from wistfully romantic to seriously somber to lighthearted good humor without ever jarring or confusing his audience. The sample of songs on this tape shows what a master showman he was in late 1964, perhaps the absolute peak of Dylan's folk performance years.

The duet with Joan Baez on "Mama, You've Been On My Mind" was a real crowd pleaser, but he could turn around and sing an absolutely devastating early version of "It's Alright, Ma" in a deliberate slowed down manner that leaves the audience breathless. Imagine how it must have seemed to hear these words for the very first time and realize that he was saying all the things everyone was probably thinking but could never put into words. Just an absolute magnificient performance. Followed on the tape by "Talkin' World War III Blues", the comic effect is enhanced by the very fact that it comes after an amazing song of utmost seriousness. When "Don't Think Twice" is sung in an exaggerated swagger, the crowd laughs not inappropriately at the fun of it all. Likewise "If You Gotta Go", which follows the amazing "Gates of Eden", gets huge laughs. Even "Gates of Eden" gets a few laughs at the grotesque images that must have seemed very novel at the time ("gray flannel dwarf", etc.). The rest of the concert must have been just as good.

Sound quality is pretty good for a 1964 audience tape. The crowd is quiet throughout (except for some hearty laughter), a true testament to Dylan's ability to keep an audience on the edge of its seat.

Now available on *The 50th Anniversary Collection 1964.*

Bringing it All Back Home Sessions

January 14-15, 1965
Released March 1965

Bob Dylan's 115th Dream (released)
Gates of Eden (released)
If You Gotta Go, Go Now (1; *The Bootleg Series*)
If You Gotta Go, Go Now (2; single August, 1967)
I'll Keep it With Mine (1; *Biograph*)
I'll Keep it With Mine (2; instrumental)
It's All Over Now, Baby Blue (1; released)
It's All Over Now Baby Blue (2)
It's Alright Ma (released)
Love Minus Zero/No Limit (1; released)
Love Minus Zero/No Limit (2)
Maggie's Farm (released)
Mr. Tambourine Man (released)
On the Road Again (released)
Outlaw Blues (released)
She Belongs to Me (1; released)
She Belongs to Me (2)
Subterranean Homesick Blues (released)
Farewell Angelina (*The Bootleg Series*)
Bending Down On My Stomick Lookin' West

There doesn't seem to be much in the way of unreleased material for this, Dylan's first "electric" album, but what we have here is pretty fantastic. There are two versions of "If You Gotta Go, Go Now", a song he had been performing acoustically for the previous year. This song is a natural for the electric format and it's a shame it isn't better known. The version released on *The Bootleg Series* is a lot looser than the single version (never released in the US) but just as much fun. The alternate versions of some of the more famous songs on this album are a real treat: "It's All Over Now Baby Blue", much better than the official version; "She Belongs To Me" and "Love Minus Zero", both looser and lacking drums, are in many ways better than the album versions.

"I'll Keep It With Mine" is the same version that appears on *Biograph*. "Farewell Angelina" took the world by surprise when it was released on *The Bootleg Series*, and really should have appeared on the album. "Bending Down On My Stomick Lookin' West" is probably only slightly better known under the title "You Don't Have To Do That". This song showed up on a compilation tape recently and can be found on the Spank bootleg *7 Years of Bad Luck*. It's only a fragment.

Bringing It All Back Home was a milestone for Dylan, but I still have some serious problems with this album. It seems too schizophrenic and lacking coherency. One side seems to be the "frivolous side" and the other the "serious side". Side two, the "serious side", almost seems as if it were made up from outtakes from the previous album, although this is obviously not so. Side one, the "frivolous side", is Dylan rocking out for the first time (ok, not really the first time if you consider that he used a backing group for the *Freewheelin'* sessions back in '62) and singing a lot of songs that don't appear to carry any deep hidden meanings (deceptively so, as it turns out). I would rather have the songs mixed up a little better so that the electric songs were interspersed with the acoustic, but I guess that's a small complaint compared to the greatness of the album.

CDs:

- **Bringing It All Back Home** (official release)
- **Biograph** (official release)
- **The Bootleg Series** (official release)
- **Thin Wild Mercury Music**
- **Seven Years of Bad Luck**

LPs:

- **Bringing It All Back Home** (official release)
- **Stealin'**
- **Ten Of Swords**
- **GWW - Talking John Birch**

POSTSCRIPT:

In 2015 Sony released volume 12 of The Bootleg Series, including a massive 18-disc Collector's Edition that contains everything recorded in the studio in 1965 and 1966. This includes the entire *Bringing It All Back Home* sessions, which brought forth many recordings that were previously unknown to the public, but mostly just alternate versions of already well known songs. The Collector's Edition also included the entire *Highway 61 Revisited* and *Blonde On Blonde* sessions. This edition was produced in a limited number and is no longer in print, but used copies can be obtained on eBay and other places. Two other editions still exist: a 6-CD Deluxe Edition and a 2-CD Best Of edition. In addition, for those who purchased the Collector's Edition, *Bob Dylan's 50th Anniversary Collection: 1965* was released. This set contains every known live tape from 1965 and was available as a download-only in MP3 format. Yet further to all of this amazing output, Sony released *The 1966 Live Recordings*, a 36-CD box set containing every known 1966 live recording. Most of these are professionally recorded along with every known audience tape. Again, the purpose behind all of these releases was to secure copyright protection due to the 50-year limit prior to having the recordings go into the public domain.

One of the big surprises from the *Bringing It All Back Home* sessions was a previously unknown full electric version of "Mr. Tambourine Man", although there were no finished takes.

Les Crane Show WABC TV, NYC
February 17, 1965

It's All Over Now, Baby Blue
It's Alright Ma, I'm Only Bleeding

This is probably Dylan's best TV appearance. It's certainly the most entertaining of all that I've heard. Not only does Dylan play two of his very best songs, and with Bruce Langhorne on electric guitar accompaniment, he also gets to talk extensively with host Les Crane and the rest of the panel. Much of this talk is hilarious as Dylan proceeds to put everyone on for the entire duration of his stay. It was clear that by this time Dylan had begun to perfect his guerilla interview techniques - turning questions back on the interviewer; poking and prodding; changing the subject, etc., and he seems to be having a good time needling Les Crane, whom he seems to like.

A little about Les Crane: he was a former DJ who became a sort of poor man's Johnny Carson and tried to compete directly with the Tonight Show and, like many others, failed to survive. Years later he had a hit single with *Desiderata* (go placidly amidst the noise...) and later had become a computer software entrepreneur as chairman of The Software Toolworks. He passed away in 2008.

About Dylan's performance: just great. "It's Alright Ma" is especially good with the electric guitar accompaniment by Bruce Langhorne. Very different from the album version which was acoustic guitar alone. "Baby Blue" has a completely different electric guitar feel to it. Dylan himself sings with great confidence and was really beginning to hit his stride here.

CDs:

- **1965 Revisited**
- **Before the Flood and After the Fire** [Luna Records]
- **I Was So Much Younger Then** [Dandelion]

This tape appears on *Bob Dylan's 50th Anniversary Collection: 1965.*

Santa Monica Civic Auditorium 1965

March 27, 1965

To Ramona
Gates of Eden
If You Gotta Go, Go Now
It's Alright Ma
Love Minus Zero/No Limit
Mr Tambourine Man
Don't Think Twice
With God on Our Side (cut)
She Belongs to Me
It Ain't Me Babe (cut)
Lonesome Death of Hattie Carroll (cut)
All I Really Want to Do
It's All Over Now, Baby Blue

This is a funny tape. In short it's a decent enough audience tape from the 1965 American tour, but it's marred by too much talking among the tapers and their tendency to turn the tape recorder off when they didn't want to keep certain songs. This was obviously someone's personal tape and I'm sure there was never any intention of having it get into circulation. Indeed, it's highly possible that the taper had no idea how sought after some of these tapes would be!

Good performances, almost identical to the much better sounding Manchester '65, and decent sound for a 1965 audience tape.

CDs:

- **Songs That Made Him Famous**
- **1965 Revisited**

Now available as part of *Bob Dylan's 50th Anniversary Collection: 1965*.

1965 Tour of England

In 1965, Dylan had reached the peak of his ability as a solo performer and his British tour, well documented in the excellent cinema vérité film *Don't Look Back*, was one of his best ever. With the release of *Bob Dylan's 50th Anniversary Collection: 1965,* which was provided as a bonus to purchasers of *The Cutting Edge: Collector's Edition* in 2015, all of the circulating shows from this tour were made available as a download in MP3 format only. Many of these shows were previously only circulating, if at all, in incomplete versions, mostly fragmentary snippets from the D.A. Pennebaker film.

The following is a list of shows currently in circulation. All of them are soundboards unless otherwise noted:

The Oval, City Hall, Sheffield - April 30, 1965
Odeon, Liverpool – May 1, 1965
De Montfort Hall, Leicester – May 2, 1965
Town Hall, Birmingham – May 5, 1965
City Hall, Newcastle – May 6, 1965
Free Trade Hall, Manchester – May 7, 1965
Royal Albert Hall, London – May 9, 1965 (audience)
Royal Albert Hall, London – May 10, 1965

The set list for all of the shows did not vary:

1. The Times They Are A-Changin'
2. To Ramona
3. Gates Of Eden
4. If You Gotta Go, Go Now
5. It's Alright, Ma (I'm Only Bleeding)
6. Love Minus Zero/No Limit
7. Mr. Tambourine Man
8. Talkin' World War III Blues
9. Don't Think Twice, It's All Right
10. With God On Our Side

11. She Belongs To Me
12. It Ain't Me, Babe
13. The Lonesome Death Of Hattie Carroll
14. All I Really Want To Do
15. It's All Over Now, Baby Blue

Of special interest:

Manchester Free Trade Hall
May 7, 1965

This great concert has long been available as a bootleg CD called *Now Ain't The Time For Your Tears*. Everything comes together perfectly here: the intimate vocals, the hypnotic acoustic guitar rhythms, the haunting lyrics, and the subtle humor - all adding up to a unique concert experience. At a time when The Beatles and the entire British invasion were influencing popular music, Dylan managed to hold an entire concert hall captivated with only an acoustic guitar and the powerful images from his timeless songs. Dylan was able to attract both the rock and roll fan and the more mature young adult who had not yet become accustomed to the full frontal rock assault. It's no coincidence that soon after this particular tour the British rock groups began to grow up a little. Witness The Beatles' *Rubber Soul*, The Rolling Stones' *Aftermath*, and The Kinks' *Face To Face* - all very mature rock albums emphasizing meaningful lyrics combined with "folk rock" instrumental backing. Some of the songs performed at this concert could be listened to as rock and roll: “If You Gotta Go”, “It Ain't Me Babe”, “Baby Blue”, etc. At the same time, Dylan's "protest" roots are fully displayed here as well: “Hattie Carroll”, “With God On Our Side”. Most important of all, his new surrealistic songs were showcased: “Gates of Eden”, “Mr. Tambourine Man”, “It's Alright Ma”. Each song moves effortlessly from one to the other without seeming incongruous in the least.

Since this is a PA recording, the sound is excellent. As 1965 performances go, this is good as it gets, which is very good indeed!

CDs:

- **Now Ain't the Time For Your Tears** [Swinging Pig & Wanted Man]

Levy's Recording Studio
London May 12, 1965

Miami Sales Message
If You Gotta Go, Go Now

This short tape was recorded in a studio in London during Dylan's 1965 tour of England, the same tour documented in the film *Don't Look Back*, and features members of John Mayall's Bluesbreakers, although apparently not with the participation of either John Mayall or Eric Clapton. Somebody is playing piano on "If You Gotta Go" but it's hard to tell if it's Dylan or Mayall. Anyway it's really nothing more than a fragment and it stops before it even gets going.

The apparent purpose of this session was to record a couple of Dylan promo spots. The "Miami Sales Message" is nothing more than Dylan in the studio improvising a short greeting to Columbia sales reps and says pretty much "thanks for selling so many of my records". Dylan argues a little bit with the session producer but finally manages to come up with a finished message of some kind. I have no idea whether or not this tape was ever actually used for the purpose intended. The short rendition of "If You Gotta Go" seems to have been for a radio spot. After a shaky start where there is much arguing (although it seems amiable) a slow version of the song is started and Dylan sings one verse. "Fade it out. Fade it out!" he yells to the control room. He doesn't seem to have been in a very good mood by this time.

This tape, though short, is pretty funny to listen to but I wouldn't consider it vital to anyone's collection. For completists only. Sound quality isn't too good either.

CDs:

- **Thin Wild Mercury Music**

LPs:

- **Ten of Swords** (sales message only)

Now available as part of *Bob Dylan's 50th Anniversary Collection: 1965.*

BBC broadcast 1965

June 1, 1965

Ballad of Hollis Brown
Mr. Tambourine Man
Gates of Eden
If You Gotta Go, Go Now
The Lonesome Death of Hattie Carroll
It Ain't Me Babe
Love Minus Zero/No Limit
One Too Many Mornings
Boots of Spanish Leather
It's Alright Ma, I'm Only Bleeding
She Belongs to Me
It's All Over Now, Baby Blue

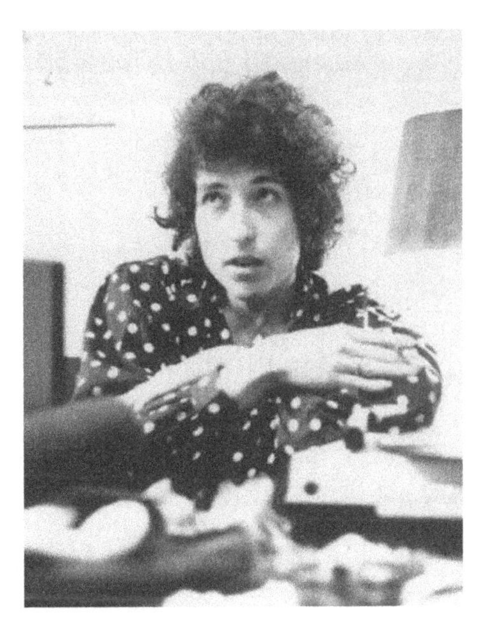

The first tape I heard of this 1965 British television broadcast sounded as if it were recorded with an open mike sitting right next to the TV speaker, and this was the recording that had been available for years as the 2-lp vinyl boot called *The BBC Broadcast*, but more recently a much improved recording has surfaced. It appears to come from an acetate, possibly direct from the BBC studios. Although there are crackles, the sound quality is still very good and well worth having.

Even though these performances were videotaped for the BBC, and were eventually broadcast in two separate showings, no video of either show is known to survive. Apparently the BBC simply reused their videotape after being broadcast and neglected to keep what turned out to be historic performances! The acetate is probably all that we're like to have.

What makes this tape so interesting is the choice of songs and the intimate manner in which he performs them. Of special interest: “One Too Many Mornings”, “Boots of Spanish Leather”, “It's Alright Ma”, and “Mr. Tambourine Man” - all great versions.

This tape is a must.

CDs:

- **The Circus Is In Town**
- **1965 Revisited**

LPs:

- **GWW - BBC Broadcast**

Now available on *Bob Dylan's 50th Anniversary Collection: 1965.*

Highway 61 Revisited sessions

June - August 1965
Released August 1965

Ballad of a Thin Man (released)
Barbed Wire Fence (1)
Barbed Wire Fence (2)
Can You Please Crawl Out Your Window (1)
Can You Please Crawl Out Your Window (2; single briefly available Sept '65)
Desolation Row (1)
Desolation Row (2;released)
From a Buick 6 (1;released, then withdrawn)
From a Buick 6 (2;released)
Highway 61 Revisited (released)
It Takes a Lot to Laugh, It Takes a Train to Cry (1)
It Takes a Lot to Laugh, It Takes a Train to Cry (2; released)
Just Like Tom Thumb's Blues (released)
Like A Rolling Stone (released)
Positively 4th Street (single, September 1965)
Queen Jane Approximately (released)
Tombstone Blues (released)

First the official album itself: A classic! There are at least three different versions of the album - the original mono, the original stereo (both mono and stereo versions have different mixes and song lengths in some cases), and the alternate version (both mono and stereo?) with "From a Buick 6" replaced by a different take (a version that is still supposed to be available in Japan). Whichever version you happen to have, this is one of the greatest rock & roll albums ever made. The backup band consisting of Al Kooper / Mike Bloomfield / Harvey Brooks / Paul

Griffin / Bobby Gregg still sounds vital today. There is such a great live-in-the-studio sound that has rarely been duplicated, even by Dylan himself, and has been copied by many. In fact the piano/organ/guitar sound of this album is *still* associated closely with the "Dylan sound", even though it may not have been entirely new at the time (The Hawks had been using this combination for years prior to hooking up with Dylan), and has been the musical basis for many bands inspired by this album (Procol Harum and Mott the Hoople, to name just two). Unlike the previous album, where the electric songs were thrown in for novelty's sake, the rock numbers here are serious, ominous, and joyful at the same time!

The unreleased (at the time this was originally written) songs are of course the most interesting. Let's take them one at a time:

Barbed Wire Fence - There are two known versions of this. The best known one has been around for a long time on such famous bootlegs as *Great White Wonder* (the original bootleg) and *Stealin'*, among others. No matter where I've heard this track it always changes tone and volume about midway through the song so that what starts out crisp and clear winds up sounding slightly muddy. The other, more rare version is very different. The copy I've heard is in stereo and has piano (sounds like Dylan playing) as the most prominent instrument. Bloomfield's wailing guitar can be heard in the background, but just barely. This is obviously just a run-through for the real thing. I'm hoping that version 1, the strongest take, will be released officially on the upcoming CD set because I'd really like to hear this song without the tonal change in the middle.

Can You Please Crawl Out Your Window - Once again there are two different versions floating about; one fairly well known and the other pretty obscure. Both versions sound very similar, but the more familiar one is definitely superior. In fact the better take was officially released by mistake under the title "Positively 4th Street" and quickly withdrawn. I was lucky enough to find a copy not too long ago when I bought what I thought was the common "Positively 4th Street" single. Shocked the shit out of me when "Crawl Out Your Window" came crashing out of my stereo instead! Those who have only heard this song on *Biograph* have been missing quite a lot and I hope this mistaken single version will find its way onto an official collection someday. By the way, contrary to popular belief that's neither an electric piano nor a xylophone being played - it's actually a celeste.

Desolation Row (version 1) - The song as it wound up on the album was recorded at a different session with different musicians and is the only "acoustic" song on the album. It's great but I prefer the earlier take recorded at the Kooper/Bloomfield sessions. This version is slightly slower and much more dramatic. It also features some interesting variations on the lyrics ("they're feeding Casanova the boiled guts of birds" rather than "to get him to feel more assured", for instance). No drums or keyboards; instead what we have is Dylan on acoustic guitar accompanied by Bloomfield on electric guitar and (probably) Harvey Brooks on electric bass. It's only a rehearsal and there may be other, more fully electric versions in existence.

From a Buick 6 (version 1) - This version is the weaker take (in my opinion) that found its way onto the official album for a brief period of time. Some of the lyrics are different, but not drastically so, and the entire musical feel is different. It starts out with harmonica and the lead guitar is more Muddy Waters than Chuck Berry.

It Takes a Lot To Laugh, It Takes a Train To Cry (version 1) - The same arrangement as performed at Newport '65, this features the full hard-rocking Kooper/Bloomfield sound ala "Tombstone Blues". This version is exciting, but I think it's one example of where the final released version is way better. The lyrics have wild variations and the original title of the song was "Phantom Engineer"!

Rough mixes for most of the "official" songs are also in circulation. These songs include "Like a Rolling Stone", "Positively 4th Street", "Tombstone Blues", "It Takes a Lot To Laugh" (version 2) as well as the alternate "Desolation Row" and the rarer take of "Crawl Out Your Window". The nice thing about these rough mixes is the opportunity to hear the endings without the fadeouts.

CDs:

- **Highway 61 Revisited** (official album)
- **Highway 61 Revisited Again** [Scorpio]
- **Thin Wild Mercury Music** [Spank]

LPs:

- **Great White Wonder**
- **Stealin'**
- **Ten of Swords**
- **Highway 61 Revisited Again** (shorter than the CD version)

POSTSCRIPT:

As previously noted, the entire *Highway 61* sessions are included in the *Bootleg Series Volume 12 Collector's Edition.* Among the many surprises is a fully electric version of "Desolation Row".

Newport Folk Festival 1965

July 25, 1965

Maggie's Farm
Like a Rolling Stone
It Takes a Lot to Laugh, It Takes a Train to Cry
It's All Over Now, Baby Blue
Mr. Tambourine Man

This is it. This is Dylan's very first electric public appearance. This was also the appearance that began a yearlong period of hostility between Dylan and his audience. According to most reports, Dylan was booed off the stage. According to Dylan himself, he had only intended to perform three songs anyway and the whole electric part of the set was impromptu. According to others (source: Robert Shelton's *No Direction Home*) Dylan was devastated by the audience's rejection of his new music and couldn't continue after the first three songs, and only came back onstage after much coaxing.

Contrary to popular belief, this isn't the Paul Butterfield Blues Band backing Dylan. It's Mike Bloomfield on electric guitar, Al Kooper on piano, Barry Goldberg on organ, Jerome Arnold on electric bass, and Sam Lay on drums. All but Kooper and Goldberg were members of the Butterfield band, so that is where the misconception comes from. The Butterfield band were also appearing at the festival, so it was natural that Dylan would suppose there would be nothing wrong with teaming up for a set.

"Maggie's Farm" and the rocking version of "It Takes a Lot To Laugh" are great but a little monotonous after awhile because of Bloomfield's similar guitar licks throughout, but the real highlight of the three song electric set is "Like a Rolling Stone", which had just been released as a single and was climbing the charts. This version is closer to the original recording than any other and comes off very good except for a few minor glitches with the organ part. The drums are very weird here, sounding more like a march than a rock song, and the ending just sort of peters out - but still a great version! After the electric set Dylan returns for excellent renditions of two of the best songs from the *Bringing It All Back Home* album. During "Mr. Tambourine Man" he asks the audience if anyone has an E harmonica and someone in the audience obliges by tossing one up on stage.

Excellent PA sound throughout, probably due to the fact that Dylan's set (among others) was being filmed for a documentary about the festival, eventually released as *Festival*. Brief portions of Dylan's set appear in the film.

CDs:

- **Live In Newport 1965**
- **Folk Rogue**

LPs:

- **Passed Over and Rolling Thunder**
- **St. Valentine's Day Massacre and More**

"It Takes a Lot To Laugh" appears on *Bob Dylan's 50th Anniversary Collection: 1965.*

Forest Hills 1965

August 28, 1965

She Belongs To Me
To Ramona
Gates Of Eden
Love Minus Zero/No Limit
Desolation Row
It's All Over Now, Baby Blue
Mr. Tambourine Man
Tombstone Blues
I Don't Believe You
From A Buick 6
Just Like Tom Thumb's Blues
Maggie's Farm
It Ain't Me Babe
Ballad Of A Thin Man
Like A Rolling Stone

I think this is Dylan's greatest concert. That's a pretty audacious thing to say, considering the vast body of live work that Dylan has presented to us throughout the years, but I really hear something special and truly magnificent in this, his first concert to feature a full electric set. It's a shame that there isn't a better tape of this event, but until an as yet undiscovered PA tape comes to light, this will have to do.

This show is legendary, and for anyone who doubts that 1965 audiences heaped great scorn on Bob Dylan and his electric crew, all they need to do is listen to this tape to hear the audience's point of view. There is so much hostility directed toward the stage that it's frightening. Coming as it does after the shocking Newport appearance with members of the Paul Butterfield Blues Band, the audience for the Forest Hills show pretty much knew what to expect, and the majority showed extreme displeasure during the electric half.

But first we have the acoustic set, which was very well received. The crowd was quiet and respectful for the 45-minute opening set, which followed a typical top-40 DJ introduction more appropriate for a Dave Clark Five concert than a Bob Dylan concert. This show featured the debut of "Desolation Row", from the *Highway 61* album that was yet to be released (only a few days away, in fact). It's a great performance and it went over very well with the crowd, who laughed appreciatively at the lyrics. It must have been amazing to sit there and hear a brand new masterpiece like "Desolation Row".

Photo © 1967 Daniel Kramer

After the well-received acoustic half came to an end with "Mr. Tambourine Man", the band set up for the second half. No doubt the crowd was gearing up for the hostility that was to follow. Another DJ (was it Murray the K?) introduces the electric set to tremendous catcalls and booing ("It's what's happening, baby"). The band consisted of Robbie Robertson on lead guitar, Levon Helm on drums, Harvey Brooks on bass, and Al Kooper on keyboards. It is essentially a marriage of the Highway 61 sound with the future Hawks sound of the 1966 tour, but it actually sounds exactly like neither. It's like no other Dylan concert we have on tape (or did have, until the recent discovery of the Hollywood Bowl concert from September 3). The electric half featured no less than the debut of four songs and a fifth ("Like a Rolling Stone") that had been released as a single a month before and played live at the Newport Festival soon after.

The crowd is so loud and belligerent at times that it becomes extremely hard to hear the music, but what can be heard is awesome. Levon lays down a muscular beat that drives the music forward and Robbie plays tough blues licks as only he can. Al Kooper pretty much plays the way only Al Kooper can, and is most effective on "Just Like Tom Thumb's Blues" and "Ballad of a Thin Man". The latter features one of Dylan's live tricks -- he vamps on the piano intro for several minutes until the crowd quiets down somewhat. The tape has most of this edited out, though. "Ballad of a Thin Man" is played very close to the album version, and by the time he's finished with it the crowd has for the most part come to realize that not only can they not stop Dylan from playing rock and roll, but that it's actually pretty damn good rock and roll too! They even clap and sing along with "Like a Rolling Stone", which to me sounds a little weak and (dare I say it?) bubblegummish. It doesn't help that Kooper attempts to play his trademark organ part on electric piano instead. It doesn't really work.

As previously mentioned, the tape is of poor quality. In fact, I think it's one of the worst sounding audience tapes I've ever heard. And yet it's one of the top four or five Dylan concert tapes of all time, and still what I consider to be his all time greatest concert. This was one of those moments where he stood on the edge of time and faced up to his place in history and found himself equal to the challenge. Had he retreated at this show into doing exactly what the audience wanted him to do, we would not be celebrating his career some 30+ years later.

CDs:

- **1965 Revisited**

Available on *Bob Dylan's 50th Anniversary Collection: 1965*, but unfortunately it's still a crummy audience tape after rumors of the existence of a soundboard tape.

Hollywood Bowl 1965
September 3, 1965

She Belongs To Me
To Ramona
Gates Of Eden
It's All Over Now Baby Blue
Desolation Row
Love Minus Zero/No Limit
Mr. Tambourine Man
Tombstone Blues
I Don't Believe You
Just Like Tom Thumb's Blues
From A Buick Six
Maggie's Farm
It Ain't Me Babe
Ballad Of A Thin Man
Like A Rolling Stone

Personnel:
Robbie Robertson (guitar)
Levon Helm (drums)
Al Kooper (piano)
Harvey Brooks (bass)

An amazing find, this nearly complete line recording documents the second of only two shows to feature the Robertson/Helm/Kooper/Brooks lineup, and the second ever Dylan concert to feature a full electric set. Like the Forest Hills concert six days earlier, this concert featured a full solo acoustic set, which was apparently well received, and a full electric set, the reception of which is hard to tell here because it's a soundboard recording and very little audience interaction can be heard. It seems likely, though, that there may have been some hostility, but probably less than at the previous concert. After all, this was an LA crowd, used to west coast folk-rock bands and possibly more open to new musical trends than east coast folk purists.

This tape first came into circulation on a CD-R (recordable CD) from Wild Wolf called *Western Electric*, which eliminated two songs so that it would fit on a single disc. The two missing songs were both from the electric set: "Tombstone Blues" and "It Ain't Me Babe". The more recent *We Had Known a Lion* from Vigotone presents the entire concert, except for the missing start of "Tombstone Blues". There is also a problem with the ending of "Mr. Tambourine Man" which appears to be the result of the original acetate or transcription disc sticking. On some tapes I have heard the sound just cuts off at that point, but on the Wild Wolf CD, there is a fade during the stick. These are the only detectable flaws in this otherwise excellent sounding soundboard tape.

As for the performance itself, it is very much like the Forest Hills concert, with wonderful versions of "Desolation Row", "Just Like Tom Thumb's Blues", and "Ballad of a Thin Man", but "Like a Rolling Stone" is just a mere shadow of the song it would become by the time it was performed during the last days of the 1966 tour. At times the keyboard playing is thin, especially on "Like a Rolling Stone". It really needed the power and imagination of Garth Hudson to make this song come alive.

I am unsure of the origin of this tape and how it came into circulation, but I suspect that it may have been in the vaults of radio station KRLA, or in the hands of a former employee, because the announcer at the end of the concert mentions that the show was presented by KRLA. It is unknown whether or not KRLA actually taped any of the shows they sponsored, but it does seem like a possibility.

CDs:

- **Western Electric** [Wild Wolf]
  Incomplete
- **Electric Black Nite Crash** [Junk]
  Incomplete
- **We Had Known a Lion** [Vigotone]
  Complete

Available on *Bob Dylan's 50th Anniversary Collection: 1965.*

Playboy Interview
Autumn 1965

There are two different versions of this interview. One is the real interview, which appears on this tape, and the other is a complete fantasy written by Bob after he disapproved of the way his words were edited for publication. That was the version that was published in Playboy. Both interviews are with Nat Hentoff.

The published interview is an incredible piece of guerilla theatre, and is likely one of the most surrealistic things you'll ever read in a mainstream magazine. The actual "real" interview is more serious and could have been great, but there's no telling what Playboy actually intended to publish. At any rate, Bob did not approve and set out to fool the magazine, with Hentoff's help, and provided something along the lines of what we would eventually see in *Tarantula*.

LPs and CDs: None that I know of, but no doubt the audio can be found on YouTube.

The Hawks Sessions
October thru December 1965, January 1966

Can You Please Crawl Out Your Window (1; fragment)
Can You Please Crawl Out Your Window (single November 1965)
I Wanna Be Your Lover
I Wanna Be Your Lover (*Biograph*)
Jet Pilot (*Biograph*)
Medicine Sunday (aka Midnight Train)
Number One
One of Us Must Know (single 1966; *Blonde on Blonde* 1966)
Visions of Johanna (1; aka Seems Like a Freeze-Out)
Visions of Johanna (2; aka Seems Like a Freeze-Out)
She's Your Lover Now (1; aka Just a Little Glass of Water)
She's Your Lover Now (2; aka Just a Little Glass of Water)

Until the release of *Planet Waves* in January 1974, the entire officially available recorded output of Bob Dylan and the Band (nee the Hawks) consisted of a mere ten songs, of which only two were studio recordings. This was a major loss considering the vast amount of material that actually existed:

1. The 1965 and 1966 studio sessions listed above. "Can You Please Crawl Out Your Window" and "One Of Us Must Know" were both released as singles and the latter was also released on *Blonde On Blonde* in 1966.
2. The entire 1966 world tour, practically all of which was professionally recorded. Only "Just Like Tom Thumb's Blues" from Liverpool was released (b-side of "I Want You").
3. The "basement tapes" which consisted of around five hours of (at the time) unreleased music, and probably much more yet to be discovered! None of this material appeared on any album until 1975.
4. The Woody Guthrie Memorial Concert at Carnegie Hall in 1968. All three songs performed at this show were released in 1970.
5. The Isle of Wight festival appearance in 1969. Four of these songs were released on *Self Portrait* in 1970.
6. A few miscellaneous surprise appearances at Band concerts, none of which have ever been released.

Until the release of *Masterpieces* in 1976 (Japan and Australia only) and *Biograph* in 1985, "Can You Please Crawl Out Your Window" remained out-of-print and very hard to find. *Biograph* not only included the above song, but it also contained two more songs from the 1965 Hawks sessions – “Jet Pilot” and “I Wanna Be Your Lover” (version two). With the release of *The Bootleg Series* in 1991, “She's Your Lover Now” was finally released, and recently “Medicine Sunday” showed up on the *Highway 61 Interactive* CD-ROM. Who knows what other surprises await us? [Note: refer to Krogsgaard's *The Recording Sessions* for more information on these sessions]

Actually, these 1965/1966 studio tracks were the first *Blonde On Blonde* sessions and give an idea of what the album would have sounded like if it had been done in its entirety with The Hawks instead of with the Nashville studio musicians. Would it have been a better album? I don't know, but it would have been very different! One of these songs did eventually wind up on the album and it doesn't sound out of place. According to Robert Shelton in *No Direction Home*, there was one mammoth 16-hour session that "yielded nothing". I don't know who decided that the material contained here represented "nothing", but somewhere along the line the decision was made to scrap plans for a Dylan/Hawks album in favor of the Nashville studio lineup. I don't regret that decision at all, because *Blonde On Blonde* is the greatest rock album of all time, but I think the finished Dylan/Hawks album would have been a pretty good album too.

The songs one by one:

Can You Please Crawl Out Your Window - A short fragment done in the slow style of the *Highway 61* version and the complete fast version, originally a single and now available on *Biograph*. The fragment of the slow version shows great promise and would have been great if finished. The fast version is of course a classic.

I Wanna Be Your Lover - the one on *Biograph* is great, but the alternate unreleased version is even better and contains some of the nastiest lead guitar Robbie Robertson ever played. It's a little annoying, however, to hear Rick Danko constantly blow the obvious chord changes. Great lines like "Rasputin, he's so dignified. He touched the back of her head and he died."

Jet Pilot - For a long time I had serious doubts as to whether it belongs on this list, but now it's pretty much proven to have come from these sessions, but to me it sounds like something left over from the *Highway 61* sessions. Not only do the tune and lyrics sound like an early version of "From a Buick 6", the instrumentation also sounds like Kooper/Bloomfield. Anyway, this is just a fragment, but what appears on bootlegs is slightly longer than what we have on *Biograph* - even though it's the same version.

Medicine Sunday - A great find and a great loss that a complete version won't be heard on the forthcoming CD set (but according to Krogsgaard's sessions notes, there wasn't a complete take of this song). This song, also known as "Midnight Train" (only because that phrase is mentioned in the first line), happens to be an early version of "Temporary Like Achilles". To my ears it would have been a vastly superior version, although (on the basis of one verse) lacking the humor of the later official version. This is probably the crux of what made these sessions get scrapped in favor of Nashville - this music with the Hawks is very somber, sort of like Procol Harum with Dylan as lead singer, if you can imagine what that would be like.

Number One - An instrumental. Was there ever a vocal track? The chord progression sounds too complicated to feature the standard Dylan-type vocal, but who knows? He might have been trying for a whole new thing here and then had to let it drop when the entire project moved to Nashville. Still a great track featuring the Hawks. Dylan apparently plays rhythm guitar.

One Of Us Must Know (Sooner Or Later) - The same track that was released as a single and later on *Blonde On Blonde*. The stereo mix on the album is slightly different than the mono single mix, but otherwise the tracks are exactly the same. Not really part of any bootleg tape, this is included on this list for completion only.

Seems Like a Freeze-Out - There are at least two versions known, and many more attempts that are not in circulation. The two that are in general circulation are a slow version and a brighter, faster version that sounds to me more like a Nashville outtake. As for the slow version, it's really incredible! Garth's organ really steals the show and Robbie's guitar is perfect. The real surprise here is the harpsichord, probably played by Richard Manuel. Dylan plays piano on this track. Contains the "nightingale's code" line. One of the real highlights of this tape!

She's Your Lover Now - Probably the absolute greatest thing Dylan's ever recorded, now officially available on *The Bootleg Series*. No other Dylan recording has as much emotional impact as this one does. It's only too bad that the song comes to a sudden halt midway through the final verse, which remains unpublished. There is another version of this song with piano only, and the final verse is complete. It wasn't until I heard the full last verse that I came to realize what happened with the Hawks take and why it just crashes to a halt - Dylan screwed up the line "now your mouth cries wolf..." (a great line in itself!) that should have been "now your eyes cry wolf while your mouth says 'I'm not scared of animals like you'".

All in all, this entire tape is absolutely essential to any Dylan collection. I think it's the best studio sessions he's ever done!

POSTSCRIPT:

Since writing this, it has been determined that some of the tracks mentioned in this article were performed by a combination of Hawks members and leftovers from the Highway 61 sessions, notably Al Kooper and Paul Griffin. Refer to the Krogsgaard's session info for more details on who played what.

Also, in reference to released Dylan/Band material, the entire encore set with Dylan is available on the expanded remaster of the Band's *Rock of Ages* live album from December 31, 1971.

CDs:

- **The Bootleg Series** (official album)
- **The Session**
- **Bob Dylan Live With The Band, Al Kooper And Mike Bloomfield**
- **Thin Wild Mercury Music**
- **The Lonesome Sparrow Sings**

LPs:

- **Seems Like a Freeze-Out**
- **Black Nite Crash**
- **Now Your Mouth Cries Whoops!**
- **Ten of Swords**
- **Barbed Wire Blues**
- Many others (one of the most heavily bootlegged tapes)

The complete sessions are available on *The Bootleg Series Volume 12 Collector's Edition*. There are many false takes and impromptu re-arrangements to the songs that reveal the extreme frustration that Dylan was having with the material and the players themselves. Most of the time, it's Dylan himself who manages to sabotage the sessions by constantly changing his approach to the song without letting the musicians know, but it was apparent that things were not going the way he wanted them to go. Moving the sessions to Nashville turned out to be a really great idea, and the sessions from that point on went very smoothly.

Allen Stone Interview 1965

This is a pretty good interview by Allen Stone, taking place in Detroit while Bob was in town with the Hawks getting ready to do a concert. Allen Stone asks some smart questions and is not overly obsequious as some DJs tended to be. He obviously was well aware of Dylan's music and expressed a genuine appreciation for what he was doing. Bob, for his part, is serious and does not try to punk the interviewer and gives intelligent answers. Levon Helm was still in the band at this point, as Bob names him along with the rest.

Bob sounds very tired and it's easy to see that he was heading toward nervous exhaustion, which would really manifest itself during the 1966 world tour. There are a lot of quotable moments on this tape, and I would recommend it for a view of what Bob's mind was like at that stage of his life. Essential.

LPs and CDs: None that I know of.

KQED Press Conference

San Francisco, CA 12/3/65

In December 1965, Bob Dylan and the Hawks gave a series of West Coast performances, the most well known of which was the Berkeley concert from 12/4/65 (see the next section for more information on this), and this press conference occurred the night before. It was organized by noted journalist Ralph J. Gleason, who was then writing for the San Francisco Chronicle. For years, the videotape of this broadcast was hard to find because it was in Gleason's personal possession until his death in 1975. I remember seeing it (and videotaping it) when it was broadcast on KQED-TV in San Francisco sometime in the late '70s. It was quite a find.

Although the entire press conference was amusing to watch, there was really no important information given by Bob (what would you expect!) and he basically punks all the reporters in the room with surrealistic sarcastic answers to their earnest questions. All in all, there doesn't appear to be much point to the event in the first place, and I'm sure most of the reporters in the room were wondering why they were there, other than the fact that Dylan was incredibly famous and noteworthy at the time.

Some of the questions from the reporters are beyond lame. Most of them obviously knew little about him. One reporter asks for the meaning of the cover to *Highway 61 Revisited* (which he gets wrong as "the one with 'Subterranean Homesick Blues'"). Dylan gives no real answer, because the question was absurd to begin with. It's just a photo. Dylan goes on to describe himself as a "song and dance man" – a quote that has become almost a catch phrase when referring to Bob.

At one point, Allen Ginsburg (who recorded the next night's show) jokingly asks, "Do you think there'll ever be a time when you'll be hung as a thief?" Bob responds, "You weren't supposed to say that!"

This is Bob Dylan at his most bizarre. For a complete transcript, see https://www.rollingstone.com/music/music-news/bob-dylan-gives-press-conference-in-san-francisco-246805.

LPs and CDs: None that I know of, but a pirate edition of the press conference can probably be found on various bootleg VHS tapes or on DVD.

Berkeley Community Theatre 1965

December 4, 1965

Tombstone Blues
I Don't Believe You
Baby Let Me Follow You Down
Just Like Tom Thumb's Blues
Long Distance Operator
It Ain't Me, Babe
Ballad Of A Thin Man
Positively 4th Street
Like A Rolling Stone

Personnel:
Robbie Robertson (guitar)
Richard Manuel (piano)
Garth Hudson (organ)
Rick Danko (bass)
Bobby Gregg (drums)

This audience tape from the electric set of the Berkeley concert is pretty amazing. The sound quality is quite acceptable and Bob and the Hawks really kick it. Levon Helm had only recently left the band and Bobby Gregg was tapped as a quick replacement, and the band was still feeling their way around this revolutionary sound, but they were well on the way. The set list is similar to what would come later, except that one song would eventually be dropped from the set (the slot occupied by "Positively 4th Street"), and some substitutions would be made ("Tell Me Mama" for "Tombstone Blues", "Leopard-Skin Pill-Box Hat" for "Long Distance Operator", "One Too Many Mornings" for "It Ain't Me Babe"), and of course the amazing Mickey Jones would be brought in for the European tour to take the music to a high level not heard before or since.

"Long Distance Operator" is the revelation here. It's the only known recording by Dylan that we have and it's just fine. Years later it would show up on *The Basement Tapes* sung by Richard Manuel. "It Ain't Me, Babe" sounds remarkably like the arrangement used for the 1974 tour! The other songs are fine, but would sound even better by the time the tour concluded. The audience is polite and attentive. No boos are evident and there is even a request for "Like a Rolling Stone" from one of the members of the audience very near the audience microphone. As a matter of fact, it is believed that Allen Ginsburg was the person who recorded the tape.

Very highly recommended!

CDs:

- **Long Distance Operator** [Wanted Man - the first title in their catalog]

Available on *Bob Dylan's 50th Anniversary Collection: 1965.*

Bob Fass Show - WBAI-FM

January 1966

This radio call-in show has no musical content, and yet it's the most entertaining Dylan tape that I've ever heard! It's just Dylan and friends paying a late night visit to New York DJ Bob Fass and, Dylan being in a particularly good mood, taking phone calls from the audience. Dylan jokes around with Bob Fass, who is one of the few media personalities who seemed comfortable with Dylan and was able to keep up with his mad humor. This show had to have taken place in January or very early February of 1966 because the White Plains concert was being plugged and that show occurred on February 5 of that year.

Dylan introduces a couple of his friends as "Harry the Hat" and "Roosevelt Gook" (which is a well-known alias for Al Kooper) and is in a constant put-on mood throughout the entire relaxed appearance. Phone calls start coming in and Dylan answers some of the strangest phone calls in radio history. Some of the calls are fairly hostile and demand that the station play some music rather than have Dylan talk. Others phone in with support for Dylan's appearance.

I listened to this tape for the first time under ideal circumstances - through headphones very late at night. This simulated as close as possible the atmosphere of the original broadcast, which was late at night on the type of FM radio station that would typically be listened to with the lights off and headphones securely in place, and gave me a feeling of being transported back in time to 1966. This happened by accident, as it turned out. It was getting late and I was going to call it a night when I thought I'd preview a little of the tape to see what the sound quality was like. I was hooked from the very start and couldn't stop listening until I'd heard the entire 90 minutes. Fascinating tape! Sound quality is excellent.

CDs and LPs: none that I know of

Denver Hotel Room
March 13, 1966

Most Definitely Not Van Gogh
Don't Tell Him
If you Want My Love
Just Like a Woman
Sad-Eyed Lady of the Lowlands

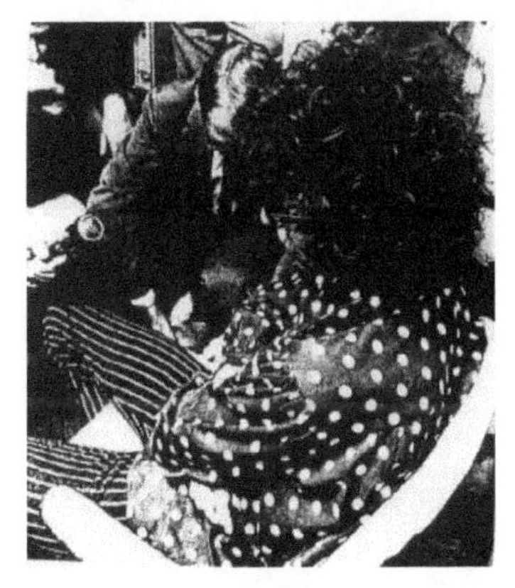

This tape was recorded in a hotel room in Denver by Robert Shelton, who also can be heard on the tape. It's Dylan and Robbie Robertson trying out new songs, two of which are "Just Like a Woman" ("best song I ever wrote", says Bob) and "Sad-Eyed Lady of the Lowlands". The other three songs have never been released, and one of them is easily up to the standards of *Blonde on Blonde*. This is a song that has no title but I prefer to think of as "Most Definitely Not Van Gogh" (Some people have taken up the habit of calling it "Positively Van Gogh", but I doubt Bob would have recycled such a similar song title when he had so many other adjectives to exhaust first). The tape is loose and there are lots of starts and stops throughout as they work out arrangements and modify tempos. At one point Bob can be heard telling Shelton he doesn't have to hang around if he doesn't want to.

Sound quality is poor, but entirely reasonable considering the unusual nature of the material: two future masterpieces and one unknown major work in the process of being born but busy dyin'.

UPDATE:

The Bootleg Series, Volume 12 now lists the songs as:

Positively Van Gogh

Don't Tell Him, Tell Me
If You Want My Love
Just Like a Woman
Sad-Eyed Lady of the Lowlands

CDs:

- "Van Gogh" and "Just Like a Woman" appears on **Seven Years of Bad Luck** [Vigotone]
- "Van Gogh" appears on **Genuine Bootleg Series Take 2** [Scorpio]

This tape appears on *The Bootleg Series Volume 12 Collector's Edition* as a bonus disc. The sound quality does not appear to be any different from the circulating tape.

The 1966 World Tour

I still believe to this day that the 1966 Dylan world tour with the Hawks represents the best live rock and roll music ever created. The music was dynamic, the music was powerful, and the music was like none other being performed at the time. The chemistry between Dylan, Robertson, and Hudson was spectacular. There was major telepathy going on there. One element that made Dylan's 1966 concerts different from anyone else's was the amazing way the tempos were deliberately slowed down rather than speeded up, as most groups had been doing in order to generate more live excitement. Dylan's songs were so dramatic that slowing them down was the only logical way to present such profoundly different rock and roll, and the effect was stunning.

Partial and complete PA tapes exist for:

- Sydney, Australia 4/13/66 (complete)
- Melbourne, Australia 4/19/66
- Copenhagen, Denmark 5/1/66
- Dublin, Ireland 5/5/66
- Belfast, Ireland 5/6/66
- Birmingham, England 5/12/66
- Liverpool, England 5/14/66
- Sheffield, England 5/16/66
- Manchester, England 5/17/66 (complete)
- Edinburgh, Scotland 5/20/66
- London, England 5/26/66
- London, England 5/27/66

Partial and complete audience tapes exist for:

- White Plains, NY 2/5/66

- Pittsburgh, PA 2/6/66
- Hempstead, NY 2/26/66
- Stockholm, Sweden 4/29/66
- Bristol, England 5/10/66
- Leicester, England 5/15/66
- Edinburgh, Scotland 5/20/66

The best and most famous 1966 boot is *Guitars Kissing and The Contemporary Fix*, which is an excellent 2-CD boot taken from the complete stereo DAT tape of the Manchester 5/17/66 concert that was originally intended for official release as *The Bootleg Series Vol. 4*. This presents a different mix than the official release (now known as *Live 1966: The "Royal Albert Hall Concert")*. Also of interest is the recently circulated Sydney 4/13/66 concert (although this date is in dispute). It presents an entire concert, with a slightly incomplete "She Belongs To Me", in excellent sound except for an unusually loud placement of Dylan's vocal and harmonica in the mix. The most surprising thing about this tape is the substitution of "Positively 4th Street" for "Like a Rolling Stone" as the final song of the second set. Only small portions of the other shows exist - Dublin's acoustic half (incomplete), five songs from the electric show at Liverpool (one of which was released on the flip-side of "I Want You" in 1966), parts of the acoustic and electric sets at Melbourne (about 45 minutes worth), one song from Belfast (released on *Biograph* - but if you believe Clinton Heylin, it actually comes from Dublin), two excellent electric songs from Edinburgh ("Like a Rolling Stone" - best version ever - and "One Too Many Mornings"), and about a third of the first

London show. This is not nearly enough considering that the entire tour was taped!

The audience tapes are mostly very poor sounding and suffer from a hostile audience reacting negatively to the electric half, which ended the show each night. Some of the halls were a little too echoey, which was pretty typical of the average rock and roll show in the mid '60s, and the band was playing way too loud for the primitive recording equipment being used (it's been said that Dylan and the Hawks were the loudest band playing in the large halls at the time). There are at least two complete shows on audience tapes: Edinburgh 5/20/66 and Bristol 5/10/66 - both poor recordings but both showing the band at their peak. The Edinburgh show is probably the best of the entire tour.

This is what currently exists for each of the PA tapes in circulation:

- **Sydney, Australia 4/13/66**
    1. She Belongs To Me (cut)
    2. Fourth Time Around
    3. Visions of Johanna
    4. It's All Over Now, Baby Blue
    5. Desolation Row
    6. Just Like a Woman
    7. Mr. Tambourine Man
    8. Tell Me Mama
    9. I Don't Believe You
    10. Baby Let Me Follow You Down
    11. Just Like Tom Thumb's Blues
    12. Leopard-Skin Pill-Box Hat
    13. One Too Many Mornings
    14. Ballad of a Thin Man
    15. Positively 4th Street

- **Melbourne, Australia 4/19/66**
    1. She Belongs To Me
    2. Fourth Time Around
    3. Visions of Johanna
    4. It's All Over Now, Baby Blue
    5. Desolation Row
    6. Just Like a Woman
    7. Tell Me Mama (cut)
    8. Baby Let Me Follow You Down
    9. Just Like Tom Thumb's Blues

- **Copenhagen, Denmark 5/1/66**
  1. Tell Me Mama
  2. Ballad of a Thin Man

- **Dublin, Ireland 5/5/66**
  1. Fourth Time Around
  2. Visions of Johanna
  3. It's All Over Now, Baby Blue
  4. Desolation Row
  5. Just Like a Woman
  6. Mr. Tambourine Man
  7. I Don't Believe You (if you believe Heylin)

- **Belfast, Ireland 5/6/66**
  1. I Don't Believe You (Heylin says this is from Dublin instead)

- **Birmingham, England 5/12/66**
  1. Ballad of a Thin Man

- **Liverpool, England 5/14/66**
  1. Tell Me Mama
  2. I Don't Believe You
  3. Baby Let Me Follow You Down
  4. Just Like Tom Thumb's Blues
  5. Leopard-Skin Pill-Box Hat

- **Sheffield, England 5/16/66**
  1. Visions of Johanna
  2. Mr. Tambourine Man
  3. Leopard-Skin Pill-Box Hat
  4. One Too Many Mornings

- **Manchester, England 5/17/66**
  1. She Belongs To Me
  2. Fourth Time Around
  3. Visions of Johanna
  4. It's All Over Now, Baby Blue
  5. Desolation Row
  6. Just Like a Woman
  7. Mr. Tambourine Man
  8. Tell Me Mama
  9. I Don't Believe You
  10. Baby Let Me Follow You Down
  11. Just Like Tom Thumb's Blues
  12. Leopard-Skin Pill-Box Hat
  13. One Too Many Mornings
  14. Ballad of a Thin Man
  15. Like a Rolling Stone

- **Edinburgh, Scotland 5/20/66**

1. One Too Many Mornings
2. Like a Rolling Stone

- **London, England 5/26/66**
    1. She Belongs To Me
    2. Fourth Time Around
    3. Visions of Johanna
    4. Leopard-Skin Pill-Box Hat
    5. One Too Many Mornings
    6. Ballad of a Thin Man

- **London, England 5/27/66**
    1. She Belongs To Me
    2. Fourth Time Around
    3. Visions of Johanna
    4. It's All Over Now, Baby Blue
    5. Desolation Row
    6. Just Like a Woman
    7. Mr. Tambourine Man
    8. Like a Rolling Stone

This is what currently exists for each of the audience tapes in circulation:

- **White Plains, NY 2/5/66**
    1. She Belongs To Me
    2. To Ramona
    3. Visions Of Johanna
    4. It's All Over Now, Baby Blue
    5. Desolation Row
    6. Love Minus Zero - No Limit
    7. Mr. Tambourine Man
    8. Tell Me Mama
    9. I Don't Believe You

- **Pittsburgh, PA 2/6/66**
    1. She Belongs To Me
    2. To Ramona
    3. Visions Of Johanna
    4. Desolation Row
    5. Love Minus Zero - No Limit
    6. Mr. Tambourine Man
    7. Positively 4th Street
    8. Like A Rolling Stone

- **Hempstead, NY 2/26/66**
    1. She Belongs To Me
    2. Fourth Time Around
    3. Visions Of Johanna

4. It's All Over Now, Baby Blue
5. Desolation Row
6. Love Minus Zero - No Limit
7. Mr. Tambourine Man
8. Tell Me Mama
9. I Don't Believe You
10. Baby Let Me Follow You Down
11. Just Like Tom Thumb's Blues
12. Leopard-Skin Pill-Box Hat
13. One Too Many Mornings

- **Stockholm, Sweden 4/29/66** (mostly fragments)
    1. She Belongs To Me
    2. Fourth Time Around
    3. Visions Of Johanna
    4. It's All Over Now, Baby Blue
    5. Desolation Row
    6. I Don't Believe You
    7. Baby Let Me Follow You Down
    8. Just Like Tom Thumb's Blues
    9. Leopard-Skin Pill-Box Hat
    10. One Too Many Mornings
    11. Ballad Of A Thin Man

- **Bristol, England 5/10/66**
    1. She Belongs To Me
    2. Fourth Time Around
    3. Visions of Johanna
    4. It's All Over Now, Baby Blue
    5. Desolation Row
    6. Just Like a Woman
    7. Mr. Tambourine Man
    8. Tell Me Mama
    9. I Don't Believe You
    10. Baby Let Me Follow You Down
    11. Just Like Tom Thumb's Blues
    12. Leopard-Skin Pill-Box Hat
    13. One Too Many Mornings
    14. Ballad of a Thin Man
    15. Like a Rolling Stone

- **Leicester, England 5/15/66**
    1. She Belongs To Me
    2. Fourth Time Around
    3. Visions Of Johanna
    4. It's All Over Now Baby Blue
    5. Desolation Row
    6. Just Like A Woman (cut)
    7. Mr. Tambourine Man
    8. Tell Me Mama
    9. I Don't Believe You

10. Baby Let Me Follow You Down
11. Just Like Tom Thumb's Blues (cut)

- **Edinburgh, Scotland 5/20/66**
    1. She Belongs To Me
    2. Fourth Time Around
    3. Visions of Johanna
    4. It's All Over Now, Baby Blue
    5. Desolation Row
    6. Just Like a Woman
    7. Mr. Tambourine Man
    8. Tell Me Mama
    9. I Don't Believe You
    10. Baby Let Me Follow You Down
    11. Just Like Tom Thumb's Blues
    12. Leopard-Skin Pill-Box Hat
    13. One Too Many Mornings
    14. Ballad of a Thin Man
    15. Like a Rolling Stone

CDs:

- **Live 1966: The "Royal Albert Hall Concert": The Bootleg Series Vol. 4** (official album - complete Manchester 5/17/66)
- **Biograph** (official album - various)
- **Masterpieces** (official album - *Tom Thumb* from Liverpool)
- **Genuine Live 1966** (8-CD set featuring all known PA recordings)
- **Guitars Kissing and The Contemporary Fix** (complete Manchester)
- **Royal Albert Hall** (Manchester electric half)
- **Manchester Prayer** (Manchester and London 5/27 acoustic)
- **Before the Crash I & II** (London 5/26-27, Manchester)
- **Melbourne 1966** (Melbourne acoustic and electric)
- **Adelphi Theatre, Dublin, May 5, 1966** (Dublin acoustic)
- **Play Fucking Loud** (various)
- **Pill-Box** (Edinburgh 5/20/66)
- **Get Loud** (Bristol 5/10/66)
- **A Week In The Life** (various)
- **Mr. Tambourine Man Volume 3** (Manchester electric)

LPs:

- **Royal Albert Hall** (various labels)
- **Zimmerman - Looking Back** (Zerocks label - best RAH)
- **Live Acetates I** (Manchester 5/17 and London 5/26)
- **Live Acetates II** (London 5/27 acoustic)
- **Stars of 66** (London 5/26-27 + Manchester and others)
- **While the Establishment Burns** (Dublin 5/2/66 acoustic)
- **Burn Some More** (more Dublin + Edinburgh 5/20/66)
- **Live in Melbourne** (Melbourne 4/19/66 acoustic)

POSTSCRIPT:

The *Live 1966 Recordings* contains every known soundboard and audience concert from 1966. This is a complete list of what is contained in the 36-CD box set:

Soundboard:

Sydney, Australia, April 13 1966
Melbourne, Australia, April 20 1966
Copenhagen, Denmark, May 1 1966
Dublin, Ireland, May 5 1966
Belfast, Ireland, May 6 1966
Bristol, England, May 10 1966
Cardiff, Wales, May 11 1966
Birmingham, England, May 12 1966
Liverpool, England, May 14 1966
Leicester, England, May 15 1966
Sheffield, England, May 16 1966
Manchester, England, May 17 1966
Glasgow, Scotland, May 19 1966
Edinburgh, England, May 20 1966
Newcastle, England, May 21 1966
Paris, France, May 24 1966
London, England, May 26 1966
London, England, May 27 1966

Audience:

White Plains, NY, USA, February 5 1966
Pittsburgh, PA, USA, February 6 1966
Hempstead, NY, USA, February 26 1966
Melbourne, Australia, April 19 1966
Stockholm, Sweden, April 29 1966

In addition, the London May 27 show has been released stand-alone by Sony as *The Real Royal Albert Hall Concert 1966.*

Basement Tapes Sessions

June-October 1967
Released June 1975

A Fool Such as I
All American Boy
All You Have to Do is Dream (1)
All You Have to Do is Dream (2)
Apple Suckling Tree (1)
Apple Suckling Tree (2;released)
Baby Ain't That Fine
Be Careful of Stones That You Throw
Belshazzar
The Bells Of Rhymney
The Big Flood
Big River
Bonnie Ship the Diamond
Bourbon Street
Bring It On Home
Clothes Line Saga (1)
Clothes Line Saga (2;released)
Come All You Fair And Tender Ladies
Coming Round The Mountain
Confidential To Me
Cool Water
Crash on the Levee (1)
Crash on the Levee (2;released)
Don't Know Why They Kick My Dog
Don't Ya Tell Henry
Don't You Try Me Now
Down on Me
The Flight Of The Bumble Bee
Folsom Prison Blues
Four Strong Winds
The French Girl
Get Your Rocks Off
Goin' to Acapulco (released)
Gonna Get You Now
Guilty Of Loving You

The Hills of Mexico
I Am a Teenage Prayer
I Can't Come In with a Broken Heart
I Can't Make it Alone
I Don't Hurt Anymore
I Forgot To Remember To Forget
I Shall Be Released (released)
I'm A Fool For You
I'm Alright
I'm In The Mood
I'm Not There
Johnny Todd
Joshua Gone Barbados
King Of France
Lo and Behold (1)
Lo and Behold (2;released)
Lock Up Your Door
Long Time A-Growin'
Mighty Quinn
Mighty Quinn (*Biograph*)
Million Dollar Bash (1)
Million Dollar Bash (2;released)
Next Time On the Highway
Nine Hundred Miles
No Shoes On My Feet
Nothing Was Delivered (1)
Nothing Was Delivered (2;released)
Nothing Was Delivered (3)
Odds and Ends (1)
Odds and Ends (2;released)
Ol' Roison the Beau
On a Rainy Afternoon
One for the Road
One Man's Loss
Open the Door Homer (1)
Open the Door Homer (2;released)
People Get Ready
Please Mrs. Henry (released)
Poor Lazarus
Rock Salt and Nails
The Royal Canal

Santa Fe (released)
See That My Grave Is Kept Clean
See You Later, Allen Ginsberg
Sign on the Cross
Silent Weekend
Song For Canada
Spanish Is The Loving Tongue
The Spanish Song (1)
The Spanish Song (2)
Still In Town
Tears of Rage (1)
Tears of Rage (2)
Tears of Rage (3;released)
This Wheel's on Fire (released)
Tiny Montgomery (released)
Too Much of Nothing (1)
Too Much of Nothing (2;released)
Try Me Little Girl
Under Control
Waltzing With Sin
Wildwood Flower
Won't You Be My Baby
Yea Heavy and a Bottle of Bread (1)
Yea Heavy and a Bottle of Bread (2;released)
You Ain't Goin Nowhere (1)
You Ain't Goin Nowhere (2;released)
You Win Again

NOTE: for a song-by-song description, refer to my review of the **Genuine Basement Tapes,** which appears in the Appendix.

These recordings represent the finest body of work ever recorded by Dylan, although I'm sure there will be much disagreement, and could stand as the peak of Dylan's career as a singer of unusual new songs. Not only did he seemingly rattle off new and ingenious songs with incredible ease, but he also had the good fortune to do it with some of the greatest rock musicians of all time, and he was also able to benefit from their collaborative efforts with some of the richest song structures of his entire career.

Listening to these songs now it's obvious to me how this material can be seen as a bridge between the excessive surrealism of *Blonde On Blonde* and the quiet mysticism of *John Wesley Harding*. Although less focused than either of those two albums, I find all of this material much more rewarding, and I think this has to do with the way these songs were recorded: friends getting together each day to blow off a little steam and just have a good time doing what they like to do best. But I think there's a little more to it, though, because the whole project has "contractual obligation" written all over it. You see, [according to Robert Shelton's book *No Direction Home*] Dylan's contract with CBS was getting ready to expire and he was all set to sign with MGM, but he still owed CBS an additional 14 songs under the terms of the contract. Well, by an amazing coincidence there were exactly 14 songs on the acetate that was distributed to various artists requesting demos of the new Dylan songs. My guess as to why these 14 songs were used as publishing demos rather than as an album by CBS is due to the fact that the MGM deal fell through and Dylan signed with CBS for another term, and by the time he had done that he already had the 14 songs ready to go and CBS didn't want to use them. So, the Basement Tapes sessions existed as a means of getting those 14 songs out of the way and delivered to CBS, and also as a deliberate slap in the face - low-tech home recordings of mostly nonsense songs; and CBS was expected to make use of it? This whole episode *could* have been the inspiration for “Dear Landlord”.

The 14 songs on the acetate were:

Million Dollar Bash
Please Mrs. Henry
Lo and Behold
Yea, Heavy, and a Bottle of Bread
The Mighty Quinn
I Shall Be Released
Down in the Flood
Nothing Was Delivered
Too Much of Nothing

You Ain't Goin' Nowhere
Tiny Montgomery
Wheel's On Fire
Tears of Rage
Open the Door, Homer

But there are plenty more of the same or greater quality. Many of the best basement songs are actually not written by Dylan at all. These were probably done for the same reason the *Self Portrait* tracks were recorded: just for warm-up and setting mike levels. Also, they liked playing together and these were probably some of the songs they knew best.

Every time I listen to the Basement Tapes I always get the feeling that I'm hearing the lost and sadly neglected recordings of an unknown artist who died as an early age and is just now becoming known through a recent discovery of a cache of obscure recordings. This is similar to the feeling I get when I see a James Dean movie or hear a Buddy Holly song - "what a tragic loss". This is odd because I *know* that nothing of the kind happened with Dylan. Still, these recordings have a timeless quality not unlike those recorded by Robert Johnson in a makeshift hotel room recording studio or early Hank Williams demos. Some of these tracks are just heartbreaking, for reasons mentioned above, and this is the only Dylan tape that affects me in this way. I would be interested to know if others feel the same way.

My favorites of the unreleased tracks? “One for the Road”, “Rock Salt and Nails”, “I'm Alright” (unfortunately incomplete), “All You Have To Do Is Dream”, “Baby Ain't That Fine”, “Song For Canada”, “Long Time A-Growin'”, “One Man's Loss”, and “Sign on the Cross”. “Sign on the Cross” in particular has been singled out by most as possibly the best thing in this collection, and at first I wasn't all that impressed but now I'm almost inclined to agree. This recording alone demonstrates what the Basement Tapes were all about, and it has that timeless tragic quality that is evident in each and every song on this collection of tapes.

CDs:

- **The Basement Tapes** (official album)
- **Biograph** (official album - contains "Mighty Quinn")
- **The Bootleg Series** (official album - contains "I Shall Be Released" and "Santa-Fe")
- **Genuine Basement Tapes** (Scorpio - 5 volumes)
- **A Tree With Roots** (Scorpio & White Bear - sonic upgrades - 4 CDs)
- **After the Crash** (2 volumes, duplicates 3 & 4 of above)
- **Lost Basement Tapes**

LPs:

- **The Basement Tapes** (official album)
- **The Great White Wonder** (the *first* bootleg! Contains the core songs – "I Shall Be Released", "Tears of Rage", "Wheel's On Fire", "Mighty Quinn", etc.)
- **Troubled Troubadour** (the complete 14 song acetate - some versions of this album feature additional songs)
- **Stealin'** (alternate version. Contains the rest of the acetate – "Lo and Behold", "Million Dollar Bash", "Tiny Montgomery", etc.)
- **VD Waltz** ("Odds and Ends", "Get Your Rocks Off", others)
- **Waters of Oblivion** (the "acetate", supposedly in really good quality. I've never seen or heard it.)
- **Blind Boy Grunt and the Hawks** (Two 2-record sets containing the recently discovered basement tracks. In stereo, although of a crude unmixed sort.)
- Many other duplications of the above albums no doubt exist.

POSTSCRIPT:

In 2014 Sony released *The Bootleg Series, Volume 11: The Basement Tapes Complete*. This fantastic collection was a dream come true for Dylan fans everywhere, and it contains the complete Basement Tapes for the first time – including many songs and performances previously unknown or even rumored to exist.

The Johnny Cash Sessions
Feb 17-18, 1969

Columbia Studios, Nashville

One Too Many Mornings
Mountain Dew
I Still Miss Someone
Careless Love
Matchbox
That's All Right Mama
Big River
I Walk The Line
You Are My Sunshine
Guess Things Happen That Way
Just A Closer Walk With Thee
T For Texas (Blues Yodel No 1)
Blues Yodel No 5
Girl From The North Country
Ring Of Fire

This failed attempt to produce an album between Dylan and Cash resulted in some interesting things, but overall I would have to say this session is pretty dismal. It's really more of a Johnny Cash session, although Dylan is certainly interested and having a good time. Only two songs performed here are by Dylan and both are old at that. The rest are songs long a part of Cash's repertoire, songs familiar to both Dylan and Cash, and for good measure one of Carl Perkins' tunes. Perkins sits in on this session, by the way.

The most successful tracks here are "One Too Many Mornings" (two versions - both are a lot of fun), "Girl From the North Country" (which was released on *Nashville Skyline*), "Big River", and "Careless Love". "Blues Yodel No. 5" is a lot of fun because it gives Dylan a chance to yodel! The rest of the tracks are mostly impromptu jams that never quite come together despite Cash's earnest attempts to get Bob to open up a little more. Dylan, for his part, seems content to sing a sort of "harmony" to Cash's lead vocals. Dylan's harmonies tend to be a little limited and would have sounded better if he hadn't even attempted to sing at all. The songs mentioned above as relative successes tend to be those where the lead vocal duties are traded off. “One Too Many Mornings”, for instance, changes keys with each different verse sung by the one or the other. The effect is nice and helps to relieve the monotony of the "chunk-a-chunk" sound that Cash is famous for.

Although a lot of fun in places, this is *NOT* the place for a Dylan newcomer to start.

CDs:

- **The Dylan/Cash Sessions**
- **Bob Dylan Meets George Harrison and Johnny Cash**

LPs:

- **The Dylan/Cash Sessions**

The Johnny Cash Show
May 1, 1969

I Threw It All Away
Living the Blues
Girl from the North Country

Dylan made a rare television appearance in 1969, sometime after the release of *Nashville Skyline*, and it was fitting that the appearance was on Johnny Cash's new hit variety series. Cash was at a career high at the time, and having his friend Bob on the show was quite a coup. I watched the show when it aired, and even though I was not yet a big fan of Bob Dylan, I appreciated what he was doing. I did own a copy of *Nashville Skyline* (and *John Wesley Harding*, the only other Dylan album I listened to at the time), so I knew "I Threw It all Away" and expected the duet with Cash on "Girl from the North Country". "Living the Blues" was new to me, but by the time *Self Portrait* came out, I was a solid fan and knew the song, not only from the album version but also from the live version from this show that appeared on *Great White Wonder*.

The performances are relaxed and assured. The duet with Cash is superior to the album version, in my opinion, if only because it seems more polished and confident. The sound quality varies depending on your source. The *Great White Wonder* version of "Living the Blues" is fairly muddy, but there is a pretty decent sounding complete tape of both performances in circulation that is well worth seeking out. If you like both of these artists, this is essential. Also, the 2-disc DVD set *The Johnny Cash Show: The Best of Johnny Cash 1969-1971* contains "I Threw It All Away" and "Girl from the North Country", but is missing "Living the Blues".

LPs:

- **Great White Wonder**

George Harrison Session
May 1, 1970

Columbia Studio B, New York

Ghost Riders in the Sky
Cupid
All I Have To Do Is Dream
Gates of Eden
I Threw It All Away
I Don't Believe You
Matchbox
True Love
Telephone Line
Honey Just Allow Me
Rainy Day Women
Song To Woody
Mama You Been On My Mind
Don't Think Twice
Yesterday
Just Like Tom Thumb's Blues
Da Doo Run Run
One Too Many Mornings
Working on a Guru
If Not For You

This tape is proof that Dylan's stature was so great in 1970 that he could book time in a major studio to sit and fool around with a famous friend and come up with absolutely nothing usable. Very few recording artists then or now could do the same. Touted as a session with George Harrison, this tape is actually part of the *New Morning* sessions, and in fact one song ("If Not For You") was at one time considered for inclusion on that album. There was actually much more material recorded at the same session, including versions of

"Sign on the Window" and "Time Passes Slowly". Other musicians include Charlie Daniels on bass and Russ Kunkel on drums. Bob Johnston plays piano on a few songs as well.

Unlike the Johnny Cash sessions that took place the year before, this was not an effort to blend the two talents into an equal collaboration. Harrison is a sideman only, and uncredited on studio logs at that, but still Rolling Stone magazine at the time made it sound like an historic meeting of the minds. What really took place here was an effort to come up with one or two original songs for the next album. I'd like to hear what they did with "Sign on the Window" and the other originals, but it's likely that nothing good ever came of them. As stated previously, the version of "If Not For You" recorded during these sessions was intended for *New Morning* but replaced at the last minute by a superior version recorded at a later date. The original "If Not For You" eventually found its way onto *The Bootleg Series*.

What we have on this tape is mostly fooling around, wasting time really, perhaps warming up for the real work at hand or relaxing afterward. Dylan runs through some older songs from his catalog, and some of these show promise: "Song To Woody", "Gates of Eden", "One Too Many Mornings". The fact that none of these songs were formally worked on, or restarted to get clean intros, shows that they were just tossed off for fun. Most of the songs are covers of songs that George Harrison might have been interested in playing: "Matchbox", "True Love". Some of these show promise, especially "Matchbox", but for the most part the music here is truly awful. "Telephone Line" might have been a good blues had it been worked on a little and finished. "Ghost Riders" is just abysmal, and Dylan shows that he doesn't have a clue how "Cupid" is supposed to go.

Sound quality is excellent, though.

CDs:

- **Seven Years of Bad Luck** (incomplete)

- **Possum Belly Overalls**
- **Yesterday**
- **Almost Went To See Elvis**
- **The Bootleg Series** ("If Not For You")

LPs:

- **Yesterday's Blues** (incomplete)

Dylan vs Weberman

January 19, 1971

This legendary phone conversation between Dylan and Weberman is a riot! Weberman is so stupid and obnoxious that it's hard to understand why Dylan would waste an hour of his time talking to this moron, but the answer soon becomes obvious - Weberman is fascinating to talk to because his sheer lunacy takes your breath away. Despite Dylan's complaints to him and repeated references to A.J. as a "pig", he continues to talk to him out of morbid curiosity. When Weberman says something at one point about some backwards messages on the *New Morning* album, Dylan can hardly believe his ears. He's completely stunned and it's hilarious to hear Weberman seriously putting forth the notion that the backwards-masked messages "when Mars invades us" and "please don't expose me" were deliberately put into a couple of *New Morning* songs. When Dylan, completely lost at this point, asks what he's talking about Weberman says "you know as well as I do because you put them there, man". This happens fairly early in the conversation and I would have said goodbye at that point, but Dylan hangs in there for more.

Weberman also had the notion that some of the songs were written for him. Dylan quickly puts that idea to rest: "I didn't even know about you when I wrote 'Dear Landlord'". Dylan also affirms that "Dear Landlord" was *not* written about Grossman. He also states that his "message" songs were really messages to himself. In other parts of the conversation Dylan says how much he admires Johnny Cash and refuses to say one bad thing about the man. He also insists that his children be left out of any article Weberman has planned and says if they are included "my wife will hit me, man". Dylan also reveals a strong animosity toward Roger McGuinn - "Fuck him. You can put that in [your article] twice."

In another amusing exchange Dylan asks rhetorically who writes better songs than he does and Weberman replies "I can name you a hundred" to which Dylan replies "bullshit!" Weberman proceeds to name some pretty lame songwriters (and non-songwriters such as Jack Elliot) along with some good ones and Dylan gives his opinions, mostly negative. John Lennon: "never!", Credence Clearwater: "bullshit!", George Harrison: "...maybe". Dylan's willingness to play this game with a twit like Weberman shows that he really gets a kick out of talking to this guy.

Weberman's political rhetoric is comically dated, dropping phrases like "White Panther", "Weather Underground", "capitalist pig", and his avowed purpose in annoying Dylan was to try to make him conform to his narrow idea of correct political thinking. The fact that Dylan is still here and all those pinhead "revolutionaries" of the late '60s and early '70s are long gone or have all jumped on the Reagan bandwagon speaks volumes. Listening to someone like Weberman talk for an hour leaves me no doubt as to why Dylan wanted to get away from the public eye for so long.

CDs: none that I know of

LPs: released officially for a short time but withdrawn

Mexico City Tape

January 20, 1973

Billy (1)
Billy (2)
Turkey
Turkey II Or Tom Turkey
Billy Surrenders
And He's Killed Me Too
Goodbye Holly
Peco's Blues (1)
Peco's Blues (2)
Billy (3)
Knockin' On Heaven's Door (1)
Sweet Amarillo
Knockin' On Heaven's Door (2)
Knockin' On Heaven's Door (3)
Final Theme (1)
Final Theme (2)
Rock Me Mama (1)
Rock Me Mama (2)
Billy-7 1
Billy-7 2
Instrumental (1)
Instrumental (2)
Final Theme (3)
Final Theme (4)

Personnel:

Terry Paul (bass, vocals)
Roger McGuinn (guitar, banjo)
Jim Keltner (drums)
Carol Hunter (vocals)
Donna Weiss (vocals)
Brenda Patterson (vocals)
Carol Hunter (guitar)
Gary Foster (flute)
Carl Fortina (harmonium)

Fred Catz and Ted Michel (cellos)
Bruce Langhorn (guitar)
Booker T (bass)
Russ Kunkel (tambourine, bongos)
Byron Berline (fiddle & vocal)
Priscilla Jones (vocal)

In 1973, Bob Dylan was hired by Sam Peckinpah to not only write songs for his new film, *Pat Garrett and Billy the Kid*, but also to act in it. Thus begins Dylan's film career as an actor. The movie had its moments, but I consider it to be a lesser Peckinpah film, somewhat below *Major Dundee* and *The Wild Bunch* – the two films I consider to be his masterpieces. Nevertheless, Dylan contributed some atmospheric songs and scored one of his biggest mainstream hits with "Knockin' On Heaven's Door". The soundtrack album that resulted from this experience was somewhat of a letdown, and added to one more placeholder in his career between *Blonde on Blonde* and *Blood on the Tracks* – the two albums most Dylan fans consider to be his masterpieces. Actually, both *John Wesley Harding* and *Planet Waves* were strong albums, but the four that came between his two masterpieces were, in general, mediocre. That said, there is much to enjoy here. "Peco's Blues", "Rock Me Mama", and "Knockin' On Heaven's Door" are certainly standouts. The rest is just okay. Hardly essential, but nice to have in your collection.

CDs:

- **Peco's Blues**

The 1974 Tour with The Band

January & February 1974

Dylan returned to regular touring after an eight-year absence. For this tour he decided to use The Band - a very wise decision! The tour started out great, if a little shaky, and finished up tight and slick but too predictable. After the first several shows where he tried out new and interesting material, and wonderful arrangements of little performed songs, he soon settled into a formulaic show that found him singing with the wrong emphasis in all the wrong places and generally sticking to a safe tried and true set list. The Band, on the other hand, just got better and better as the tour progressed, and they are really the only reason to listen to any of the later shows. Dylan's acoustic sets, except for the first half dozen shows or so, are completely wasted and, to these ears, unlistenable.

Every show was recorded, either by the audience or the stage crew - or both. Two complete (or very nearly complete) soundboard tapes are in circulation: Oakland 2/11/74 evening and Los Angeles 2/14/74 afternoon (missing the first song). In both cases, it's obvious that the source is from 90-minute cassette, because the Band songs that happen to be playing at the end of the 45-minute mark where the tape would run out are suddenly cut. These are very small flaws to compensate for outstanding sound and performance quality. Two partial soundboard tapes are also circulating: Boston 1/14/74 (afternoon show) and New York City at Madison Square Garden 1/31/74 (evening concert). In both cases the tapes are the first 90 minutes only and include the astounding Band sets as well. In addition, there is a *Before the Flood* outtake tape that has been recently bootlegged as *Stem the Tide* (notice the similarity in titles!). The majority of the songs on the BtF outtake tape are from the final Los Angeles shows in mid February. Musically these shows were very powerful, but artistically pretty drab. My recommendations would be for the early shows only, in particular the first Chicago 1/3/74, the incredible Philadelphia 1/6/74 afternoon show, and Toronto 1/10/74 - all decent audience tapes. Until the complete soundboards for ALL 1974 shows are circulated, these will have to do.

CDs:

- **Love Songs for America** (Boston 1/14/74)
- **Before and After the Flood** (New York City 1/31/74)
- **The Poet and the Players** (New York City 1/31/74 + Oakland 2/11/74)
- **Paint the Daytime Black** (Los Angeles 2/14/74)
- **Phantoms of My Youth** (various)

LPs:

- **Stem the Tide**
- **St. Valentine's Day Massacre** (double and triple)
- **Love Songs for America** (*NOT* the same as the CD - Florida 1/19/74)
- **Oakland 1974**

POSTSCRIPT:

At this time all of the shows, either complete or featuring only the Dylan sets, are in circulation. Perhaps we can expect another complete live set in 2024, as with the 1966 live box?

The Friends Of Chile Benefit Concert
May 9, 1974

Felt Forum, Madison Square Garden, New York

Deportee
North Country Blues
Spanish Is The Loving Tongue
Blowin' In The Wind

This is without a doubt the very worst Dylan performance I've ever heard! I found it hard to believe that I was listening to the same man who wrote and sang so many great songs, and yet it's true. Supposedly Dylan and Phil Ochs had been drinking a lot of wine throughout the day and Dylan was just barely able to stand up straight by the time of the performance. At one point, so the legend goes, he fell off the stage.

"Deportee" is sung by Arlo Guthrie and both "Spanish Is the Loving Tongue" and "Blowin' In the Wind" feature Dylan joined by Guthrie, Dave Van Ronk, Phil Ochs, Larry Estridge, Melanie, and Pete Seeger. Such an unlikely combination (for 1974) didn't in itself hold out much promise. Dylan's only real solo number is the rarely performed "North Country Blues", and even this number is massacred by Dylan's very weird delivery.

This tape is a pretty good audience tape, but I can't recommend it to anyone but the most diehard Dylan collector.

CDs and LPs: none that I know of

The S.N.A.C.K. Benefit Concert
March 23, 1975

Kezar Stadium, Golden Gate Park, San Francisco

Are You Ready For The Country
Ain't That A Lot Of Love
Looking For A Love
Loving You Is Sweeter Than Ever
I Want You
The Weight
Helpless / Knockin' on Dragon's Door
Will The Circle Be Unbroken

Neil Young (piano, guitar)
Tim Drummond (guitar)
Ben Keith (pedal steel guitar)
Levon Helm (drums)
Garth Hudson (keyboards)
Rick Danko (bass)

This benefit concert (S.N.A.C.K. stands for Students Need Athletics, Culture and Kicks) was organized by Bill Graham in 1975 and was broadcast over the radio, and therefore there are many nice tape copies in circulation. This one time only mixture of Dylan/Band/Young was the featured act in a full day's concert that featured many local San Francisco bands, such as Santana and Jefferson Airplane. The appearance of Neil Young and company was merely rumored and Dylan's performance was a complete surprise. Completely unrehearsed, some of this music is great, but mostly it's just haphazard and rough. Dylan debuts "I Want You" live, but unfortunately he can't be heard for most of the song. Mostly what we hear is Rick Danko shouting the chorus. Hearing the Band without Robbie Robertson is weird at first, but Ben Keith makes up for it very nicely. The oddest thing on this tape is the “Helpless”/”Knockin'” medley where Dylan substitutes "knockin' on the dragon's door" for "knockin' on heaven's door". I have no idea what he meant by it! The entire set is approximately 45 minutes.

CDs:
- **Ballad Of A Blue Poet**
- **Duets**
- **Live In San Francisco 1975**

LPs:
- **SNACK!** (Reputedly an audience recording)

The World Of John Hammond

September 10, 1975

WTTW-TV Studios, Chicago Broadcast December 13, 1975 and simultaneously by WBAI-FM radio, NYC.

Hurricane
Oh, Sister
Simple Twist Of Fate

Personnel:

Rob Stoner (bass)
Scarlet Rivera (violin)
Howie Wyeth (drums)

Another Rolling Thunder warm-up, but this time an advance peek at Dylan's new band. The *Desire* album hadn't yet been released, but the single "Hurricane" was already being played on the radio, so most of the audience was probably already familiar with the song when he launched into it on this television tribute to John Hammond taped for PBS. Using a very small backup band consisting of Rob Stoner on bass, Howie Wyeth on drums, and Scarlet Rivera on violin, Dylan performed mature, fully realized versions of "Hurricane", "Oh, Sister", and "Simple Twist of Fate". I think it would have been spectacular to have an entire concert with this minimal band. This tape is highly recommended.

CDs:

- **Songs for Patty Valentine**

LPs:

- **Blood Takes** (also contains original Blood tracks)
- **Passed Over and Rolling Thunder** (double album, half of which consists of **Blood Takes**)

- **Joaquin Antique** (probably the same as **Blood Takes**?)

Rolling Thunder Revue 1975

Starting in October of 1975, Bob Dylan took to the road for another tour of the US. This time it was different, though. Rather than tour with the Band again, or another solid outfit of that caliber, he chose to put together a ragtag group of musicians of varying quality, some of whom he had just recently used during the recording sessions for *Desire*, and some that were old friends and colleagues that could put on a show of their own with Dylan being the main attraction of the Revue. Some of these friends included Joan Baez, Bob Neuwirth, Roger McGuinn, Ramblin' Jack Elliot, Ronnie Blakely and others. The core group of musicians included Rob Stoner, David Mansfield, Howie Wyeth, Steven Soles, T-Bone Burnett, Scarlet Rivera, and special guest Mick Ronson!

The first leg of the Rolling Thunder tour concentrated on New England and Canada. Most of the venues were medium-sized and often unannounced; the idea being to surprise the fans with a spontaneous performance. The second leg in 1976 branched out into other parts of the US, concentrating on the South and the Southwest, and was more formal and closer to a standard rock concert, although still maintaining the Revue format. A potential third leg of the tour would likely have targeted the West and Midwest, but that never happened for any number of reasons. I am only going to talk about the first leg of the tour, which had a very different flavor from the second half and was much more intimate.

The complete 1975 itinerary is as follows:

October 30 - Plymouth, MA
October 31 - Plymouth, MA
November 2 - Lowell, MA
November 4 - Providence, RI
November 6 - Springfield, MA
November 8 - Burlington, VT
November 9 - Durham, NH
November 11 - Waterbury, CT
November 13 - New Haven, CT
November 15 - Niagara Falls, NY
November 17 - Rochester, NY
November 19 - Worcester, MA
November 20 - Cambridge, MA
November 21 - Boston, MA
November 22 - Waltham, MA
November 24 - Hartford, CT
November 26 - Augusta, ME
November 27 - Bangor, ME
November 29 - Quebec City, Canada
December 1 - Toronto, Canada
December 2 - Toronto, Canada
December 4 - Montreal, Canada
December 7 - Clinton, NJ
December 8 - New York City, NY

I am not going to win any new friends by admitting that the Rolling Thunder Revue is my least favorite Dylan tour. I find most of it unrelentingly drab and smug, with Bob Neuwirth especially rubbing me the wrong way. I'm sorry, but he has no business being up on the same stage with Bob Dylan. The rhythm section is perhaps the worst that Dylan has ever used in a professional capacity, although individually they are fine musicians. The problem for me is the sameness that permeates every song and becomes extremely annoying. Case in point: "Lay Lady Lay", which just plods along with the same start-and-stop motion throughout. The duets with Joan Baez are irritating, for the most part. To top it all off, Dylan used the tour as an opportunity to make a four-hour home movie that is mostly unwatchable.

Having said all of that, there are a few shows that are worth checking out, especially the very early ones. The two Plymouth shows are probably the most interesting, despite the poor audio sound quality. The Providence show has decent sound, so that would also be a good starting point. Others worth checking out, if only for the decent audio, are: Boston 11-21-75 (evening), Cambridge, Montreal, and Worcester – all of which had songs featured in excellent quality on *The Bootleg Series Volume 5*. I should also point out that Mick Ronson is a most welcome addition and provides some of the most interesting musicianship.

Overall, the *Desire* album is a much better representation of the sound that Dylan was going for.

CDs:

- **The Bootleg Series Volume 5: Bob Dylan Live 1975**
- **It All Came Crashing Down**

LPs:

- **Believe What You Heard**
- **Bangor, Maine**
- **Dark As a Dungeon**
- **Passed Over and Rolling Thunder**

Appendix

The following articles original appeared on the website known as *Bringing It All Back Homepage*, which began in 1994 and continues to this day. They appear just as they did when they were originally published, warts and all.

About This Site

Bringing It All Back Homepage started back in June 1994 when I was still using Netcom as my internet service provider. Here is the original announcement on rec.music.dylan dated June 27, 1994:

> Well, I don't know if it's really the first or not, but I haven't run across a complete Dylan home page yet. Giuseppe Valetto has a page devoted to a text analysis of Dylan's lyrics, and there may be a few other things out there that I haven't run across yet, but my server will contain, among other things: Olof's yearly chronicles; tape and concert reviews; Adam Powers' FAQs; news of upcoming events; concert schedules (when available); and whatever else will fit and whatever I have time for. One thing I lack is sufficient disk space, otherwise I would offer to keep sounds and pictures online. Maybe later.
>
> Still under construction, and available now for your perusal, is the "Bringing It All Back Home Page". If you have Mosaic or Lynx, use this URL: ftp://netcom11.netcom.com/pub/howells/dylan.html. Contributions and suggestions welcome.
>
> --
>
> John Howells
> howells@netcom.com
> ftp://netcom11.netcom.com/pub/howells/howells.html

Netcom didn't do a very good job of providing WWW service, sticking their customers with an unreliable FTP method that was totally inadequate, so I eventually moved the site to my personal home page on Silicon Graphics, where I worked for awhile. Eventually the site wound up at its present location - punkhart.com.

When I started this site, there were no other Dylan WWW sites on the web. Mine was the first. However, soon after starting my own page, others began to pop up, (Ben Taylor's **Ragged Clown** page and Karl Erik Andersen's **Expecting Rain**, both of which are excellent). Soon, other excellent pages started to surface, such as Bill Pagel's indispensible **Boblinks** and Larry Yudelson's **Tangled Up In Jews**. As these and other pages began to show up, I started creating links to them. I also created links to other home pages dealing with artists related to Dylan.

My original intent in creating this site was to gather together all of the material scattered throughout the net dealing with Bob Dylan. Some of these resources were lyrics sites, Usenet articles that I had saved, some original articles written by myself and others, pictures, sound bites, and whatever else I could find. The amount of material found on the net has grown tremendously in just the short time this site has been active, and it's impossible to include it all here. Nor would I want to. When someone else has a resource on their server, I create a link. If I have a resource someone else wants to reference on their site, they create a link to my server. That's the way it works. If you see something I have that also appears on someone else's site, chances are it's actually a link to that site and not a duplication.

What This Site Is NOT

It's not a fan club page, nor is it officially endorsed by Dylan or his camp. They may or may not approve of what I'm doing here. They may even ask me to stop, although I certainly hope that never happens.

It's not a clearing house for buying and selling merchandise. I'm not in the business of selling bootlegs, if that's what you're looking for. You might be able to find links to other people who do sell merchandise, but it ain't me babe!

It's not a lyrics server. I have some lyrics here, such as unpublished or rare alternate versions of some songs, and I have links to some sites that may or may not carry some lyrics that you're looking for, but I don't have time to sit down and transcribe the lyrics to every song ever written by Dylan. Even if I had the time to do that, I wouldn't want to because there are already books that you can go buy or check out of the library that contain all of Bob's published lyrics.

Reprinting the contents of these books would be copyright infringement.

John Howells
October 2002

Discovering Bob Dylan

How I became a fan, an appreciation of Al Kooper, and other sundry items

I became a Bob Dylan fan by way of Al Kooper. Let me explain.

You see, I was an Al Kooper fan before I even knew he had played with Bob Dylan. I had heard Dylan on the radio but didn't really appreciate him. I was among those who thought he couldn't sing and that his songs were too weird. Secretly, though, I liked hearing "Like a Rolling Stone" and "Positively 4th Street" when they played them on the radio, but I didn't tell my friends that. In all honesty, I'm pretty sure the very first time I was aware of Dylan was hearing "Bob Dylan's 115th Dream" being played on AM radio back in 1965 and wondering who that was. I was struck by the line "I asked the captain what his name was and how come he didn't drive a truck" and thought it was the funniest song I had ever heard, but to me it was just another novelty tune - not unlike all those Ray Stevens songs I kept hearing around the same time. Someone told me that was Bob Dylan, so I filed that away for future reference. Later I found out he had written the Peter Paul & Mary hit "Blowin' in the Wind" and the new Byrds single "Mr. Tambourine Man", plus a whole slew of other big hits. I was impressed by his songwriting, but that voice. Couldn't get past that at the tender age of 13.

Fast forward to 1968. I had just recently discovered a phenomenon called free form underground radio on the FM dial. There were few stations on the FM dial at that time, and those were either classical or foreign language, but a few renegade rock stations starting popping up. In my area it was the legendary KMPX-FM in San Francisco (By the way, if anyone reading this happens to have any tapes of KMPX from the mid to late '60s, please let me know!). Suddenly I was hearing all sorts of music that top-40 AM radio would never play:

The Mothers, Velvet Underground, Pink Floyd, the Blues Project - pretty much anything they felt like playing. One day I heard a song that blew me away. It was just one person singing with a string quartet, but the nature of underground radio was such that they would play sometimes hours of music without telling you what was played, or they might give the rundown at the end. You really needed to pay attention to the order of the songs played if you wanted to know what you just heard. Anyway, it took a few more times of them playing that song before I found out who the artist was. It was a song called "The Modern Adventures of Plato, Diogenes, and Freud" by Blood Sweat and Tears. Now I had seen that album in the stores and didn't know anything at all about it, so I went to buy it. Looking at the back cover I see all these horn players. Hmmm, jazz. Being 16 years old at the time, jazz was the music my grandparents listened to. I wasn't sure about this, but what the hell, I had to have that song. Well the Blood Sweat and Tears album turned out to be the first mature rock album I ever bought and opened my eyes up to other styles of music. The album simply stunned me, and the song I had bought it for turned out to be not even the best tune on the album. On first listen I realized I had already heard about half of the album on KMPX and liked what I heard without knowing who it was. I studied the liner notes more carefully now. Who was this lead singer with the unusual voice? It appeared that this guy Al Kooper was the brains behind the whole thing, singing all but two of the songs and writing most of the material as well as having a hand in arrangements. The more I listened to the album the more I was convinced it was a masterpiece, and I still feel that way today. It's easily one of the best albums of the 1960s.

KMPX continued to play the album, although I never heard any of it on "regular" radio, and one day after playing something from the album, the announcer said "Blood Sweat and Tears. Al Kooper and Steve Katz, formerly of the Blues Project...". Ding! I knew about the Blues Project but didn't know that Al Kooper came from that group, so I went out and bought all the Blues Project albums the next day. Fortunately for me, they were all in a bargain bin. The Blues Project albums, in particular their only studio album "Projections", cemented my admiration for Kooper. (I didn't realize it at the time, but there was a connection between a lot of what I was hearing on FM radio, and it was producer Tom Wilson. He produced Dylan, the Blues Project, the Mothers, and the Velvet Underground all in roughly the same time period.) What else did Kooper do? I managed to find out, I forget how, that he played with Dylan on the Highway 61 Revisited album. Now I had to hear that, so I borrowed it from a friend. Hmmm, Mike Bloomfield was on the album too. I had been hearing lots of the Paul Butterfield Blues Band on my newfound FM radio station, so I was well aware of how heavy Bloomfield was. And with Al Kooper too, another heavyweight. Wow. This Dylan guy must be pretty good after all, but isn't it folk music? What are these blues guys doing on an album like that? I soon found out. It was like walking into a dark room and turning on the light. Suddenly everything was clear and bright. This album ROCKED! This album was underground. This album was the real thing, like a shot of the hard stuff after drinking milk all my life. I felt like I had aged 10 years and now had the wisdom of a mature adult. No more teeny bopper crap for me now!

So that was it. No turning back. From there it was Blonde on Blonde and every album before and since. Blonde on Blonde just simply eclipsed everything I had ever heard before. As for Kooper, I still listen to that first BS&T album every now and then and am still blown away by it. It doesn't seem to have aged a bit. His work with that band was highly innovative, and in my opinion helped to change the course of pop music in the late '60s and into the '70s. I'll always be grateful that through him I was led to the amazing work of Bob Dylan, and I'm glad that he played a major role in helping to shape the sound that defined Dylan in 1965.

John Howells
September 2007

The Genuine Basement Tapes
Volumes 1-5

(Note: This article was written long before the Official Bootleg Series Volume 11 was released in 2014. This release contained, for the first time, all of the Basement Tapes known to exist in complete and official form. When this article was written, the closest we came to a complete collection of these amazing recordings was the five-CD series known as The Genuine Basement Tapes. There were other bootleg releases throughout the years leading up to that (as will be discussed in the following article), but this five volume series of releases represented the most complete set yet available. A complete official release was still just a far-fetched dream that was unlikely to ever occur. The article appears here exactly as it originally appeared, and indeed the way it still exists on the site itself.)

Introduction

In 1975 Columbia released its official version of *The Basement Tapes,* and at the time it was thought that all of the songs from that session were in circulation. However, the inclusion of "Going To Acapulco", a previously unknown recording, raised the suspicion that there might have been many more songs as yet uncovered. This suspicion turned to reality about ten years later when a new batch of tapes appeared and were subsequently bootlegged as two double LP sets called *Blind Boy Grunt and the Hawks I & II.* These records not only presented entirely new material, they also contained a few of the standard tracks in new stereo mixes. These mixes were of a crude nature that betrayed the primitive recording equipment used and put an end to the speculation that the basement tapes were actually recorded in Columbia's studios (yes, I had actually heard this rumor!). The new tracks also showed a new side of Dylan and the Band. There is considerably more goofing off and the atmosphere is more relaxed than what was apparent on the "core" tracks that we were all familiar with (more on this later).

Finally, within the past few years we have seen the discovery of an additional few hours of unknown basement tapes. All of this material (the Dylan portion at least) has been released on five CDs in the series called, appropriately enough, *The Genuine Basement Tapes*. Assuming that we now have the complete collection of basement tapes at last, and barring any further surprises, this seems like a good time to discuss this material in its entirety.

What was the purpose of these sessions? At various times Dylan and members of the Band have claimed that they were "just for fun", and certainly it shows that they were having fun. It also seems apparent that one purpose may have been to get some new songs published. After all, fourteen songs were distributed on acetate to various artists throughout the world, and in 1967 we began to hear new Dylan songs being covered by the likes of the Byrds, Manfred Mann, and Peter, Paul and Mary. But I don't think either one of these explanations will suffice.

First the "just for fun" theory: sure they were having fun, and anyone who has ever been in a band with almost daily rehearsals knows that there is a need to cut up and let off steam. But there are times when Dylan seems very serious about getting something down on tape and even tells Garth Hudson at one point "you don't have to record this, Garth. You're just wasting tape". So then maybe the purpose is to make some publishing demos. But then why record so many non-originals?

One other theory is that the sessions were actually rehearsals for the Guthrie tribute at Carnegie Hall, or for an aborted concert tour. Unlikely on two counts: first, were they going to perform without a drummer? Levon Helm had not yet rejoined the Band; second, Dylan had just recently broken his neck and was in no condition to be going out on an extended concert tour of any kind.

Well, I have my own theory. In 1967, Dylan and his manager Albert Grossman were in the midst of negotiations with MGM Records, who were very eager to sign Dylan to a long-term contract, but (according to Robert Shelton's book) Dylan still owed Columbia fourteen songs. Now it could be an amazing coincidence that the original basement tapes acetate consisted of fourteen songs, but I doubt it. These fourteen songs make up the core of the basement tapes and are as follows, probably more or less in the order intended by Dylan (but who knows?):

```
Million Dollar Bash
Yea Heavy and a Bottle of Bread
Please Mrs. Henry
Down In the Flood
Lo and Behold
Tiny Montgomery
This Wheel's On Fire
You Ain't Goin' Nowhere
I Shall Be Released
Tears of Rage
Too Much of Nothing
Quinn the Eskimo
Open the Door, Homer
Nothing Was Delivered
```

These are the most famous songs from the basement tapes, and the first to be bootlegged. All of the above appeared on one of the most famous of the early boots, *Troubled Troubadour*. About half of these songs appeared on *Great White Wonder*, arguably the world's very first bootleg record album.

I think Dylan and company were planning to release this material as Dylan's final album for Columbia before joining MGM. Partly because Dylan was still recuperating and deserved a rest, and partly because he just didn't care about delivering a professional studio quality recording, the songs were done at home in the most relaxed setting possible. As a result, Dylan recorded his greatest body of work.

So why wasn't this material released until 1975? The deal with MGM fell through (and they collapsed a few years later anyway) and Dylan had a new contract with Columbia, and so *John Wesley Harding* was released instead. The basement tapes songs couldn't go to waste, so they were sent out to various artists for demo purposes. But then why didn't Dylan just re-record the basement tapes songs with the Nashville musicians for *John Wesley Harding*? I don't know. Maybe by that time he was bored with the whole project, or maybe he still held out hopes of releasing a definitive *Basement Tapes* album.

The music is all available here on five CDs called *The Genuine Basement Tapes*, and genuine they are. No overdubs and no cleaning up - just the way they were recorded. Some tracks cut off just as they get going, others begin in the middle of verses, and others are merely tryouts that never got beyond the initial run-through stage. Some of it is in very clear mono, and some is distorted and full of hiss, but mostly the sound is superb. Many people have complained about the stereo sound, with Dylan's voice on one channel and most of the instruments on the other (much like the early Parlophone Beatles albums), but I actually like this sound myself. I get to hear Dylan's voice in isolation and Garth Hudson's organ is much more prominent. Also, some of the harmonies that weren't apparent on the official album and early bootlegs can now be heard for the first time.

The release of the basement tapes came in three stages. (I don't mean to imply that the songs were recorded in three separate stages - but that they came to the public in distinct batches). The first stage consisted of the fourteen songs forming the core plus the other songs that were in circulation at the same time, including "Odds and Ends", "Clothesline Saga", "I'm Not There", "Get Your Rocks Off", "Apple Suckling Tree", and others. These songs went into circulation because they were being made available to recording artists throughout the world who might be interested in recording new Dylan songs. I'll call these the "original archives". The second stage consists of the songs discovered in the late 1980s and soon after released on the *Blind Boy Grunt and the Hawks* albums. Most of these songs were either traditional or cover tunes, but some are still of unknown origin. In Clinton Heylin's book *Bootleg: The Secret History of Rock and Roll,* he tells us how this batch of tapes was uncovered. A friend of Robbie Robertson gave or loaned the tapes to a record store owner in the Pacific Northwest and from there the tapes were bootlegged. Apparently the original owner of the tapes didn't know what a gold mine he had. I'll call these the "Robbie Robertson archives". The third stage consists of the newly discovered tracks, which surfaced at the same time the *Bootleg Series* collection was being assembled by CBS/Sony. This collection of songs is the weirdest of the lot and features mainly covers of traditional folk and blues tunes, but there are a few alternate takes of some of the more familiar "original" songs thrown in for good measure. Since these songs are believed to come from the Garth Hudson archives, I'll call these the "Garth Hudson archives". I wonder if we can look forward to a stage four release? Maybe Rick Danko's widow is still sitting on a stash...

Genuine Basement Tapes Volume 1

Personnel:
Bob Dylan - guitar, piano, harmonica, vocals
Robbie Robertson - guitar, drums, vocals
Rick Danko - bass, fiddle, vocals
Richard Manuel - piano, drums, vocals
Garth Hudson - organ, piano
(Levon Helm also appears on some tracks)

Volume one consists entirely of songs (from the Robbie Robertson archives) discovered about ten years after the release of the "official" Basement Tapes album (hereafter called *OA*). Some of these songs feature Dylan on 12-string guitar and others feature him on piano. All are very impassioned performances.

All You Have To Do Is Dream

I don't know if this song is an original, but it definitely has some clever lyrics ("if the farmer has no silo, and his fuel cost is running high, well that's just how much I would love you, if you'd only let me try"), plus the arrangement appears to be more worked out than most, leading me to believe that this was possibly one of the songs intended for future release. Apparently they never finished a suitable version. Too bad. The second version also appears on this volume.

I Can't Make It Alone

Mostly improvised, this song is a nice minor key blues and has a lot of potential, but it's definitely not finished. Dylan on piano, I believe.

Down On Me

This is just a brief pass at an old gospel standard later made famous by Janis Joplin. Nice harmonies. This recording, like so many others in this collection, demonstrates that Dylan and the Band were a unit and not just a singer with his backup group helping out.

Bonnie Ship the Diamond

Apparently a traditional English or Scottish folk song about whaling expeditions. Dylan on 12-string guitar and very rough voice. Excellent organ from Garth Hudson.

One Man's Loss

This is one of my favorites, even though it's one of the poorer sounding recordings in the bunch, because for much of the beginning of the song you can't hear Dylan's voice, but once it gets going and you can hear him better, the song can be appreciated as a nicely improvised blues. Nice lyrics: "one man's loss always been another man's gain, one man's joy always been another man's pain". Dylan on piano. As usual, Robbie's guitar adds so much without really making you aware of it.

Baby Ain't That Fine

Nice ensemble country singing at its twangiest. Another example of how Dylan and the Band collaborated vocally. This song reminds me of Dylan's later “Wallflower”.

Rock Salt and Nails

Nice slow country tune written by Bruce Phillips with great lyrics and wonderful vocal. "If the ladies were squirrels, with their high bushy tails, I'd fill up my shotgun with rock salt and nails". This is the type of song that the boys were singing at these sessions!

A Fool Such As I

Made famous by Elvis Presley, Dylan later redid this song at the *Self Portrait* sessions and Columbia subsequently released it on the notorious *Dylan* album. This version is different, though, and is much slower and more relaxed.

Stones That You Throw

An old Hank Williams song from his Luke the Drifter days, this morality fable is a sort of "drawling blues" obviously done on the spur of the moment. No one for sure really knows how the song goes, but Bob gets the lyrics right, apparently, and the sing-along chorus is fabulous: "A tongue can accuse or carry bad news, the seeds of distrust it will sow. So unless you have made no mistakes in your life, be careful of stones that you throw". Performed very tongue-in-cheek.

Hills of Mexico

This is actually none other than “On the Trail of the Buffalo” and goes under many different titles. Unfortunately this version stops just as it gets started, with Bob saying "you don't have to record this one, Garth, you're just wasting tape". Well, I would have liked to have heard the rest! As with many of the songs on these tapes, the original key is abandoned and it starts over in a new key. It could have been great, but maybe the mood just wasn't right.

I'm Alright

It's really a shame that this is only a fragment because it sounds like it must have been one of the best songs recorded at these sessions! One verse and chorus is all we get before the tape chokes. A lot of other really outstanding songs are aborted in the same way. "I'm a three time loser but I'm alright". Who wrote this?

One Single River

The actual title is “Song for Canada”. One of my favorite songs on volume one. One of several songs written by Ian and Sylvia. Dylan must have been listening to their records quite a lot at the time, and they're some of the best songs on these sessions! Not having been familiar with them before hearing them here, I had assumed them to be Dylan originals. Now I'm going to have to seek out some of their recordings because I'm very impressed by the quality of the writing.

Try Me

"Try me little girl, we can raise a family". Dylan on piano. Excellent melody and chord progression. Dylan almost goes into falsetto during the "try me"'s. The song is essentially complete. Garth shines on organ.

One For the Road

No, not the one made famous by Frank Sinatra, but apparently a totally improvised song which will break your heart. The lyrics seem to be nonsense and exist only to fill in for what would be the real words, if they ever existed. Slow country blues with more excellent Richard Manuel harmonies. The chord changes alter slightly toward the end - to great effect. One of the best tracks on volume one. Very dynamic.

I Don't Hurt Anymore

Another country standard, originally recorded by Hank Snow 1951. More ensemble singing from the band. Really nothing more than an initial run through and not as good as some others on the same disc.

People Get Ready

Curtis Mayfield's classic gospel song, sung entirely in harmony by Bob and the boys. Dylan returned to this song at least twice more in his career (*Renaldo & Clara*, and *Flashback* film soundtrack). Musically beautiful. Dylan on 12-string guitar.

Won't You Be My Baby

A fragment, unfortunately. This cuts off just as it starts to get cooking with a Garth Hudson solo. Very tough, brittle guitar and bluesy organ, combined with Dylan's piano and vocal. Richard Manuel on drums. Excellent!

Don't You Try Me Now

Another great blues. Great vocal by Bob. I believe he plays piano on this one too. Sample lyrics: "You might think you're having a good time, but wait 'til later on when your troubles start".

All You Have To Do Is Dream

Version two of the same song that opened this disc. This time out it's more refined and polished, but I prefer version one myself. When Robbie begins his solo, it's so loud that it literally sounds like a completely different instrument. It's very startling. This could have been a single.

You Say You Love Me

Not listed on the cover, this song features the Band without Bob Dylan. Richard Manuel sings lead during the chorus and you can barely make out Robbie Robertson during the verses. There is a better take of this on the vinyl collection *Blind Boy Grunt and the Hawks* volume one, but it's not available on the CD.

Long Time A-Growin'

This disc closes with one of the very best vocal performances ever given by Dylan, or by anybody for that matter. This is the Irish folk song that he sang back in 1961, slightly updated with guitar and organ, and with fragmented altered lyrics. Slow and relaxed with Bob gliding effortlessly through the melody, you've never heard anything like it before. He also plays 12-string guitar. This one is worth the price of the disc alone.

Genuine Basement Tapes Volume 2

Personnel:
Bob Dylan - guitar, piano, harmonica, vocals
Robbie Robertson - guitar, drums, vocals
Rick Danko - bass, fiddle, vocals
Richard Manuel - piano, drums, vocals
Garth Hudson - organ, piano
(Levon Helm also appears on some tracks)

Volume two consists mostly of those songs available in 1967 and subsequently released on the official Basement Tapes album (hereafter called *OA*), but many of these versions have never been heard before by the general public, even though they have been known of for years. This is the core of the Basement Tapes. The nice thing about this disc is that is tends to present the multiple takes more or less in order, so that for the first time we actually have both versions of *Quinn the Eskimo* and all three takes of *Open the Door Homer* on one disc. Also, the multiple versions present further evidence that these songs were probably intended to be released as part of an album at one time or another.

Odds and Ends #1

A different take than the one on the *OA*, but not much different except that the ending is more ragged.

Nothing Was Delivered #1

Much different than the *OA* version. This one is more uptempo with a drum track. Just a fragment, though. There's a more complete one later on.

Odds and Ends #2

The *OA* version, minus the piano which was actually overdubbed in 1975 (prove me wrong!). Otherwise, identical to the album track.

Get Your Rocks Off

One of the legends of the original Basement Tapes. Long available on various vinyl bootlegs, most notably *VD Waltz*, this one is a pretty funny blues number with everyone having a real good time. Covered by Manfred Mann, of all people. The lyrics are hilarious.

Clothesline Saga

Same as on the *OA*, except that the flub at the beginning was cleaned up for the album. It's intact here. One of the highlights from the session.

Apple Suckling Tree #1
Apple Suckling Tree #2

Version 1 appeared on the *OA* and version 2 is only slightly different, being just a little bit more sloppy than the first one. Both are very good and Garth really shines. Has anyone noticed that the tune is almost identical to “Froggie Went A-Courtin'”?

Going To Acapulco

Before the release of the *OA*, this song was completely unknown. Here it is again, this time in a slightly different mix which emphasizes Richard's backup vocal and Garth's organ.

Gonna Get You Now

It's funny that this would appear here, because it really belongs on volume one, seeing as it was one of the songs discovered only recently. One of the minor songs from the sessions, still very enjoyable.

Tears of Rage #1
Tears of Rage #2
Tears of Rage #3

All three versions of “Tears of Rage”, including one (version 1) in waltz time. One of these versions appeared on the album, but the most famous of them (version 2) did not. Compare for yourself and see which one you like best. Version 3 is the one that appeared on the *OA*.

Quinn the Eskimo #1
Quinn the Eskimo #2

Version 2 appears on *Biograph*, but it was really version 1 that was the more famous of the two. "Waitin' on you", Bob says at the beginning, apparently waiting for Garth to begin his famous flute-like organ riff before beginning the first verse. I suppose they thought the second run through was more polished. Until version 2 appeared on *Biograph*, the only official version of this song was the live one from the Isle of Wight concert that appeared on *Self Portrait*! In fact, that was the only live rendition of the song that Dylan has ever done. A huge hit for Manfred Mann in 1967.

Open the Door Homer #1
Open the Door Homer #2
Open the Door Homer #3

Three versions of this song, all pretty similar. The most famous one (version 1) appeared on the *OA*. It was also the best. The others show obvious signs of the song still being worked out and there are some pretty rough edges. It's strange that the song started to collapse after take 1, unless the order here is confused.

Nothing Was Delivered #2
Nothing Was Delivered #3

Version 2 is the famous official version and version 3 is the full rock version complete with drums. The *OA* version is the best one, and it appears here in a slightly different mix.

I'm Not There (1956)

One of the true wonders of the Basement Tapes sessions, and the very best song on this CD. After years of hearing this song only in low quality sound, we finally have a brilliantly clear version to listen to. The lyrics are still mostly indecipherable, but at least we can clearly hear the mumbles for a change! Although it's available in stereo on other bootlegs, it's in mono here. There's also a slight glitch at the beginning which sounds almost like a skip, but I suppose it could have been deliberate on the bootlegger's part. Truly one of the best unreleased Dylan songs ever recorded. I'd still like to know where the "1956" in the title comes from.

Don'tcha Tell Henry

At one time very rare because it had never before appeared on a bootleg, this drunken romp is a lot of fun. Don't expect it to sound like the *OA* version as sung by Levon Helm, though. This one is so loose that you wonder how they can keep from falling down the whole time the song is going! Somebody plays trombone. Garth plays bass on the organ.

Too Much of Nothing #2

This is the most famous version of the song, but it wasn't the one released on the *OA*. There was much complaining when the album came out because this version was replaced by a lesser known take (more on that later). I can't get too upset about it, though, because with the GBT series we have it all!

Genuine Basement Tapes Volume 3

Personnel:
Bob Dylan - guitar, piano, harmonica, vocals
Robbie Robertson - guitar, drums, vocals
Rick Danko - bass, fiddle, vocals
Richard Manuel - piano, drums, vocals
Garth Hudson - organ, piano
(Levon Helm also appears on some tracks)

Volume three features more of the "original" songs, but with a few extra newly discovered songs thrown in for good measure. Despite the wealth of wonderful material, this disc is the one I like the least, primarily because of the poor sound. Whether by design or accident, the entire disc is in mono and features a lot of hiss at times. I know that there are stereo versions of some of these songs available, and so the decision to master them in mono makes for some pretty poor mixing results. Garth Hudson can't be heard as he should and some of the harmonies are buried. Still this disc is essential because of the material presented.

OA refers to the "Official Album" released by Columbia in 1975.

Million Dollar Bash #1

An alternate version which is unusual for the presence of harmonica. Otherwise not much different from the *OA* version.

Yea Heavy and a Bottle of Bread #1

A more relaxed alternate take. Also not much different from the final version.

Million Dollar Bash #2
Yea Heavy and a Bottle of Bread #2
Please Mrs. Henry

These are the *OA* versions. Different mixes, and unfortunately in mono.

Crash on the Levee #1

Version 1 of this song, more popularly known as “Down In the Flood”. Different tempo than the *OA* one.

Crash on the Levee #2

The familiar *OA* version. Different mix.

Lo and Behold #1

The first version of “Lo and Behold” sounds very similar to the *OA* version, but it's only slightly less together and there's a point where Dylan stumbles over the lyrics and cracks up. Lots of fun, nevertheless.

Lo and Behold #2

The *OA* version. Different mix.

Ferdinand the Imposter

Rick Danko sings this song and Dylan takes no part. Too bad it's just a fragment, because it sounds like it would have been a great song. Fades out slightly before the abrupt end which was clearly evident on the vinyl boot.

Tiny Montgomery
This Wheel's On Fire
You Ain't Goin' Nowhere
I Shall Be Released

All the same versions as on the *OA*. Lots of hiss during "I Shall Be Released", making it one of the poorest in fidelity since the original *Great White Wonder*. Fortunately we have it on *Bootleg Series 2*. Both "You Ain't Goin' Nowhere" and "This Wheel's On Fire" sound dramatically different than their *OA* counterparts. "Wheel" was vastly improved for the *OA* and "Nowhere" has, I believe, a guitar overdub that isn't evident on this mix.

Too Much of Nothing #2

Supposedly a stereo mix of the most famous of the two takes, but not the one on the *OA*. Still, it's *NOT* in stereo on this disc and has a fair amount of hiss.

Even a Tomato

An instrumental from the Band. I don't know what the title refers to. Levon Helm rejoined the Band after the Dylan material was recorded, so he appears on this track.

Santa Fe

One of the songs only rumored before the release on *Bootleg Series*. Lyrics are mumbled and obviously improvised. This seems to have been an excuse for Dylan to sing the very nice melody. With a little work it could have been a good song.

Silent Weekend

The best thing on this disc! Another long rumored song, this one almost made it to the *Bootleg Series* before that set was trimmed down from four to three discs. If it isn't Levon playing drums, then it must be Richard. Doesn't really sound like his style to me, though. Excellent singing from Dylan and fine backup from Danko. Rockabilly at its finest.

Too Much of Nothing #1

The *OA* version. Many people were disappointed to hear this instead of the other one when the album came out, but I like this one just as much. I remember being very surprised when I first heard it because the melody and chords are so different from the one I was used to. This is very worked out and proves to me, beyond a shadow of a doubt, that there was more to these sessions than just having a lot of fun. This is a serious attempt to produce a polished song. Possibly another proposed single?

Sign on the Cross

Next to "Silent Weekend", this is the real reason to own this disc. "Sign on the Cross" is simply one of Dylan's very best performances ever. Everything about this seven minute gem is perfect, from Garth's organ swells right down to Bob's drunken monologue. I think it's interesting to note that the basic structure and melody of this song was recycled many years later for the Dylan/U2 collaboration "Love Rescue Me". Even though a stereo mix exists, this track is in mono. Still worth it, as it sounds very loud and clear.

Genuine Basement Tapes Volume 4

Personnel:
Bob Dylan - guitar, piano, harmonica, vocals
Robbie Robertson - guitar, drums, vocals
Rick Danko - bass, fiddle, vocals
Richard Manuel - piano, drums, vocals
Garth Hudson - organ, piano
(Levon Helm also appears on some tracks)

Starting with volume four, the rest of the unreleased basement tapes (the Garth Hudson archives) began to go public. What we have here are some of the most entertaining songs in the whole collection. They're also the poorest sounding with lots of distortion and occasional dropouts from time to time. Still, there is some very good material here. In fact, I would have to say that volumes 4 and 5 are my favorites of the series. Bob and the Band are having a lot of fun here. The fun is contagious.

OA refers to the "Official Album" released by Columbia in 1975.

You Ain't Going Nowhere #1

A real surprise! The lyrics are ***nothing*** like the released version, either on the *OA* or on *Greatest Hits 2*, which was a little different in itself. The lyrics here are a crackup! Sample verse:

Just pick up that oilcloth
cram it in the corner
I don't care if your name is Michael you're gonna need some boards
get your lunch, you foreign bib
you ain't goin' nowhere

It's sung in a talking drawl similar to “Lo and Behold” and “Bottle of Bread”. I wish this version had been released on the *OA* instead of the more well known one.

Bourbon Street

Apparently recorded at the same time as “Don'tcha Tell Henry”, this features the same drunken sound complete with trombone and organ bass pedals. This song is a little bit of a disappointment after having heard of it for years in lyric form only. Even though incomplete, it appears to be substantially finished all the same.

All American Boy

A great talking blues with Rick helping out with comic asides. Written by Bobby Bare and a hit for Bill Parson in 1959. Lots of fun.

Wild Wood Flower

Written by A. P. Carter. This doesn't really sound that much like one of the basement tapes at all. In fact, it sounds more like something from the *Self Portrait* era. Sound problems (left channel has dropouts). Floppy Nashville style drums and somebody blowing a blues harmonica in the background, doesn't really sound like the rest of the basement tapes. No keyboards.

See That My Grave Is Kept Clean

The Blind Lemon Jefferson song that Dylan did on his very first album. This sounds like another *Self Portrait* era recording. The voice sounds like the one he was using on *Nashville Skyline* and *Self Portrait.*

Comin' Round the Mountain

Yep, "she'll be coming round the mountain when she comes". Sure sounds like a *Self Portrait* outtake, but the voice does sound more in line with basement tapes plus the backup vocals could be the Band. Who knows?

Flight of the Bumblebee

Just some fooling around. Don't know where this song comes from, or if it even exists as a real song at all. Mostly just an uninteresting blues jam.

Confidential To Me

This is more like it. Definitely Garth on organ and probably Robbie on drums, although it could be Richard. The piano could be Dylan. Pretty sloppy, but the spirit is right. Written by Dolinda Morgan and recorded by Sonny Knight in 1956.

I'm a Fool for You

Great song with great possibilities. Falls apart at the bridge because of key change problems. Too bad. This is a real good example of how a song can get ruined by too much rehearsal and why Dylan always liked to get everything in the first take. The song starts with great feeling and the Band is completely with it up until the time it falls apart because Bob calls out the wrong chord. They try to pick it up again, but it never gels. The words don't appear to mean anything, but the feeling gets across just the same. Further proof that at this stage in his musical development, he was much more involved in melody and chord progressions than he was in lyrics.

Next Time on the Highway

Great rockabilly. Great singing and playing. Pure basement tapes excellence. Dylan seems to be uttering obscenities toward the end!

The Big Flood

Actual title is "Tupelo". Another talking blues, with a real blues feel for a change. Dylan growls low and mean. Written by John Lee Hooker.

Don't Know Why They Kick My Dog

Also known as "Everytime I Come To Town" and "You Gotta Quit Kicking My Dog Around", this is a lot of fun. They're apparently trying to work out the arrangement, but I don't think it would have become an actual released recording at any time, but who knows? I have heard conflicting things about the origin of this song. First, I've been told that it's an old political song written by Oungst-Perkins and recorded in 1916. Then I've been told that the song originated by Gid Tanner and the Skillet Likkers as "You Gotta Quit Kickin' My Dog", circa 1934. I'm not sure which is right, perhaps both are correct.

See You Later, Allen Ginsberg

Just fooling around with variations on "See You Later, Alligator". Lots of laughing.

The Spanish Song #1 & #2

More fooling around. Also known as *Luisa*. Bob and the boys in their south of the border mode.

I Am a Teenage Prayer

One of my favorites. "Take a look at me baby, I'm your teenage prayer". Rick Danko (or is it Richard Manuel?) tries and succeeds in cracking Bob up with variations on "teenage prayer" (teenage hair, teenage bear). Just silly stuff, but I love it!

I'm in the Mood

Another John Lee Hooker song, this one from 1951. This appears to have been recorded at around the same time as the above four songs. It's amazing how much of this disc sounds like the type of thing the Beatles were doing during their *Get Back* sessions two years later.

Belshazzar #1 & #2

This one has sound problems that didn't exist on the tape. The left channel drops out for the first few 10 seconds or so, and then it comes on with very low volume. Great song and one of the best performances in the whole collection. Even though two versions are indicated, there is really only one here and the first run-through was just an abortive attempt in the wrong key. Written and recorded by Johnny Cash in 1957.

Bring it on Home

"Richard, take a verse", says Bob. "What's the song?" says Richard. "Any song!" says Bob. Just more fooling around. A variation of Bo Diddley's “Bring It To Jerome". This is an excellent demonstration of Bob's ability to improvise-on-the-spot lyrics. Fades out.

The King of France

Some distortion on this on, and Bob's voice is very hard to hear. Electric piano (unusual for these sessions), drums. It fades out too soon.

If I Lose, Let Me Lose

Written by Ralph Stanley. This is Levon Helm singing with the rest of the Band and Bob is nowhere evident. Apparently another of the Band tunes recorded during or immediately after these sessions.

Originally the signature tune of Charlie Poole & The North Carolina Ramblers.

Genuine Basement Tapes Volume 5

Personnel:
Bob Dylan - guitar, piano, harmonica, vocals
Robbie Robertson - guitar, drums, vocals
Rick Danko - bass, fiddle, vocals
Richard Manuel - piano, drums, vocals
Garth Hudson - organ, piano
(Levon Helm also appears on some tracks)

This is my favorite of the five volumes, mainly because everyone seems to be having so much fun. Like volume 4, this one contains some of the more obscure outtakes from the basement tapes sessions and comes (possibly) from the Garth Hudson archives.

OA refers to the "Official Album" released by Columbia in 1975.

Four Strong Winds

Another Ian and Sylvia song which Neil Young performs from time to time. Richard Manuel on harmony.

The French Girl #1 & #2

Yet another Ian and Sylvia song. Dylan later came back to this song during the Grateful Dead rehearsals in 1987. The version numbers refer to the fact that there is an initial run-through that peters out and then it's restarted again in a different key. Good song with a very nice melody.

Joshua Gone Barbados

An Eric von Schmidt song that has a calypso feel. The lyrics apparently refer to a strike among the cane field workers.

I Forgot to Remember to Forget

Also recorded by Elvis Presley, Johnny Cash, etc. Nice slow version, but the vocal is a little hard to hear. Written by Sam Kesler and Charlie feathers.

You Win Again

Hank Williams tune. Probably recorded at the same time as the above.

Still in Town

Written by Johnny Cash and recorded for his "I Walk the Line" album. One of Bob's best vocals from these sessions.

Waltzing with Sin

Great great song. There was really an attempt to get this song right. Beautiful performance by all involved. Wonderful vocal.

Big River

One of my favorite Johnny Cash songs. There are actually two takes. The first is a single verse only, but then they stop and start it over in a different, much more rocking and compelling tempo. Bob really sings the hell out of this one. At the end, Bob wonders if there's any more room on the tape.

Folsom Prison Blues

Another Johnny Cash song. They must have been in a certain mood, I guess. He still does this one occasionally. Sound problems on this one, with the left channel completely dropping out for much of the song. This doesn't occur on the original tapes, so it must be a fault in the CD mastering.

Bells of Rhymney

The Pete Seeger song. One of the least successful songs on this collection, in my opinion. Sound is pretty distorted.

Nine Hundred Miles

Sound on this one is horrible. Lots of distortion. It's hard to imagine that this was recorded at the same time as the other tracks on this disc. Fortunately it's just a brief fragment. There is some weird screeching violin and what sounds like a double bass along with floppy drums. I wouldn't be surprised to find that this isn't the Band at all. Maybe this is the famous Einstein on electric violin we've heard so much about? (sorry Craig :-))

No Shoes on My Feet

Usually referred to as "Goin' Down the Road Feelin'" Bad. Dylan on piano. A bit of distortion. Some of the lyrics are similar to "Worried Blues".

Spanish is the Loving Tongue

Charles Badger Clark song. This is a favorite of Dylan's, having released two official versions and also recorded it live at the Friends of Chile benefit in 1974. This one is just okay, with a weird affected vocal style.

On a Rainy Afternoon

Distorted. One of those long rumored songs known only by the lyrics. Has potential. The lyrics are different from the published ones, so maybe there's another take or two lying about?

I Can't Come in with a Broken Heart

Too bad this is so incredibly distorted, because it sounds like it was one of the more worked out songs and could have been very good if completed.

Under Control

This is another of my favorites. Great rockin' groove. Great vocal. Hard to make out the lyrics, but the feeling is just right.

Ol' Roison the Beau

Great New Orleans country twang. One of the greats. The bass is slightly distorted, as it is on many of the tracks on volume 4 and 5. This song makes me want to get drunk and sing along!

I'm Guilty of Loving You

Just a fragment of what sounds like might have been excellent if finished. A lot like something Van Morrison might do. Very soulful.

Johnny Todd

Probably a traditional English folk song. This cuts in so close on the previous song that it leads me to believe that someone screwed up during recording and accidentally erased over the rest of "I'm Guilty of Loving You". Either way, this song doesn't do much for me.

Cool Water

Bob Nolan song. God, this is great! Bob's best vocal on this volume. The backup vocals are all great too. One of the true wonders of this collection.

Banks of the Royal Canal

Brendan Behan prison song also known as "The Auld Triangle". Apparently a one-time-only take, because the arrangement changes slightly as the Band starts to adjust to the melody. Bob sounds very relaxed and pulls off one his best performances. Just fantastic.

Po' Lazarus

Just a fragment, and a fitting end to the entire series.

The Story Behind Self Portrait

The Sessions

Basic sessions began in Nashville on April 24, 1969 and concluded March 5, 1970.

This information courtesy of Michael Krogsgaard.

April 24, 1969 (Nashville):

1. Living The Blues
2. Spanish Is The Loving Tongue

Personnel:

Charlie McCoy (bass)
Pete Drake (steel guitar)
Robert S. Wilson (piano)
Kenneth Buttrey (drums)
Charlie E. Daniels (guitar)
Fred F. Carter Jr. (guitar)

April 26, 1969 (Nashville):

1. Take Me As I Am (Or Let Me Go)
2. A Fool Such As I
3. I Forgot More Than You'll Ever Know
4. Let It Be Me
5. Running

Personnel:

Charlie McCoy (bass)
Norman L. Blake (guitar)
Pete Drake (steel guitar)
Robert S. Wilson (piano)
Kenneth Buttrey (drums)
Charlie E. Daniels (guitar)
Fred F. Carter Jr. (guitar)

May 3, 1969 (Nashville):

1. Take a Message to Mary
2. Blue Moon
3. Folsom Prison Blues
4. Ring of Fire

Personnel:

Charlie McCoy (bass)
Pete Drake (pedal steel guitar)
Fred Carter Jr. (guitar)
Robert S. Wilson (piano)
Norman Blake (guitar)
Doug Kershaw (fiddle)
Kenneth Buttrey (drums)
Charlie E. Daniels (guitar)

March 3, 1970 (New York):

1. Pretty Saro
2. Little Sadie
3. Dock Of The Bay
4. Went To See The Gypsy
5. In Search Of Little Sadie
6. Belle Isle
7. Universal Soldier
8. Copper Kettle
9. When A Fellow's Out Of A Job
10. These Hands
11. It Hurts Me Too

12. The Boxer
13. Spanish Is The Loving Tongue
14. Woogie Boogie

Personnel:

Al Kooper (organ or piano)
David Bromberg (guitar)
Emanuel Green (violin)

March 4, 1970 (New York):

1. Went To See The Gypsy
2. Thirsty Boots
3. Tattle O-Day
4. Railroad Bill
5. House Carpenter
6. This Evening So Soon
7. Days Of '49
8. Annie's Going To Sing Her Song
9. Early Morning Rain
10. Wigwam
11. Time Passes Slowly

Personnel:

Al Kooper (guitar and keyboards)
David Bromberg (guitar)
Emanuel Green (violin)
Alvin Rogers (drums)
Stu Woods (bass)

March 5, 1970 (New York):

1. Alberta
2. Alberta # 2
3. Little Moses
4. Alberta # 1
5. Come A Little Bit Closer
6. Come All You Fair And Tender Ladies
7. My Previous Life

8. Gotta Travel On
9. Went To See The Gypsy
10. Time Passes Slowly
11. Come A Little Bit Closer
12. All The Tired Horses

Personnel:

Al Kooper (guitar and keyboards)
Emanuel Green (violin)
Alvin Rogers (drums)
Stu Woods (bass)
David Bromberg (guitar)
Hilda Harris. Albertine Robinson, and Maeretha Stewart (vocals)

After the basic tracks were recorded in New York City, the tapes were flown to Nashville, Tennessee for overdubbing. These sessions took place from March 11, 1970 through April 3, 1970.

Personnel:

Charlie McCoy (bass)
Kenneth Buttrey (drums)
Bob L. Moore (bass)
Fred Carter Jr. (electric guitar)
Charles E. Daniels (guitar)
Bubba Fowler (guitar)
Karl T. Himmel (sax, clarinet. trombone)
Ron Cornelius (guitar)
Bill Walker (leader & arranger)
Rex Peer (trombone)
William Pursell (piano)
Gene Mullins (baritone horn)
Dennis A. Good (trombone)
Frank C. Smith (trombone)
Martha McCrory (cello)
Byron T. Bach (cello)
Gary van Osdale (viola)
Lillian V. Hunt (violin)
Sheldon Kurland (violin)
Martin Katahn (violin)
Marvin D. Chantry (violin)
Brenton B. Banks (violin)
George Binkley (violin)

Solie I. Fott (violin, viola)
Barry McDonald (violin)
Carol Montgomery (vocals)
Dolores Edgin (vocals)
June Page (vocals)

The Story Behind the Album

One of the oddest chapters in Dylan's career was the recording and release of the legendary album *Self Portrait*, released in 1970 to almost uniformly negative reviews. Many critics and fans thought they were on the receiving end of a massive joke, or if not a joke then a seriously deteriorated Dylan who had finally lost all touch with reality. Or perhaps Dylan was just out of ideas? The lead track from the album certainly seemed to indicate that with its repeated chorus "all the tired horses in the sun, how am I supposed to get any riding done?", which sounded a little like "how am I supposed to get any *writing* done"!

Various reasons for the seemingly poor quality of the album were given, including the idea that all the songs were scraps left over from *Nashville Skyline* and *New Morning* sessions (the latter album would be released *after Self Portrait*, but many of the songs on that album featured the same musicians on many of the *Self Portrait* songs, so the sound would fit). Since so many of the songs on the *double album* were apparently filler (four songs from the Isle of Wight festival, different versions of some songs on the same album, lifeless jams, etc.), the skimpy artistic nature of the album was clearly highlighted.

And the title of this mess was *Self Portrait*! This was supposed to define Bob Dylan? With its cubist self portrait on the cover (the original cover was reported in Rolling Stone at the time to be a picture of Bob standing in the window of an abandoned tenement building - wonder whatever happened to that picture?), and with the straight faced comical pictures of Dylan hanging around a barnyard with chickens, the visual impact of the album was jarring. To hear the sound inside was even more jarring.

What follows is a sort of insider's look into the making of this album. Rather than taking quotes from reviews, I chose to use actual quotes from people involved in the making of the album, or those close enough to Dylan to know what may have been going on in his mind during this strange period.

From Bob Dylan: An Intimate Biography *by Anthony Scaduto, 1971*

At the same time, Dylan had just completed another album. The reports coming out of Columbia were too incredible: Dylan had put together an album tentatively called *Blue Moon*, filled with his interpretations of other artists' works, songs by Rodgers and Hart, Paul Simon, Gordon Lightfoot, and a large number of the old traditional country and folk things he had been doing back in Minnesota. Bob had cut a couple of dozen songs in New York and had to discard many of them because they simply didn't turn out well at all. He then went to Nashville for some help from the country boys, but things were only slightly better down there.

When the album was finally released in June, 1970, the most insane rumors seemed to be true: Bob Dylan had put out a *product*, a two-record set mysteriously called ***Self Portrait***, filled mostly with the works of others and some examples of Americana, produced in a style that appeared to be almost Mantovani music, dreary enough to pipe into elevators or corset shoppes. You laughed when you first heard it - Bob Dylan trying to turn his nasal twang into a bass baritone, in the style of Johnny Cash. It seemed to be a huge joke. Bob Dylan as commercial popular songwriter and singer, a one-man Simon and Garfunkel. Or, perhaps, the Dylan Brothers - his version of Simon's "The Boxer", Dylan dubbing harmony with Dylan, sounded so lame at first hearing that it had to be a parody of Simon, except that Dylan was spending a lot of time with Simon in New York and out on Fire Island, and parody doesn't make sense.

... Dylan is somewhat defensive about the *Stone* interview, while sounding absolutely certain about the worth of ***Self Portrait***: "It's a great album," he said to me. "There's a lot of damn good music there. People just didn't listen at first."

notes:

The quote from Dylan indicates that he was surprised at the negative response and felt at the time that the album was a genuine worthy effort. The Rolling Stone review is worth seeking out. It features a round table discussion between several prominent Rolling Stone critics and pretty much trashes the album without mercy. [JH]

From No Direction Home: The Life and Music of Bob Dylan *by Robert Shelton, 1986*

I told Dylan that ***Self Portrait*** confused me. Why had he recorded "Blue Moon"? He wouldn't be drawn out, although obviously he had been stung by the criticism. "It was an expression," he said. He indicated that if the album had come from Presley or The Everly Brothers, who veered toward the middle of the road, it wouldn't have shocked so many.

notes:

Again, an indication that Dylan was serious about the nature of the album and was disappointed at the criticism. [JH]

Roger McGuinn interview with Ed Ward in Rolling Stone, 1970

EW: Does the latest Dylan puzzle you any?
RM: Not at all. I understand it thoroughly.
EW: Really?
RM: Well, I'm more on the inside of it than most people because we were supposed to work with Dylan at the time. I got a call from Clive Davis, president of Columbia, saying, "How would you like to work with Dylan?" and we'd previously discussed doing albums with other Columbia artists and so I said, "Sure thing, let's get together. Just tell me when and where." So I called Dylan and he wasn't there, but he returned the call and said, "Did Clive Davis call you about doing an album?" and I said, "Yeah, but I don't know what we'd do. Do you have any ideas?" and he said, "No, I haven't thought about it myself. Maybe if you come in with some of the old stuff and I do too that'll be all right." I think he meant some of his old stuff, so it would be all his publishing. So I said, "Well, the only thing we could

do is go into the studio and see what happens, right?" And I asked him if he had any material to spare and he said no, that he was kind of hard up, that he hadn't been writing as much as he used to and I mentioned that we all get fat and lazy and he laughed. And we wound up the conversation by saying that we'd be in touch with each other, nothing definite.

So we got to New York and did a couple of gigs - Felt Forum and Queens College - and that took care of the weekend. By Monday we were still in town, but waiting for some kind of word. Finally the guys took a 12:00 plane back to the Coast. And at 1:00 I got a call from Billie Wallington, a friend of mine at Columbia, and she said that the session was in Studio B at 2:30. Well, I explained to her what the situation was, and she called Dylan and he was pissed off that we didn't have the courtesy to sit around and wait for his phone call. Well, the crux of it all was that Clive was supposed to come down to the show the night before but he didn't show up, and we could have settled it all right there. The other thing was a political thing with Bob Johnston. We'd fired him as our producer, right, and Bob Johnston, as producer, is responsible for notifying the musicians of the time of the session within 12 hours. It's a union regulation. He knew where we were, but he didn't call us and Clive didn't call us. Like I say, it was political.

What I think it would have amounted to is that we would have been backup musicians for Dylan, like the Band, on a couple of cuts on his new album, which he never mentioned to us. He said it could be a separate album, the Byrds and Dylan, and I asked him what kind of billing we'd get on it and he said well, he didn't know, but Clive assured me that we'd be getting at least 33 percent billing on it.

I would have liked to have done it, if it had worked out at all. In view of the circumstances, I'm just as glad that we didn't get on...this...particular...album...that came out, because it was poorly prepared, that's my opinion. He came into the studio prepared to use a lot of outtakes from ***Nashville Skyline*** and a lot of the Isle of Wight stuff, which is just a remote, just a live recording rather than anything musically good. The New York stuff, "Wigwam" and a lot of those, are pretty good.

So I understand the album thoroughly. I understand why there are repeats to fill time because he didn't have enough new material to do it, why he used a lot of old folksongs that everybody's known for 10 or 12 years.
EW: Why is he claiming he wrote them?

RM: He's probably taking publishing on them as re-arrangements of public domain material. It's a standard trick. I've done it myself. But I usually make a few changes. "Old Blue." That's one.

notes:

The above is an insight into why the album may have turned out as poorly as it did. If the original concept had been to have Dylan record some traditionals with the Byrds, it would have been truly great, but because of confusion and misdirection it never happened, and Dylan was forced to rely on outtakes from *Nashville Skyline* instead, the first indication that this is indeed what he may have been planning in the early stages. The mystery for me is how he could have ever thought this would result in a decent album. [JH]

Bob Dylan interview with Kurt Loder in Rolling Stone, June 1984

KL: It always seemed to me that you where sort of infallible in your career up until ***Self Portrait*** in 1970. What's the story behind that album?
BD: At the time, I was in Woodstock, and I was getting a great degree of notoriety for doing *nothing*. Then I had that motorcycle accident, which put me outta commission. Then, when I woke up and caught my senses, I realized that I was workin' for all these *leeches*. And I didn't wanna do that. Plus, I had a family, and I just wanted to see my *kids*.

I'd also seen that I was representing all these things that I didn't know anything *about*. Like I was supposed to be on acid. It was all storm-the-embassy kind of stuff - Abbie Hoffman in the streets - and they sorta figured me as the kingpin of all that. I said, "Wait a minute, I'm just a *musician*. So my songs are about this and that. *So what?*" But people need a leader. People need a leader more than a leader needs people, really. I mean, anybody can step up and be a leader, if he's got the people there that want one. I didn't want that, though.

But then came the big news about Woodstock, about musicians goin' up there, and it was like a wave of insanity breakin' loose around the house *day* and *night*. You'd come in the house and find people there, people comin' through the *woods*, at all hours of the day and night, knockin' on your door. It was really dark and depressing. And there was no way to *respond* to all this, you know? It was as if they were suckin' your very *blood* out. I said, "Now wait, these people can't be my fans. They just *can't* be." And they kept comin'. We *had* to get out of there.

This was just about the time of that Woodstock festival, which was the sum total of all this bullshit. And it seemed to have something to do with *me*, this Woodstock Nation, and everything it represented. So we couldn't *breathe*. I couldn't get any space for myself and my family, and there was no help, nowhere. I got very resentful about the whole thing, and we got outta there.

We moved to New York. Lookin' back, it really was a stupid thing to do. But there was a house available on MacDougal Street, and I always remembered that as a nice place. So I just bought this house, sight unseen. But it wasn't the same when we got back. The Woodstock Nation had overtaken MacDougal Street also. There'd be crowds outside my house. And I said, "Well, fuck it. I wish these people would just *forget* about me. I wanna do something they *can't* possibly like, they *can't* relate to. They'll see it, and they'll listen, and they'll say, "Well, let's get on to the next person. He ain't sayin' it no more. He ain't given' us what we want", you know? They'll go on to somebody else. But the whole idea backfired. Because the album went out there, and the people said, "*This* ain't what we want," and they got *more* resentful. And then I did this portrait for the cover. I mean, there was no *title* for that album. I knew somebody who had some paints and a square canvas, and I did the cover up in about five minutes. And I said, "Well, I'm gonna call this album ***Self Portrait***."
KL: Which was duly interpreted by the press as: This is what he is...
BD: Yeah, *exactly*. And to me it was a *joke*.
KL: But why did you make it a double-album joke?
BD: Well, it wouldn't have held up as a single album - then it *really* would've been bad, you know. I mean, if you're gonna put a lot of crap on it, you might as well load it up!

notes:

By 1985 Dylan was in a revisionist mode and confessed something that I had long suspected anyway: that the album was a deliberate joke. Perhaps at the time he didn't really want to believe it, but by this time Dylan was no longer interested in defending the album on its own merits and was ready to admit that he put it out to test the limits of his fans' credulity. [JH]

From Record Collector magazine, September 1992 - "In the Studio: Al Kooper on Dylan"

RC: How did that [Blonde on Blonde sessions] compare with the sessions for the next album you worked on with Bob, ***Self Portrait*** in 1970?
AK: I don't know what he was looking for on ***Self Portrait***. We'd just go in and do 'cover' songs, all day long.
RC: Wasn't it obvious to everyone that the stuff you were cutting wasn't up to scratch?
AK: By this time we were really good friends, so his charisma had worn off for me. He was just this guy, you know, not some superhuman. But the other people on the session were really excited just to be there, and so everyone approached it with the enthusiasm they would have done if it was a new Dylan song they were doing.

notes:

So, according to Kooper they were recording the cover songs all along and nothing here to indicate that there was any actual original material being worked on, which is contrary to what Dylan will say later on. More on this later. [JH]

From Record Collector magazine, September 1992 - "In the Studio: Charlie McCoy on Dylan"

RC: The last album you did with Dylan was ***Self Portrait***. Do you have any idea what he was trying to create out of that strange mixture of covers and new songs?
CM: In my estimation, Bob had already decided by that point that he wasn't going to work with Bob Johnston any more - for what reason, I don't know. Bob Johnston brought us a tape full of demos that Dylan had done - just guitar or piano and vocals - and on a lot of the songs, Kenny Buttrey and I simply overdubbed drums and bass. Dylan did do a couple of sessions here for that album, but he wasn't here for the whole thing, by any means.
I'm not sure, actually, that ***Self Portrait*** was a 'mutual agreement` project. Either Dylan told Bob to just go ahead and finish it up, by taking those

demos and patching them up; or else maybe Bob Johnston still had to come up with some more tracks to complete his production contract with Dylan, and he just did them off his own bat. We never knew what the deal was.

notes:

Hmmm. The mystery deepens here. McCoy claims that they were really just overdubbing acoustic demos that Bob delivered and that he was rarely in the studio for much of the album. This makes great sense to me, because an awful lot of the album sounds like it may have been done in this way. Possibly the sessions that Kooper attended were different and Bob really played in the studio with the rest of the musicians, but I can see where songs like "It Hurts Me Too", "Alberta", and others may have been demos with later overdubs. [JH]

From Rolling Stone, November 26 1970 - "The Man Who Did Self Portrait" (David Bromberg article)

"On the ***Self Portrait*** album I was sitting right across from Dylan and I played whatever came to mind and there was hardly any discussion. On the new one [***New Morning***] there were more musicians in the studio - Dylan had the songs pretty well worked out beforehand. What they did was sit me in a corner where I had dobro, mandolin, mandocello, electric guitar, acoustic guitar and nylon string guitar. Usually I did rather than the solo things on ***Self Portrait*** was a lot less obvious things. Most tunes were first takes, sometimes second, because Dylan likes a spontaneous sound. Maybe the best thing I did on the album was not to play too much."

[*Bromberg describes meeting Dylan and making vague plans to record together*]
"...I didn't hear from him for about a month and then he called me up about two o'clock one afternoon and asked me what I was doing. He said he was going to test out these studios and would I like to come along, and I said sure. It turned out we had to be in the studio in half an hour and that was the beginning of the sessions for ***Self Portrait***."

Bromberg remembers the sessions as "stream of consciousness things" - one song after another for hours, and he was sick with a high fever. He would work all day, go home, fall asleep and wake up in time to go back to the studio.

"I didn't remember anything we'd done until after the album came out. It was really a challenge, for instance, working on *Little Sadie*. You can tell if you listen to it that he's improvising almost everything he does and even he doesn't know what he's going to do next. All I can say about him is he's a good man, I get good vibrations from him, I like to play with him. That he's a genius, I don't question for a minute."

***notes*:**

Bromberg's statement that Dylan was testing out studios would indicate that he was less interested in putting down great music and more interested in finding a good sounding studio in which to record his next album. Maybe Dylan didn't consider ***Self Portrait*** to be anything more than a warm-up for his next "real" album? The description of Dylan improvising throughout the sessions certainly rings true when you listen to the album.

From Biograph notes, 1985

Self Portrait, Dylan explained recently, "was a bunch of tracks that we'd done all the time I'd gone to Nashville. We did that stuff to get a (studio) sound. To open up we'd do two or three songs, just to get things right and then we'd go on and do what we were going to do. And then there was a lot of other stuff that was just on the shelf. But I was being bootlegged at the time and a lot of stuff that was worse was appearing on bootleg records. So I just figured I'd put all this stuff together and put it out, my own bootleg record, so to speak. You know, if it actually had been a bootleg record, people probably would have sneaked around to buy it and played it for each other secretly. Also, I wasn't going to be anybody's puppet and I figured this record would put an end to that...I was just so fed up with all that who people thought I was nonsense."

notes:

Now Dylan was revising the story once again. He now claims that the tracks were warm-ups for the *real* material they were going to do.

As Paul Williams asks in *Performing Artist: the Early Years*, where is this material? Is there a whole bunch of unknown recordings laying around that no one knows about? It's doubtful for several reasons. First of all, if this material exists why hasn't it been talked about by the musicians involved in the sessions? Second, Dylan's typical "good stuff" from the time was pretty mediocre, so I wouldn't hold out much hope for anything better than what we hear on *Nashville Skyline* or *New Morning*. But this leads me to what I've suspected all along: that *Self Portrait* was a collection of warm-ups recorded during sessions for both of those albums. The statements by Kooper and McCoy would seem to contradict this, though. [JH]

So, there you have some of the background surrounding Dylan's strangest album. If anyone has any more quotes by people involved with the sessions, or any other material that may shed light on what went on during the recording of this unique album, please drop me a line!

UPDATE: With the release of *Another Self Portrait* (volume 10 of the *Bootleg Series*), this seems like a good time to re-evaluate this period. One thing *Another Self Portrait* shows is that there was always the potential for Dylan to make a great album, but he either chose not to or was thwarted by circumstances beyond his control. Looking at the session details at the beginning of this article, it seems clear that the material that eventually wound up on *Self Portrait* spanned from the tail end of the *Nashville Skyline* sessions to the very beginning of what would become *New Morning*. The fact that songs from both album sessions show up on *Another Self Portrait* further emphasizes the connection. *Self Portrait*, therefore, was a sort of placeholder, and perhaps it was never intended to be a "real" album. The early sessions in Nashville were really more *Nashville Skyline* sessions, even though that album had already been completed. "Living the Blues", "Take Me As I Am", "I Forgot More Than You'll Ever Know", "Let It Be Me", "Take a Message To Mary", and "Blue Moon" were recorded at these sessions. Those songs, along with the ones that didn't make the final album, would have made an interesting follow-up to *Nashville Skyline*. There are bootleg versions of several of these songs without the eventual overdubs, and they sound quite nice.

However, it's likely that the feeling was that Dylan didn't need another album just like *Nashville Skyline*, and so Dylan set out on a different path. He took to New York (see the comments from David Bromberg above) and informally recorded some demos of traditional and modern folk songs with minimal accompaniment. These sessions, with just Bromberg and Al Kooper, in early March, make up the best material on *Another Self Portrait* and show what the album could have been. This material is so good that it's unlikely to me that Dylan intended to do anything other than make a great album along the lines of *John Wesley Harding* or the unreleased *Basement Tapes*, but somehow the misguided notion of sending the unfinished demos to Bob Johnston to overdub in Nashville led to one of the most disastrous decisions of his career (although later Dylan would try to spin this as a deliberate attempt to alienate his fan base).

The New York sessions, with the minimal accompaniment supplied, would have made a great single album, but for whatever reason the decision was made to also use the Nashville songs from April and May. The two sounds did not merge well, in my opinion, and to make matters worse it was also decided to use some of the Isle of Wight live tracks for filler. At one time the plan was to release Isle of Wight as a live album, but that was nixed when it was decided the quality wasn't good enough. Instead, we get *Self Portrait*. Luckily, now we get the entire Isle of Wight concert as a bonus to the 2-CD *Another Self Portrait*, so we can hear it in its proper context.

So, to sort this all out, there were three different potential albums here: a set of country standards; a set of traditional and modern folk standards; and a live album with The Band. At the same time, toward the end of the *Self Portrait* sessions, a new sound was emerging which would become *New Morning* - probably released much sooner than anticipated due to the anger unleashed at *Self Portrait*. I would love to someday hear all of the Nashville and New York sessions without the massive overdubs, which ruined this great material.

ISIS and the 1974 Tour

A Song About Marriage

"This is a true story!" - Bob Dylan shouts at the beginning of at least one live rendition of "Isis" during the 1975 Rolling Thunder Revue tour. The question is, which true story is he talking about? Another introduction has him saying "this is a song about marriage", which naturally leads everyone to conclude that the song is about his real life marriage to then wife Sara Dylan. My opinion, and has been ever since the first time I heard the song, was that it's really about his 1974 US tour. Hearing him state that the song is a true story only confirmed it for me.

When I first heard the album *Desire*, the 1974 tour with the Band was still fresh on my mind. I remember how disappointed I was that the reunion did not last and that another album and tour did not immediately follow. The conclusion I reached was that the tour was something of a bust for all concerned and didn't really turn out the way they had expected. Also, I had the distinct impression that the tour had put a strain on Dylan's relationship with his wife and family. After eight years of relative serenity and down-home family life in Woodstock, away from the hassle of big city life and the hardships of dealing with the music industry, getting back on the road for even a single tour seemed to tempt the demons all over again. How easy would it be to avoid the drugs and the depravity of life on the road during a high profile big time rock stadium tour? Was he doing this over the objections of his wife?

A High Place of Darkness and Light

The 1974 tour was initiated in large part to promote his new album, *Planet Waves*. After several years of low profile and inactivity, and after eight full years of not touring and appearing live on very rare occasions, Dylan suddenly found himself ready and able to take to the road again, and he also found himself ready to commit to a real major recording, for the first time since the release of Blonde on Blonde in 1966. To do this he decided to reunite with the Band, his greatest accompanying group, and news of this was greeted among fans as a dream come true. For years the few available recordings of Dylan with the Hawks, as they were known prior to the release of *Music from Big Pink*, were highly esteemed by collectors and any bootleg studio or live recordings were eagerly sought out. It was assumed that the few recordings that were officially available would be all anyone would likely ever get from this historical combination of musicians. So, needless to say the news that Dylan and the Band were going to get back together again for an album and a tour was greeted with high expectations. The most startling news, however, was that Dylan had left his longtime record label after twelve years to sign with David Geffen's Asylum label. This was quite a coup for Geffen, since Dylan was the undisputed king of Rock in the 1970s, in spite of the fact that he never sold all that many records in comparison to his peers. Nevertheless, Dylan had the respect of music critics and a very large fan base, and his influence was felt practically everywhere. There was every indication that the resulting album would be a huge bestseller and that the tour would be a sellout throughout the nation. Indeed, tickets were available only by mail order and not everyone who wrote for tickets got them. Most venues were sold out right away. This was a big event - Bob Dylan was back! The cover of Newsweek, a new record contract with a new label, a new collaboration with one of the most respected bands, the promise of all the old songs coming to life again along with new material - the expectations were very high.

The Cold in the North

Bill Graham was the person most responsible for the 1974 tour, seeing as he was the one who approached Dylan with the proposal in the first place. Dylan agreed and determined that it was a good time to return to the public eye. In fact, the album was called *Planet Waves* because he felt he was in a good place with the planets favorably lining up and so forth (apparently Bob was influenced by Astrology at the time). The tour started out well enough in Chicago in January 1974. The first several shows were rough but wonderful. He played songs he had rarely attempted before: "Hero Blues", "As I Went Out One Morning"; new songs like "Tough Mama" and "Nobody 'Cept You"; and old Dylan/Hawks favorites such as "One Too Many Mornings", "I Don't Believe You", "Leopard-Skin Pill-Box Hat", and of course "Like a Rolling Stone". Dylan was in good voice and the Band played with passion and purpose, if sounding a little under-rehearsed at times. Over time, as the Band became tighter and certain songs that didn't appear to go over as well as others were dropped, a certain formula began to emerge. Also, tempos became brighter and Dylan's vocals changed to a more shouting style that seemed inappropriate at times. Some of the more interesting songs disappeared and the more obvious ones remained. Dylan's acoustic sets began to take on an air of "let's get this over with as soon as possible", and by the end of the tour it was just business as usual for everyone involved. They probably couldn't wait to finish the whole affair. On top of that, the album sold less than expected, and even though it was number one (Dylan's first of three consecutive albums to hit the top spot), it was remaindered in large quantities. Cut-outs could be found in most bargain bins within months of its release - the first and perhaps only Dylan album to hit the bargain bins in such a manner. Asylum had obviously pressed far too many copies and the number one status was most likely due to units shipped rather than actual copies sold. After the promised live album, *Before the Flood* (which was also overstocked), Dylan's contract with Asylum was ended. It turns out that the deal with Asylum was only for two albums and I'm not sure who's idea it was to pass on a renegotiated deal, but ultimately Dylan wound up signing with Columbia again and has remained there ever since.

There Was No Jewels, No Nothin'

What is "Isis" really about? It is about many things. It is about marriage, but what sort of marriage? Taken on one level, it could be about the marriage between a man and a woman. On another level it could be about the marriage between art and commerce. Given the latter idea, the song seems to be about how the singer lost his muse and eventually found it again after a long and arduous journey that seemed to take him nowhere, but in the long run brought him back to where he started. The song is cleverly modeled after "The Trail of the Buffalo". The parallels are obvious: in "Trail of the Buffalo" the narrator is approached by a trail boss and offered a job skinning buffalo. The offer sounds tempting but the trip soon turns into a nightmare and the narrator regrets his decision to join up but is powerless to leave and must see it through to the end. The idea of Dylan and the Band as modern day Buffalo skinners and either Bill Graham or David Geffen as the trail boss is amusing.

With the idea in mind that the song is primarily about the 1974 tour, let's take a look at the lyrics and examine the clues:

> I married Isis on the fifth day of May,
> But I could not hold on to her very long.
> So I cut off my hair and I rode straight away
> For the wild unknown country
> Where I could not go wrong.

Isis could represent his muse, which he couldn't hold on to, i.e. he lost his inspiration. After the frantic pace of the 1966 tour and all it entailed, Dylan went into seclusion following the motorcycle accident that caused him to take some time off for recovery. I'm reminded of his retreat to Woodstock after his crash and how he did indeed literally "cut off his hair".

> I came to a high place of darkness and light.
> The dividing line ran through the center of town.
> I hitched up my pony to a post on the right,
> Went in to a laundry to wash my clothes down.

He "hitched up his pony to a post on the right" where "the dividing line ran through the center of town". Is it stretching it too much to believe he's telling us he embraced the conservative philosophy of the Right and rejected the politics of the Left during his Country phase? Perhaps in embracing traditional family values he had hoped to find peace of mind. The *John Wesley Harding* album seemed to reflect a newfound religious awareness, and *Nashville Skyline* celebrated the joys of love and marriage.

> A man in the corner approached me for a match.
> I knew right away he was not ordinary.
> He said, "Are you lookin' for somethin' easy to catch?"
> I said, "I got no money."
> He said, "That ain't necessary."

The proposition is put forth, and the journey is about to unfold. Is the stranger Bill Graham? David Geffen? Dylan himself? What could be more lucrative than a comeback tour? All he had to do was go out on stage and sing his old songs. Everything would be provided for.

> We set out that night
> For the cold in the North.
> I gave him my blanket,
> He gave me his word.
> I said, "Where are we goin'?"
> He said we'd be back by the fourth.
> I said, "That's the best news that I've ever heard."

Chicago and Canada in winter must have been pretty cold. He expected to "be back by the fourth". Since he married Isis on the fifth of May, the journey is expected to bring him full circle back to his muse. The promise in store for him is that he will reconnect with everything he had lost when he lost Isis.

> I was thinkin' about turquoise, I was thinkin' about gold,
> I was thinkin' about diamonds
> And the world's biggest necklace.
> As we rode through the canyons, through the devilish cold,
> I was thinkin' about Isis,
> How she thought I was so reckless.
>
> How she told me that one day we would meet up again,
> And things would be different the next time we wed,
> If I only could hang on and just be her friend.
> I still can't remember all the best things she said.

All of the treasures and rewards that would await him when the tour commenced, but most of all he was thinking about getting back to that place where he was "so reckless". Going back on the road was all about taking chances once again.

> We came to the pyramids all embedded in ice.
> He said, "There's a body I'm tryin' to find.
> If I carry it out it'll bring a good price."
> 'Twas then that I knew what he had on his mind.

The Egyptian theme of Isis and Osiris seems a little strange in a locale where the weather is cold and icy. Egypt is not noted for its ice storms. Instead, this strange landscape seems to be very American. I'm reminded of the Grand Tetons in Wyoming. Also, remember the "Trail of the Buffalo" source material. "He said there's a body I'm trying to find, if I carry it out it will bring a good price" - the body of the "old" Dylan who was ripe for a comeback. Also, his body of work which would be "exhumed" during the tour. He revisited his protest songs for the first time in a long while. Remember what a surprise it was when he played "Blowin' in the Wind" at the Concert for Bangladesh? He had practically disowned that song after 1964.

> The wind it was howlin' and the snow was outrageous.

We chopped through the night
And we chopped through the dawn.
When he died I was hopin' that it wasn't contagious,
But I made up my mind that I had to go on.

Things were starting to get difficult and the road was getting rougher. It had become a matter of having to "chop through the dawn". He had to complete the tour, even though it didn't turn out the way he had hoped. Perhaps he wasn't really ready to go back on the road, or perhaps he just needed to do it on his own terms. Maybe he didn't really need his partner after all.

I broke into the tomb, but the casket was empty.
There was no jewels, no nothin', I felt I'd been had.
When I saw that my partner was just bein' friendly,
When I took up his offer I must-a been mad.

But when he got the casket (containing the corpse of what he used to be?) it was empty. Whatever he had hoped to find was not there, and so the major disappointment of the entire affair.

I picked up his body and I dragged him inside,
Threw him down in the hole and I put back the cover.
I said a quick prayer and I felt satisfied.
Then I rode back to find Isis just to tell her I love her.

The tour ended and the "old" Dylan is now buried. This is a strong indication that the partner was Dylan himself - the other side of him that thought it would be a good idea to exploit his own past for profit. Time to get on with the new. Time to reconnect with his muse, now that the past is gone.

She was there in the meadow where the creek used to rise.
Blinded by sleep and in need of a bed,
I came in from the East with the sun in my eyes.
I cursed her one time then I rode on ahead.

She said, "Where ya been?" I said, "No place special."
She said, "You look different." I said, "Well, not quite."

She said, "You been gone." I said, "That's only natural."
She said, "You gonna stay?" I said, "Yeah, I jes might."

Isis, oh, Isis, you mystical child.
What drives me to you is what drives me insane.
I still can remember the way that you smiled
On the fifth day of May in the drizzlin' rain.

The reconnection with the muse complete, Dylan is now ready to record *Blood on the Tracks* and embark on the more relaxed and more artistically rewarding Rolling Thunder Revue tour of 1975. This time he would know what he was doing and would be completely in charge.

John Howells
December 2002

I Don't Know, But I've Been Told

Reader Comments

Last update: May 20, 2017

howdy; just dropped by on my first web browse on aol; (my first web browse ever). looks pretty cool. see ya around rmd. --jnb p.s. drop me an email at p00518@psilink.com just to let me know i did this properly and you received it; thanks! bye (how do i get out of this message box?....
jules n. binoculas

This site works a *lot* better than the old netcom one, I must say. Makes for a much less frustrating experience.
Ross Whitwam

Hi! I have been Netscape-less for a couple of weeks, and just dropped by. Like your background, seem to recognize it somewhat.. I was looking at Ben's and your site for a transcription of the Cynthia Gooding interview from Folksinger's Choice. I saw it not. Might be a project for someone some time..
Karl Erik Andersen

Hallo Why dont you put some QuickTime clips of Zim on Here for Mac men.? I would love an EMail if you know where i can obtain a video of Renaldo and Clara!!
david@cradduck.demon.co.uk
Ps. Great page.

John- You probably realize this: your setlist for the 11/17 Unplugged show omits "Broken" as song #6 in the set, following "Hazel". Have you received a copies of the shows yet? Let me know if you would like them. Best, M.A. Zingg Providence, RI
mazingg@ix.netcom.com

Yeah, is this a bulletin board where I can post things? If so, how do I subscribe to it? My address is dsc9bam@imc210.med.navy.mil Thanks, Moe
Moe

---

i found your concert tour recording page today, (I have previously been a fan of your home page), the concert page is a great help to those of us who are knew to collecting tapes and boot CD's.
Larry Medcalf

John, I have only been on the Net for a couple of weeks, I think I tried to access your pages from the address on the HWY61CD-ROM but it was an old address, finally got through from a link from Karl Erik's page. Liked the stuff on Tarantula, films, interviews etc. - the kind of

stuff I like to read! I have been taking a look at rmd and your name seems to come up quite often lately??? I don't really know what this 'feud' is about, would you care to explain? I think all the links between various pages are good, and can only help people seeking information and "relief" from serious Dylan disabilities ... Keep up the good work .... Tricia J
Tricia Jungwirth

I found your web site through a mention of another site (Tangled Up In Jews) in the dylan newsgroup. I'm glad to find all I can about Bob, so I think your site is great -- I am relatively new and I would be interested in doing something like this. Any refs or hints on how to set up a home page etc.? Either way, "keep on keepin' on"
Bill Ward

I very much like this site. I found out about this site from the mailings list available from MIT.
jpbrooks@netdoor.com

How I found out about this really uncool page: Reading thru the rec.music.dylan or whatever that newsgroup is called, I got to some of your posts with the http ... in the signature. So I went to have a look. What I'm looking for is a site where I can download the Dylan lyrics. Can that be done anywhere? Cheers,
Chris http://www.eurassi.co.za/ chris@rupeden.eurassi.co.za

---

found your page from the highway 61 cd-rom i just said good luck
geoff 27th july 95

Howdy. I like this. This is cool. I heard about it on the ArloNet Web page. (Arlo, as in Arlo Guthrie.)
Jamie H Davis

I discovered this cite while visiting the ArloNet. Interested in Dylan, Woody Guthrie, Leadbelly, Charlie Chaplin
Stan Cook

Would it be possible to get tour info? Those of us in Phoenix missed out on the last tour. Keep up the good work.
Rich Bailen

I ain't lookin' to compete with you Beat or cheat or mistreat you Simplify ya classify ya Deny defy or crucify you All I really wanna do Is baby be freinds with you
John Wesley Harding

I'm frustrated at not being able to get a text version online of the BD pages from the All Music Guide. I don't want to buy the guide just for thgose 2 pages. Any ideas? Thanks. John
John Nemerovski

Pathed through to BIABHP via Expecting Rain... could you let me know how to get onto HWY61-L ? Do I need a special password? MajorDylan on AOL thanks for your help.. keep up the great page ..
Major Galloway

Love to see some information on upcoming concerts and appearances, tour information. Anybody willing to tab some songs
anonymous

Hey man this is an awsom site i love dylan...where can i get that wall paper please wrtie me back at jwwol@conncoll.edu thanks
Jonathan W. Wolf

I'm a Dylan Freak in UK and just got a copy of Netscape from work. First subject I searched for was this. I will comment after a few days when I have time to look through it all. Its nice to see this sort of thing available, No one else could play that tune you know it was up to me
Geoff Steele

Just keep going, bring more stuff on Dylan to this page. Everyone should learn about Dylan.
j-bread@nwu.edu

Mr. Howells, Hi there. Nice looking page! I've had a couple of difficulties with it, though: 1. The page takes a *very* long time to load, for those of us who are getting by with 14.4 connections and don't have a "direct" net connection. 2. My browser doesn't support tables (which aren't part of HTML 2.0, I believe), so I can't get at any of the neat stuff listed in the table section of your page. Wish I could! Thanks for listening ...
Aaron Snow

I got the adress from ftp.cs.pdx.edu However I would like to know know if there is any where i can get dylan's harmonica solos. They are not at nevada.
niki

I was happy to see this page. I'd like to see a kind of "letters page" with interviews and other comments. thanks again
solomon

---

how'd i get here? fairly simple, i guess. from yahoo's art/entertainment to 'author author' to the TOC to kerouac to levi asher to bob dylan...not too complicated, just follow the links... out of the stuff i have seen out and about i like your dylan page! lugar
hollyja@hiwaay.net

In 1966, while I was a student at the California College of Arts and Crafts, I had the opportunity to photograph Dylan, Michael McClure and Allen Ginsberg outside of City Lights. I was twenty-one at the time and living with my parents in Walnut Creek. When the time came to leave for the photo session, my mother said, "You haven't finished mowing the lawn." "But mom," I pleaded, "I'm going to photograph Bob Dylan!" "I don't care if you're going to photograph the Pope, buster, get out there and finishing mowing the lawn." I finished the lawn and made the session. A full page photo of that session appears in the liner notes on "Biograph." Nothing but the best, Dale Smith
Dale Smith

I linked to this site via the Allen Ginsberg site. Thanks from another Dylan fan.

Rob Beckham

---

thanks.. i found you through the ULTIMATE BAND LIST.
do you by chance know where i can find " Senior (tales of yankee power) " transcribed?
michael
[*I was unable to respond because Michael didn't leave his email address - JH*]

I DON'T KNOW HOW I GOT HERE BUT IT IS NICE. UNCLE ROBERT(B.D.) IS THE GREATEST, A TRUE LEGEND.
COLBY

Could you tell me how close Greenwich village is from Parsons Art school.My friends and I really interested in the arts and want to be in a place where we are surrounded by artsy people for spring break.Thankyou.
vic

I like the depth of your BD page. Always a fan, I just did a searh for "Bob Dylan" and your page was the first that came up (Netscape Infoseek).
jackie

Excellent page - I'll be back to browse at length! 'Saw Bob last night in Little Rock - my second show here and the better of the two. Bob was EXCELLENT - voice in very good form, and in a good mood from all signs. 'Did an acoustic Tambourine Man that brought tears to my eyes. Much other premium stuff also - he's getting better of late. 'Same band as on the Unplugged set. Anyway, thanks for your trouble with the page - I'll check in as I can. Catch this tour whatever you do!
- Dean in Little Rock

I want to suggest an Upcoming Events item be added to this page (i.e. concert info, albums, etc.)
Rich in AZ.

I found this page, because I am in need of some urgent B Dylan info. I need to know the name of the Cat on the cover of 'Bringing it all Back Home'. Can anyone help me?????
Please E-mail to the following address jao@easynet.co.uk.
Kind Regards,
Jamie
[*The cat's name is "Rolling Stone", according to Shelton's bio - JH*]

I found this page while reading the biography on Allen Ginsberg. The information on Bob Dylan came up on the blue net page request. I have found the information very interesting and informative. I have found the information very insightful into the life of ginsberg and I have always enjoyed Dylan.
Joe Chatley

---

i am james a pennebaker don allan pennebaker is my half brother.. my father's john paul first marrage... i was searching references for my last name and found you
small net isn't it

James A Pennebaker

I am searching for a Dylan song that I do not know the name of. I've heard it before, but cannot recall any of the words. I do know that my future son-in-law is wanting it to have the words calligraphied for his first born son.
Does that give any clue to the name of the song? I can't ask him because I could not surprise him with it.
Help if you can.
Thanks.
Victoria
[*the song is most likely "Forever Young" - JH*]

Encyclopaedia Britannica Online points to your web site following a search for Bob Dylan.
John Hall

I think You are the "Jokerman"!
Palle Tenfalk

Does anyone have the complete lyrics of "Last Thoughts On Woody Guthrie"? This poem can be heard on the three disc set, "Bootlegs". The set can be bought in the stores, so it is fairky common. This is the most incredible lyrical feat I have ever heard, unrivaled by even Dylan himself. I would really appreciate if anyone could help me.
Thanks
Dan Walsh
[*This should be in Lyrics - JH*]

I would like to know where I can get song tablatures on Dylan's work.
Thanks,
Jake
[*There's a link to a site in the lyrics section - JH*]

Hello there, I'm a Bob Dylan fan and would like to know if you have the lyrics to HURRICANE AND SUBTERRANEAN HOMESICK BLUES.
Jack
[*Jack didn't leave an email address, but if you're reading this, try one of the links in the "lyrics" section under "miscellaneous information". Failing that, buy the book* ***Lyrics***. *- JH*]

John, I'm new to the 'net but not to Dylan. I've been a fan since '67, have listened exhaustively to all the commercial recordings, and have seen a number of live shows since my first in Philadelphia (Jan. 1974--drove all night from Pgh. to get there). My first attempt to use the internet was to search "Dylan" and entered rmd newsgroup and downloaded FAQ, which is where I found your name and address. FAQ then referenced this web page, and here I am. I still to much of a novice to critique you page, but I must say it's pretty exciting, having been a "closet" fan for so long, to find this world with so many other fans and so much info. I feel quite greatful that you've put in the effort to organize this info. Thanks much.
Tom Lace

Great page. I found it using Yahoo. I do have one question, though. I'm looking for some information on the city and venue of some recordings of Dylan concerts in '95 (6/15 and 6/24 to be specific). If you know of any way to find this info, please get back to me. thanks a lot, and keep up the good work!
Mike Allred

Hi, there,
Nice site. _Thank you.
Perhaps some links to pix
Later,
Dan

I have a friend that is obsessed with dylan, he got me into listening to him and i like him and his lyrics, but i'm not quite obsessed, nor will i ever be. anyways, dylan has actually some actual content in his work(s). i don't have alot of music with actual meaning in it. i listen to his lyrics as carefully as i can to see what he's trying to get across. i was just wondering if you could get more of his lyrics put on the net. i would like to actually read what he sings and analyze it. thanks...
marc akin

I have Bob Dylan's Freewheelin (vinyl) it is still in plastic. Wondered if it is worth anything. Bought it ata garage sale for $5.00.
Does anyone on this site want to buy it? Is there a page that collectors hang out for Dylan stuff?
I collect Beatles and Kingsmen items, just saw the album and figured what the heck.
baumanj@ziavms.enmu

John: I have a copy of the Berkeley Dec.4 1965 Berkeley Community Theatre tape, but it only contains the electric set. Do you know if tapes or cds of the full show (i.e., acoustic and electric) exist out there somewhere. I'm not asking you to locate them for me, just asking if you know if a tape of the complete show has been reported.
Lou Leary
[*I only know of the electric half in circulation - sorry. JH*]

Hello,
This home page is lacking of a special area to some massages that come from Bob Dylan 's lyrics.
thanks for the space, Walter Kindro Andreoli, Brazil,South America.
Walter Kindro Andreoli

Nice setup for the page- easy to get places without wading through what you don't want. But- I didn't find setlists, that was what I was looking for. Oh well
Anonymous

I think your page is terrific! I heard about it from the Leon Russell home page/under "Mike's Links." I'm a Leon fan - worked for him for 10 years. Check out his page - it's just getting started. http://members.aol.com/leonrussel/leonaol.htm
Thanks!

Diane Sullivan

Do you have any current concert dates? I found this by shear determination. You can E-Mail me at COB@BLUEMARBLE.NET
MELINDA K. S.

My first letter on the internet! I will probably be visiting this page quite a bit in the future, no doubt. Like what I see so far. Keep up the good work!
Sigurjón

Dear Sir:
i found this to be a very informative and excellent web site on Bob Dylan. i found this web site through Yahoo. I have a question though, can you please tell me from which Bob Dylan albumn the song 'Positively 4th Street' is from? i can't seem to find it anywhere :(
please reply!
Henry Wang
[*"Positively 4th Street" is on Biograph and Greatest Hits I - JH*]

Your section on Dylan rocks man. I'm just a kid sitting in studyhall out exploring. Keep on rocking. Later
Anonymous

Hi! I have a page consisting of reviews I've written of many of Dylan's albums; I've put in a link to your site and I would appreciate it if you would put in a link to my page. The address is: http://homebrew.geo.arizona.edu/dylan.html
Thanks!
--Wilson

John:
I just looked at your new review page and it's great. I came across your Web site two years ago and it led me to a complete copy of 'The Genuine Basement Tapes' which still after nearly 30 years sound fabulous. Your new comments about TGBT's certainly rings true to me. I've heard that there may be about 50 more basement songs somewhere. Any confirmation on these? Also, I expect to receive in the next day or so a copy of the recently released "Guitar Kissing & The Contemporary Fix". I've had a vinal copy of "Zimmerman: Looking Back from the Royal Albert Hall" since 1967. Susposedly, this 2CD set has one acoustic and one electric session. Do you know if the acoustic one is the same as was on the vinal?
Thanks and I'll watch your new page grow!
Hugh Bollinger
[*The CD referred to above is the complete Manchester 5/17/66 show in true unbelievable stereo. Some of the acoustic set has never been released before -- JH*]

Aloha,From Hawaii!!!
My name is Kitrick Short and I might have a site you might link to ,I created a Homage to The Band set of sculptures and gave each of them one. Please check out my page and we can creat links to each other. I have a link from the Bands page and thats where I saw your link. My homage page URL is http://www.maui.net/~kitrick/hmge.html
My home URL is http://www.maui.net/~kitrick

Hope these pages inspire you!
Peace & Aloha!!
Kitrick

I found this address in some other Dylan page, but I can't recall which.
What I'd like to know is where can I find more than a one or two paragraph biography of Dylan on the Web? Any clues.
Take care.
Gary Ostroff

I found your site after downloading software to run CD Links from Voyager. I did everything they said to do and have the hardware,etc. they said I needed but it didn't work. Enjoy what I see of your Dylan site; haven't seen him since 8-29-94 at Michigan State Fair. He's still kicking and if he never writes another word no one will ever top him.
Mike

First of all !! Sorry for the mistakes, but i'm an italian student from Torino.
I'm a new surfer of the net and I'm looking for about all the stuff about "the times they are a-changing" 1963 Please ! could yoy send me anything about that ?
I'll have a "little examinatios" at university next week.
Bye from Torino.
I've found this site =>netscape search=>infoseek=>T.Dixxon Page
Paolo

I found this sight through rock links, and I think its great. I had to copy William Shattner singing tamborine man.
Bob_Arruda

Your page just keeps getting snazzier every time I come over for a visit....seeing the real you at last...
sj

Great page. I love it! Especially Captain Kirk doing Tamborine Man. I found a link to your page on a Village Voice page. It's definitely going on my hotlist. I haven't yet visited all the links on your page yet but I'm looking forward to it.
Thanks
Greg

To whom it may consern,
In what Dylan song was the line "It doesn't take a weatherman to know which way the wind blows" in it?
KD
[*The answer is* ***Subterranean Homesick Blues*** *- JH*]

Rock on. Very rarely do you find cool people like yourself who love Bob enough to give him a sort of shrine via internet. I'd even like to see more, like maybe soundbites of some of his reare and relatively unknown stuff. For example, maybe some audio files of "No More Auction

Block" from The Gaslight in Greenwich Village, or "Ramblin' Gamblin' Willie. Anyway, thanks for contributing to the memory of the greatest performer and stylist of the century.
ryan vaughn

I just wanted to let you know I've just put up my own website at
http://members.aol.com/smashprod/mansfield.html and have included some links to your Dylan site. If you're interested in putting in links to my site, I would be very appreciative.
Yours, David Mansfield (Rolling Thunder, etc.)

Hi,
My name is Arleigh Hertzler, and I am a freshman at Grove City College in Pennsylvania. I am a huge Dylan fan, and have a few bootlegs (some on vinyl) but I was wondering if someone could tell me how to get copies of some of the boots listed in the page. I love the page, and will visit often!
Arleigh Hertzler

It's been a while since I visited your page, but it's changed a bit since then. I like the "new" look (which may be an extremely old look, for all I know).
I've got a list of the CDs I listen to while here at work on my WWW page, and every mention of Bob has a link to your page!
Keep up the good work!
Theron Trowbridge

Great story, "Homer." Made me laugh and feel giddy.
Saw the URL in today's HWY61-L Digest. Recent subscriber. Longtime Dulan fan.
But I'd not even heard of Homer before. Must not be THAT big a fan, afterall.
Thanks for doing this page.
bwithers@mindspring.com

Hello...
Actually I have this Homepage bookmarked. I really like this page. The best part of course is that it has so many links toother Dylan sites. By the way, nice new look. It's snazzy. Is there any way I could bribe ya to let me link this page to my homepage? ^_^ Anyways, keep up the great work... I can't wait for his next album. I already have about 42 of his albums, but it never seems to be enough. : D
Best Regards...
Douglas Larke.

I am glad that Bob has his on pages also on the Internet. Here in Finland there are many who love him. despite his bad gig in helsinki some years ago.
Pekka Huttunen

Thanks for providing such a valuable Dylan page - I particularly liked your review of unrealesed tapes. Your page is a fitting tribute ot a genius and a source of valuable iformation.
Regards,
Brian

I really think the page is rather well done. I reached it thru the Bob Dylan FAQ pages, which I reached from the Mammoth Music Meta-List.
Joydeep

I searched Lycos for Bob Dylan and went right to Ragged Clown where I found the link to you. I am impressed with your integrity, your dedication to Dylan and your finess with the web design. Great job.
As fo rmyself I am a fifty one year old web surfer. I saw Dylan first live in Seattle in 1964 with Joan Baez. I have seen him in concert a few other times. The most recent about ten years ago with the Dead in Eugene. That was special.
I don't like big concerts much. Have most of Dylan's music to listen to at home.
Thank you for your energy.
Peace, mac

I'm very happy ,becouse I found this site.
And very suprised for many data!!
I hear his song everyday.....
I want to write more but I do not know English so much sorry
I want to see this site again
good knight

John
Congratulations for this superb web presentation of the man.
We saw him at Break for the Border in London a few months ago and he was magnificent - as good as ever.
How can we keep tabs on his future UK visits ??
Also does anyone know of any published Video performances ...
Well done ... Bernie Kiernan

How can you be so all alone? Everybody must get........
Now why did I draw a blank. Could be the era has passed. You know, I just keep trying to bury it. I thought perhaps you might like to read the poem I started back in 1978, when jerome (my brother in Bobbie D) died. With any luck you'll get it and even be able to retrieve it. In the meantime, you know, Dylan is getting really old. Doesn't it amaze you, that restlessness that come from having done it all and needing to do nothing more than dabble from here on out.
Everybody must get lost Everybody must get found
In Jesus' Name, brother.
Mark & Chris Miller
[*The poem didn't make it through the mail...JH*]

I was looking for info regarding the album "John Wesley Harding - like what songs are on it, when did it come out, simple stuff that I can't seem to find on your page (or even any links).
Jeff
[*Funny, I had no trouble finding information about that album in the* Discography *section...JH*]

---

did you hear about the dylan show on may 16 in mich? About 200 people rushed the stage during "Highway 61" It was great! Bob kept on playing!
Anonymous

---

please print more pictures
have a music section with guitar chords etc.
have a quiz or crossword
joe davitt

Heard about this site from article in THE DETROIT NEWS paper on May 9, 1996 on May 9, 1996. Sounded interesting -- thought I'd take a look see.
Anonymous

I shot the picture on the cover of Greatest Hits. The first one.
A Grammy winner for me, and proud I am too. I'd love to sell original prints of this image...perhaps your browsers would be interested?
Have them contact me at lartique@mindspring.com
I found yer page on purpose
Rowland Scherman

Great graphics, John!
John Howells, Sr.

I THINK YOUR WEB PAGE IS GREAT AND I JUST SURFED TO FIND IT. I AM WRITING TO ASK IF YOU COULD HELP ME FIND SOME INFO. I AM LOOKING FOR ARTISTS WHO HAVE DONE DYLAN'S "TANGLED UP IN BLUE". I KNOW THE INDIGO GIRLS DID A VERSION BUT I CAN'R FIND ANYONE ELSE. ANY SUGGESTIONS? PLEASE HELP!
HEATHER TUCKER
[*Check out* ftp://ftp.neda.com/pub/dylan/olof/covers/by-song.html *for information on Dylan covers by song title. - JH*]

---

hello i was refered to your site while browsing in a book store (barnes & noble)some internet book of music sites? well i just have one question, i've been trying to get it answered for some time now it's "what song is bob playing on the piano in the movie don't look back , right after the store front guitar window scene where bob says "we don't have those kind of guitars in the states." soon after he's in a little smokey room with a black guy, bob's banging away on this little piano mumbling some type of very appealing gospel number, but also very hard to hear exactly. do you know what i'm talking about? if so, do you know what song it is?
Beast,
Bill
[*Please refer to* ftp://ftp.neda.com/pub/dylan/olof/1965 *for a possible clue. - JH*]

This is great stuff, man! Actually, I too just started tooling around with the internet. Of course, Dylan was the first and most desired site for me. I look forward to checking in with you in the future. Thanks! Remember, God Knows.
Randy Tolen

The article about the Basement tapes is fascinating. Just as a historical perspective in 1967 I was in my final year at grammar school in England. I had a good friend who had gone to university a year ahead of me in London. He returned home....and here the problem starts, because I don't know when this was. Before 'great white wonder certainly. Maybe early 1968,

or even Chriatmas 1967. Anyway he had purchased, for £20 which was then a fortune (l.p.s were £5) an acetate in a plain brown cover. It was the first bootleg I had ever seen ! He bought it from under the counter in a record shop on Carnaby st. from a guy who knew he was a Dylan fan. It contained 12 of the 14 original basement tape songs. Not Tiny Montgomery and Lo and Behold but the other 12. I omly mention this because it sort of proves that great white wonder was preceeded as a bootleg by something else available to the public at a price with the basement tapes on. Certainly he was not connected with the publishing business and had no access that way. It's just that I've never heard or read about this acetate anywhere else but it was on sale in London.
cheers
Dave

---

hi,
all the web sites are ok until somebody can provide me with the traveling wilburys words, arrangement and chords of Nobody's Child, and turn to more than ok web site.
aarno

I figured I would finally, after months of delay, send you a little message saying how much I've appreciated the work you've done on this site... it has been very informative and, above all, very interesting. The Bringing it All Back Home Page has been on my hotlist for months on end. Just a word of encouragement for a fellow Dylan fan...
On a side note, I heard a rumor that Dylan will be releasing a new CD this summer. Maybe called Have You Seen Dignity?, something like that. Is there any truth to this? If you could send me a quick note telling me what you've heard I would be very appreciative.
Keep it up,
Jamie Lipton

Looks good. I'll be back.
Marq

As the master himself has said, "People don't do what they believe in, they just do what's most convenient and then they repent". Well,I believe in Dylan's lyrics and music. He's said that he's dined with kings and he's been offered wings, but he's never been too impressed. I think he wrote that before the wonderful medium of the internet came to be...Wouldn't you agree?
Mitchell Jessie

It's been a while since I listened to that Golden Throats tape you made for me so long ago so I was very pleased to hear once again WS's radical (is there any other word?) interpretation of Dylan's masterwork. Of course to breathe new life into a song that was already perfect required a depth of artistic courage which Mr. Shantner knew only too well, having plumbed those depths many times in his various artistic outings. The final screaming rage into which he falls in fadding moments of the song speak volumes about his state of mind during the session and nicely prefigures the anger that we were going to see erupt during the last few years of the 70's as punk music. Thanks again for providing a taste of this landmark artistic event for all to sample.
Anonymous

Looks like a good site. I found it while searching for stuff on Hibbing, Minnesota. I was going to Hibbing JC when Bob was a senior in HS. I havn't really looked around to see if anyone has written much about things I know he was interested in then ('cause we talked about things a few times in, as I recall, his English teacher's class) and I also remember him being with some friends and my sister at a cabin on a lake north of Hibbing. Anyway, I will poke around and see what I find....
Richard Lake

I think this web page is an excellent idea! Perhaps you could include a section where readers could describe personal experiences from past Dylan concerts . You could select the ones that you find to be particularly interesting ! I, for one, would look forward to some personal insights.
Anonymous

Nouvel utilisateur d'internet, mais vieux fan de Dylan, je découvre votre site et mesure à cette occasion l'étendue de mon ignorance à propos de ce dernier, alors que je pensais tout de même en conaitre un rayon sur le sujet...
Il me faudra surement plus d'une session pour faire le tour du sujet, mais je tenais d'ores et déja à vous adresser ce témoignage d'admiration. Bravo et continuez !
(All this french to say your site is just great. Keep on keeping on !).
PS: How do i do to register in the newsgroup ? thank's by the way...
jean-hugues pierson

IM 32 AND I HEAR THE DYLAN''S MUSIC FOR 20 YEARS HES MY FAVORITE....AND I GOT ALL HIS RECORDS.... DYLAN WILL NEVER DIE.........HES MY MASTER.....HES THE REAL AMERICAN POET...
XAVIER COELLO

Love the Web site. Keep up the good work!!
Jawbum4@aol.com

Very good site indeed!
Saw Dylan in Stockholm recently. Very good and very long concert (2 hours). Can't think of anything to say now really (it's early morning here in Sweden...).
I'll be back some other time with (hopefully) interesting comments...
Found this page thru a "beat-site"...
Hejdå!!!

Hi John! Your site is very impressive. It´s easy to see that you´ve put a lot of work into it. But with all due respect why have´nt you yet mentioned anything about ´Feeling Minnesota´, the ´Jimmie Rodgers tribute´, ´Stormy season´, the upcoming Jimmy Hendrix and Woody Guthrie tribute concert´s in one of your feature´s?
But I guess you should be able to sleep since no other site´s I know of have mentioned anything about any of this either.
All the best wishes John & you can be positive about me droping by once in awhile. Thanx for existing.
Your´s truly sion. 27 august 1996.

I am very impressed with your Dylan web page, and I am greatful for the fact that you obviously appreciate Bob and his music, and that you apparently have a lot of spare time to devote to this project. Your hard work and dedication to fact, I commend. Keep up the good work!
crapsman@ix.netcom.com

I was walking by a pawn shop once and saw Dylan in the front window playing a drum set. I went inside to say something to him but when I approached he went into a coughing fit that lasted about a minute. I split.
Nice site-- keep it up.
David O'David

---

everyone focuses on dylan's past. historical archives are essential, but how about what the old pop poet rocker is doing these days? Current photos (gray locks, wrinkles and all), and what he's producing NOW!?
attila nagy

---

hey! This site is the coolest. Being a new Dylan fan (of age 16) I found this a great place to get more info, pics, etc. Well done! I enjoyed the misheard lyrics section I was actually singing some of them (especially that line from 'Just Like a Woman', that's a tricky one!). Ok, keep up the good work, and keep publishing those fantastic pictures!
Petra

John,
Thanks for the page.Stumbled across it via The Band site. Looks interesting....I'll be back !!!
Tony Hayward

For your info re how people found this site: I was surfing thru the Literary Menagerie site from the U of Miss and I clicked Allen Ginsburgs name. The name Bob Dylan was in the body of text, so being a long time fan of Dylan, I couldn't resist hot linking over to your site. It looks very kewl and interesting. Looking forward to going thru your site.
Suzanne

Information no one probably knows:
Bob just received a nomination for the Nobel Prize in Literature. Oddly enough, his friend, Eric Anderson (the musician) who lives in Oslo, had been asked to perform at the awards ceremony this year before B. knew he was nominated.
His tours are arranged very last minute which is why it is hard to get advance information. The publicity is minimal and sometime the tours are arranged in a week's time.
Bob occasionally peruses the net and has seen the stuff out there about him.
Sadie

I have been reading on the BEAT-L subscriber group the last two days about the rumor concerning Bob Dylan winning the upcoming Nobel Prize for literature. Any confirmation of this? Thanks,
Dave Breithaupt

Folks or Folkies,

My interest and preference probably are aimed further back than Bob Z. Dylan. I never understood wild enthusiasm about his rough voice but sometimes poetic lyrics. I gather he liked Dylan Thomas' works enough to appropriate his name; Thomas had a wondrous voice and delivery plus evocative topics. Further, and for what it's worth, I think early Joan Baez recordings, pre-Zimmerman, were better than later, as if their mixing lowered the purity and beauty of her work.
It all seems remote now. I still seek the early gold. Maybe this is a voice in the wilderness.
William H. Sickels

I didn't understand something in your commentary on the Genuine Basement Tapes. Is the version of Quinn the Eskimo on Greatest Hits not the pre-Biograph version from the Basement Tapes Sessions?
Adam Mahler
[*The version that appears on Greatest Hits 2 is the live version from the Isle of Wight that previously appeared on "Self Portrait" - JH*]

Dear sir or madam;
I entered your e-mail site by looking up 'rolling stone magazine', so I do not know which sex you are, hope you don't take offense to that. I enjoyed reading your interview from Rolling Stone.
Can I ask you for some advice/help? I am doing a report for a class on the similarities between Bob Dylan and Ice Cube. I think that there are many similarities between the two; they are both spokesman for their generations, and they both let the listening public know their views in a poetic form.
Do you know anything about Ice Cube? Do you think that you may be able to help me in any way? You seem to be an expert on the distinguished Mr. Dylan so I figure you might be a good interview for my paper.
Thanx for ANY input you can give to me;
Matt Simpson
My address is: JOHNSIMP@STUDENT.FLINT.UMICH.EDU
Thanx again

Like it!
Especially the William Shatner piece! Let me know if that originated from you or where I might find similar material!
Saw Bob last year here in Jacksonville, FL (see e-mail address- real original, eh?), the show was great! As if it would not be!!
Well, again, Great Job! Keep it up!
P.S. If you are interested, I do have a seriously under construction Home Page. If you want to check it out:
http://www.jaxnet.com/~ronjax95/
All comments welcome!

Hi !
I am a swedish Dylan fan and I think your page is very good. On my hompage (http://WWW.Privat.Katedral.SE/~nv95joja/) I'm going to have som Dylan stuff. Now, I wonder if you have some suggestions of what
I can have on my homepage. Please vistit it, i've already done some.
/joel jacobsson

I found your Dylan-site through a Norwegian free copy computer-magazine called "Datamagasinet". One of the journalists recommended this and another site called "Expecting Rain" http://www.expectingrain.com/ I haven`t checked out the other Dylan sites, but I like Bringing it all back home. Good luck, and keep up the good work!
Arnsten Linstad

All I can say is THANKS! I'm glad someone besides the pot-smoking crowd appreciates Dylan like I have learned to. My father teaches his lyrics in American Literature class in a small high school, and that is how I got interested in the man who could compose a song like "Gates of Eden" or a masterpiece tougue-in-cheek short like "Jet Pilot." What a guy!
Matt

I just thought that you have a neat home page set up here. It's nice to see other fans setting things up for our fearless poet. Keep it up, I hope to put one together myself
ella

In my opinion, you should have the date of last update placed in a prominent spot on your opening page. Makes things much easier for us, the audience
Otherwise, great site!
Dave

Dear Mr. Howells,
All of this WEB stuff is still a bit of a mystery to me, so I hope this gets through. I have enjoyed your comments on RMD for a couple of years. I I seldom post, but rarely a week goes by I don't check in. I found your site at the newsgroup. Not only is yours the first, it is the best. However, I do find Bob Links very useful. I visit your site often. Please keep up the good work. I first discovered Dylan through a friend in San Marcos, TX. I think he played Freewheelin for me right after its release. I was not impressed. Was not a folk fan at the time. I worked at a 250 watt daytimer in that small college town at the time, and it was Sub Homesick Blues that hooked me. Been a fan ever since. Dylans early work (and recent work) has changed my mind about folk. Have always loved rock. BOB is the finest album of the genre. I don't share your love of Basement Tapes, but like the album. You comments on BT were very enjoyable.
Sincerely
David B. Smith

Hats off to Bob Dylan.
Tony Danesi

Greetings: I have owned the name www.bobdylan.com for some time now thinking of putting up a site but too busy with other projects. Simply put the URL www.bobdylan.com is for sale right now, any takers? I will sell it right now for $3,500.00
regards
Scott David

---

i was wondering if any one new where i could get a hold of the tape dylan made of the #1 songs of the 60's. do you know where i might be able to get a copy? thanks a bunch

jeffrey snowbarger
p.s. i'm seeing the man on nov. 22 in south bend,in

I recently just got on to the Dylan web sites and i think all of this is great abd keep up the good work
Dustin Blome

Nice site.
Thanks
Nigel Green

Hello, I'm a fan of Dylan from Romania. I have a home page at www.sorostm.ro/utzu. Please check it out and tell me what do you think. I found out about your page from Bob Links. Your page is cool. Unfortunately we don't have access to much Dylan information here in Romania. The master never give a concert here.
Thank you,
Utzu

Great Page! I'm relatively new to the internet. I got here through boblinks.
John Burkhart

I think that Dylan Is A God. I am a scientist, and really seriousoly one.
A.Wilson

---

licence plate spotted "dylnfrek". n.y.s.cool!!
Anonymous

Hi Johnny boy, i really love the web page, good job. I am only 17 and soon to be 18...but, dear god i wish i was around when the BOB MAN first sung LIKE A ROLLING STONE !!! I 'm amoung those who love bobby's great and unique voice...i can't believe some people hate his voice...how can that be ??? BALLAD IN PLAIN D...it..it just made me cry, "tears blinding my site".
O.k... well bye there.
friendly Robyn !

Hey
Your site looks very nice so far. I have not seen it all yet. I have been a fan of Bob for about 20 years, and i had the great pleasure to see him at Molde International Jazz Festival July 96. It was a fantastic consert, and Van The Man also appeard on stage.
Dylan fans, send me an e-mail and tell me if you agree that Infields is one of the best albums ever.
So long
sveinjo@namdalsnett.no

Could you please send me an e-mail on the following question?
In Europe it is impossible to get the film: Renaldo & Clara, by Bob Dylan.
Maybe you could help me out?
Please answer.
Robje Verstappen

[*Sadly, the answer is no. It has never been officially released anywhere in the world on video - JH*]

Great site, Inever found of best.
I never found chords, Why?
I have a bootleg of a concert of Dylan in Italy on 1987, if you are in interest about information send me a message.
Thanks, Gabriele Contoli

Long live Dylan! Love the site...thanks for keeping us up to date! Anyways...the only thing I have to do now is find some way of getting a copy of George Jackson...It seems impossible to get a hold of!
Douglas Larke

So we have Cpt. Kirk doing Tambouring Man, why not Elmer Fudd?
anonymous

I am trying to research the date that Bob Dylan FIRST appeared at Gerde's Folk City, New York City.
I believe it might have been April 11th 1961.
Any help would be really appreciated.
Geoff.
Webmaster@ScopeSys.com

To whom it may concern,
Great web site! I'm kind of new at computers and just happened to fall upon your page, I was wodering how I could get there right away. I was also wondering if you have chat sessions and when.
Thanks
Ben Alkin

Thanks for your web site. As a long-time Bob Dylan aficionado, I really enjoyed it, and will be coming back often for research. I hope you'll come visit my website at:
http://www.circle.net/~scandler
Sincerely,
Sam Candler

---

hey bobby remember the last time we had great fun in the tavern in pratteln, you were dam pissed and me too. this techno music is just boring crap, we prefer to sing together with you totally out of tune as usual "joey" see you next time hounting billy the kid (he was not that bad) cheers Urs, Hugo and my love Sandra

---

I like this page!!!!
Wonderful design!
Check this pages also:
http://www.geocities.com/Broadway/3389/
http://www.geocities.com/Broadway/3389/retro.htm http://www.joviform.pt/~nsilva

Regards,
Nelson

---

first fifteen minutes on the net and i'm finding dylan lyrics.....what do you think i think about this page??
thanks

John,
I see you implemented a toolbar. Neat-o. I've relocated my website, btw. It's now:
http://www2.digimag.net/~flintcrk/
Everything else is pretty much the same except the hit counter doesn't work. I've included a mention of your toolbar in my technical notes in the "About" section...
All the best,
Joe Cliburn
flintcrk@digimag.net

I would like to know more about dylan's religious side where can i find info. about this topic on the net
Sobhy Sonbol
[*Try* Slow Train Coming - *JH*]

NEW BOB DYLAN BOOK IN THE WORKS!!!
WE ARE PUBLISHING YOUR STORIES!!!
There's a brand new Dylan book on the way. Don't say it, "Oh great, not another book tracing his Hibbing roots, Greenwich Village folkie years, etc" NO WAY!!! We've been there and done that. Don't get me wrong, that was all fascinating stuff THE FIRST TIME AROUND!!! But, it's high time the story of Dylan was told from YOUR point of view. After all, YOU buy his music, YOU go to his concerts, why shouldn't YOU speak out? If you want to see YOUR story in print AND get a FREE copy of the new book to show off to your friends, send us your letters!!! Letters about elaborate schemes to get backstage after a show, letters about following his tour bus into oblivion, getting an autograph, taking his order in a restaurant, setting up his sound equipment. Where were you when you heard your first Dylan song and how did it affect you? Did you ever have the tenacity to jump onstage and risk security backlash to boogie with The Legend? Ever had any photographs taken of you with Bob?! ! WE WANT IT ALL!!! Become part of this beautiful tribute to the man who has touched our souls like no one else
Send your stories by e-mail to:
kmaughan@dbtech.net
Or by snail mail to:
Dylan Stories
P.O. Box 20721
Tuscaloosa, AL 35402-20721
WE LOOK FORWARD TO HEARING FROM YOU!!!

I'll start by saying hi and thanks. Thanks for making the web someting interesting for me. I really enjoyed your page and will now become a frequant visiter whenever I have the time. I'm 18 live near Montreal,Canada I'm an avid Dylan fan with more than a few questions; Do you know why he left 'Abandoned Love' off of 'Desire'? And do you know any songs directly linked to Jack Kerouac? If you or someone who visits your homepage could answer these questions for me it would be greatly appreciated. Thanks again...

Charlie Murdoch (SThiel@rocler.qc.ca)

I have a small question that is at the center of a dispute that I thought someone running a Bob Dylan web site ought to be able to answer. A friend and I disagree about who actually performed "Blowin' in the Wind" first Bob Dylan or Joan Baez. I am fully aware that Dylan wrote it and that certainly makes it more likely that he performed it first but you never know. If you could answer this question for us that would be greatly appreciated. You can email me if you like and if you could send a carbon copy to:
sagreenl@blue.weeg.uiowa.edu
that would be great. I look forward to hearing from you, thanks again.
-- Craig Ortner
Macalester College
[*It was definitely performed by Dylan first. Anyone disagree? - JH*]

---

thanks, l,am enjoying everything l,am reading on bob. my concern is bob coming back to toronto?
f bryan

---

wanted to know where to get set lists for this spring tour.Saw him at indiana -bobby still got it.
Greg
[*Check out* BobLinks *homepage. Lots of setlists there. - JH*]

Great site! I really appreciate your extensive information on the Genuine Basement Tapes. I have been looking for these for a long time and have had no luck. Are they still available? Could you possibly point me to a source for these disks? I'd really love to have them, or at the very least get copies of them on tape. Thanks a lot and keep up the great work.
Mark Watkins

Whats up with stormy season;is it or isnt it
Doc Johnson
[*Beat's me - JH*]

---

dig, expecting rain is gone,watta dregany dylan chat rooms?e-mail me
nat z. punx

Hello again -
I think a link to the 'All Lyrics' pages is something many will apprechiate - but I don't think there's anything to be found that justifies the additional '(all lyrics!)' - or is there?
regards
Stefan

Hi. I was wondering if you know the track listing to the Bob Dylan 'import' CD "Highway 61 Revisited Again". I have tried to find the listing of the CD on the web to no avail. Thank you in advance for your help.
Heath
heo96001@uconnvm.uconn.edu

Hi-
I've been scouring the web tonite, trying to track down a swap for a dub of "The 5 volume basement tapes". I'm in the middle of Greil's book & need the whole set! I managed to find the "unofficial tape Library" but it seems the guy who runs that has burned out & closed shop for an indefinite period. Any suggestions? I don't have any dylan to trade with anyone, but all Elvis Costello & some Neil Young.
Thanks, Bill Brown brown23@gate.net

I'm looking for a source for the Dylan CD-ROM that came out 2 or 3 years ago. I don't see it mentioned in this Web site though it got pretty good reviews at the time.
Thanks,
Art

---

really enjoy the page.would like to see more space devoted to "the times they are a changing" era
bulldog

Does anybody out there have a source for purchasing "Bob Dylan's Greatest Hits Vol. 3"? I have a friend who is having trouble locating it.
Great homepage. You must put a lot of work into this.
Thanx....
Jeff..... jeffumla@sprintmail.com

---

please i;ve made my home page dedicated to dylan only now i search for nice dylan background music waves i have but du u know where ik can find midi files of dylen and who are not payed on a roland piano but from dylan self ? please.. mij ho is www.worldonlin.nl/~bertmidd and u see whats missing :-)) by.
bert fromn holand

I think this page is really happpenin' man, keep up the great work.
justine

I would like information on where I could sell my mint condition album, The Freewheeling' Bob Dylan. It is the Monaural version cl-1986. It is valued at $15,000. any information on how to sell this album would be greatly appreciated. If you kow of any interested buyers please have them contact me.
Thank you
Kullabali@mns.com

---

this site has been really helpful See, i have this research project i have to do about Dylan (my English teacher is a big Dylan fan) and i wanted to do more than just his life history. I really wanted to find out what it was that made him so great and i really thank and commend you for your site
aNAWIM

Hey! Where's the Bob Dylan Birthday Bash Button on your home page?
Happy Birthday Blessed Bob!
jangus@asis.com

John,
Could you tell me where I find the pages for the free tapes.
Was it Simon Cyberg? in USA. He sent me a few tapes now I can't find his pages!
Bob
[*That would be* http://freelib.org/dylan/freelib.html, *although I see that it's temporarily closed for renovation. - JH*]

Thanks,
I just recently discovered this site and wanted to thank you for providing such a great service.I've spent hours just browsing and reading articles and interveiws.Olaf's Chronicles has proven invaluable in making sure shows I have traded for are complete.also reading about each year of his tours is also very interesting.Thanks again for taking the time to provide this great page,
Take Care,
Cliff Timmons

(just a quick comment)
on the day in which i heard about bob's hospitalization, it was very reassuring that i could find such a well-planned and well-organized informative site. thank you.
egg

I just wrote a tribute song to Bob Dylan hoping that he recovers. If you like it go ahead and link it.
High-Priest of the Silver Crow
http://www.geocities.com/Athens/Forum/2480/slvrcrow.htm
Simon Seamount

DYLAN, DON'T YOU DARE DIE, GOD DAMN IT!! WE LOVE YOU!! tAKE OUR LOVE, OUR VIBES, AND OUR WAVES!!
HAPPY SAILING AND THANKS FOR 30 YEARS OF BLISS!! TRULY.
CARIBBEAN SAILORS FROM THE VIRGINS TO VENEZUELA!!!!
Caribbean Sailors

Just a short comment. Found out about this site from the CNN news report about Dylan's illness. Will check it out.
Dave

---

great job on links for the hospitalization update. thanx.
had a chance to read Invisible Republic yet? nice essay in current Newsweek on general topic of hidden roots of county, w/specific discussion of Marcus on Bob, etc.
again, thanx for a nice job
stuart levitan

---

thanks for providing the hospital updates.
sbarnard@geocities.com

Wow!!! I love this place. Thanks for putting it here. I probably missed reading it somewhere along the line, but I've always wondered who the female is on the cover of the Freewheelin' album?
Sorry if this a dumb question.
Thanks!
Brian Hollabaugh
[*The woman on the cover of the album is Suze Rotolo, Dylan's girlfriend at the time. - JH*]

Hi; Love your site. Great review onthe Basement Tapes. Do you know anyone who will trade tapes for them? I have alot of Springsteen and will do the ususal 2-1 otherwise. Thanks for your help.
Allen (lbrawer@aol.com)

Dear Mr Dylan!
I am writing on behalf of my husband Mr. Oystein Lervik and his colleague atwork Ms. Lill. They are both fans of Mr. DYlan and are very sorry to hear about his hospitalization. they would appreciate if the following message is passed on to him.
"When thing go wrong, So wrong with you, It hurts me too."
Have a speedy recovery and all the best to you.
Greeting from
Oystein Lervik and Lill. Oslo, Norway!

I WAS WONDERING IF YOU COULD TELL ME WHERE I COULD FIND A FULL Biography on Bob Dylans life with dates and his connection to the counterculture during the 60's and Vietnam War. There seems to be a lack of information on this part of his life on the Web I'm doing a report on him so it would help a lot
Thanks
Holly

Hello,
I hope that this letter will arrive (or least it's contents) to Bob Dylan. Firstly I want to say that I'm happy that my prayer came true and he's healthy and he don't still went to meet Elvis like he said. I was happy to hear also that in september (my birthday month) he'll release a new album:"Time out of mind".
I'm 25 years old and I'm a poet who was influenced from Beat Generation (especially from Alan Ginsberg). Bob Dylan is my idol and in his credit I discovered so much values and they are very close to me today (like that and like Woody Guthrie, Arthur Rimbaud) and of course all Bob's music that gives me complete life. I did read a lot of biographys about his life and because it I know very well about his GREATNESS.
A year ago when I published my first poems book, many peoples told me that they saw the effect from Bob Dylan, especially in my Protest Songs (like against who assasinated my Prime Minister, Yizhak Rabin). I wish to send you my book but I wrote it in Hebrew, there is a poem who I wrote it in dedication for Bob Dylan.
I never forget his concert in my land, Israel. I saw him in Haifa port (20.6.93), it was been my only and first opportunity to saw him on stage meantime, but I wish and promise to myself to see him again.
Sincerely,
Oudi (My friends nickname me "ouDylan").
P.s. I discovered this site while visiting Cnn's report about Bob Dylan's health

Oudi Ben-porat

Dear Bringing It All Back Home Folks:
Thank you very much for keeping all of us up to date on Dylan's recent health problems. I had a very hard time getting the straight story until I found your website. Keep up the good work.
Yours,
Karl

I'm on the mailing list 'About Townes' (Van Zandt) where I read a short comment on Dylna's health. I nearly panicked and at once looked for further information in the web. So I found your homepage via Altasvista. I'm very pleased with the very new articles on Dylan (at least more actual than German newspapers that only spent a few lines on Dylan's infection). Continue your good work!
Yours,
Christof

John,
I found the site the first time I really got to grips with the net (and naturally loooking first for my hero since 1964). It's a brilliant site and I agree with the guy who wrote how great it is to feel connected with all those other, aging and young Dylan fans around the world. Especially now, when BD was hospitalised, and I could hear the latest news. I was at both of his shows in Israel and hope he'll be back here again.
Keep up the good work!
Diana

No feedback really, other than its a great web page. I do have a question though. Is there any
where I can find someones analisys of the lyrics to the "Changing of the Guard".
Thanks
Jay

Found you by searching for "The Genuine Basement Tapes".
Any suggestiopns as to how to come by them? I hear rumors
they are no longer available.
Thanks,
Leo

Very nice site!!!
looking forward to find mre lyrics of dylan's songs...
liran

Hey there,
Just wanted to let you know...I added you as a link to my "solo" web site..
http://members.aol.com/Lambchild3/index.html
I'm currently recording a Christian "folk-rock" album...

Thanks & Peace,
Eddie Lambchild.

---

the broken words site at columbia University doesnt work anymore! great site though. would love more lyric analysis stuff.
paras

Searching for info - can you help? Found an album with Bob Dylan's name written on it (do not know if it was signed by previous owner, autographed, whatever????). The record cover is for a two-album set, totally blank with no images, graphics, by-lines, etc. Inside are two 33 1/3 records without labels, apparently never labeled. Playing the records, they are Bob Dylan's but I would have to spend some time to ID the different songs on the records. Can you help to identify source or supply any infor? Or can you direct me to a web page to find out. Thank you. Enjoyed your page.
Beverly Stouffer
[*Probably* Great White Wonder. *See* http://www.punkhart.com/dylan/disco/gww.html *and* http://www.punkhart.com/dylan/disco/gww-listing.html *for more information. - JH*]

The british band Magna Carta went on concert in Holland in June 1st, and they made a small tribute to Dylan. Read the full report at:
http://www.geocities.com/Broadway/3389/reports.htm
Nelson

Congratulations !!!
It is a masterpiece and I think for us will be more than useful, will be a lot of fun !!! For the first time I've such approach with Dylan's material. I have been following him for 20 years, and wher I used to live in Brazil - Rio de Janeiro, news from him or anything related to were very rare.
By the time I moved to San Diego I got more info, but now with the internet . It is so excited to be part.
I e-mail to tzr@pitt.edu to be part of the web but I did not understand yet how things work. Please help me be part of this in a way I can always know whats going on. I also have looking for the movie Reinaldo & Clara, but I did not find. Do you know something? I read the biography by Robert Shelton and On the road from Larry Sloman.
I will be waiting from an answer from you.
A brazilian fan.
Carlos Augusto Vidigal

Dear Dyan Page Maintainer,
The Malaspina Great Books Program has designated your page as a Great Books Five Star Site.
Your site is linked to entries in our database at:
http://www.mala.bc.ca/~mcneil/dylanb.htm
A list of other five star sites is at http://www.mala.bc.ca/~mcneil/fivestar.htm
Thank you for your important WWW resource.
Yours Sincerely
Russell McNeil, Ph.D.
Malaspina University-College
Great Books Home Page
http://www.mala.bc.ca/~mcneil/template.htx

GREAT SITE. GREAT INFORMATION.
HAVE BEEN A DYLAN FAN SINCE EARLY,EARLY 1960'S. YOUR SITE WILL CATCH ME UP AND KEEP ME UP TO DATE AS TO WHAT IS HAPPENING TO THE "LEGEND".
SAW DYLAN AT LOON MOUNTANIN, NH ON SUNDAY. HE WAS AS GOOD AND SOLID AS EVER.
RICHARD BOISSEAU

---

do you know where i can get any movie clips of dylan? they must me avi file type.
thanks
brook

Bob Dylan is a lyrical and musical genuis. No one can compare. He is one of the largest influences in rock and roll. He will live on 4 E*V*E*R. (dig the web site)
Herman

Hi, I am interested in purchasing a video of the film "Renaldo and Clara". Do you know how I might be able to accomplish this? Thankyou for your consideration.
Ana

Just saw the show last evening at Pine Knob in Michigan... Really hot show. It's the sisxth show I've seen, and I'd say one of the best. Booby rocked, and I really liked the backup band behind him this time. The audio system was also the clearest I've heard him on, with the notable exception of when he opened up for the dead in DC. Just thought I'd add my view.
Ezra Reis
"I ain't gonna work on Maggies farm no more!!"

Hello:
I enjoy your page and check you out often. Thanks for the great info!
I tried to click on the Wall of Sound link to Dylan's new track list and it cam e up with:
HTTP/1.0 400 Bad Request
regards,
David Voytek
[*I just tried it and it seems to be working - JH*]

Who is Bob married to and is she the mother of Jakob? And I've looked everywhere and I can't find a picture of her. Do you have a picture of her?

Could you please link me from your sight? I have a web site called The Kerouac Quarterly. I am being linked sometime soon from Levi Asher's site. I am at:
http://www.freeyellow.com/members/upstartcrow/page1.html

I was register in the Dylanweb as #25. So far I have no answer,once I understand that I can access to you anytime. I have been surfing through this site It is simply a taste of what I was expected. Congratulations for uor job. Please enroll me at your site.
Thank You.
Carlos Augusto Vidigal.

Site#25
Brazilian Fan

Just want to say thanks for this site - I've skimmed it a few times, and everytime I find some new fascinating bits of knowledge (the Al Kooper page, for example, which may be old, but it's good, as Neil says in Pocahontas). Just saw Bob in Toronto on August 7 and I hope you have a chance to catch him, because the Man is On Fire again, for the first time in quite a while.
Thanks Again. Bill (up in Ottawa, Canada)

I am desapointed, there is nothing very much interesting on your web site ....
Beaupre@worldnet

Hey,
I think your page is awesome, I just recently turned sixteen and I had been listening to dylan almost all my life and i heard about your web page from a friend he said it was the best on the web so i checked it out
AARON

Hi folks,
nice site. Might be of interest for you: I found a site with inexpensive and good quality Bob Dylan posters (and much more) at http://www.concertposter.com.
Bye,
Stefan

I tried to access your Dylan, Oh Dylan pictures, but was given the error 403 forbidden. I have aol. I would like to see and possibly copy some of these pics. If you can help, please e-mail me back.
Great site. Bob rules

I browsed through your dylan page and thought it was amazing. I'm a huge dylan fan myself but i do have one question i hope you can answer. What album, if a ny, is the song "born in time" on. I was wondering if you could be as kind as to e-mail me the answer.
Thankyou.
[*The album in question is* **Under the Red Sky** - *JH*]

BOB!!!!
Thank You, Thank you, Thank you for a real good time. I only got to catch one show, but thanks for Tangled up in Blue. I don't know if you personally will get this, but thank you for keeping it going. If it weren't for you, Merle, Grisman, Hunter and countless others I just don't know what I would do.
Jessa McCloud

I am looking for information on Bob Dylan (and other artists of his caliber) and the relation that their music has to poetry. I was hoping that if people know where I can get this information that they would send it to me. I am doing this for a grade eight unit on poetry and would appreciate the help. Thanks.
phosmar@redeemer.on.ca

I've now added the chords to all the TOOM songs to my page.
http://hem.passagen.se/obrecht/backpages/
Eyolf Ostrem

You'll find another excellent (german) review of the new album at
http://www.spiegel.de/spiegel/kultur/40242.html. It's from the weekly german newsmagazine Der Spiegel.
Herbert Adam

I am looking for info on the Dylan movie, Renaldo & Clara, do you have any sources for purchasing the original 5 hour version fo the film on video or any other format! I enjoyed your site! I found it through a "Beat" link. Thanks.
Evan

Wonderful site. I'm not sure how I got here. I started with a search on "Joan Baez" and here I am a few pages later. What I need is a short bio on Bob Dylan (and a few dozen others) for my Sixties site at:
http://www.geocities.com/SoHo/Studios/2914
Can you steer me to a biography. Do you know anyone who'd like to DO it? Anyone who's already done it and would let me use it?
Thanks,
Lisa

I would like to find a copy of Dylan's concert movie, "Renaldo & Carla". I've searched around town and on the internet. Shirley some one markets this great movie. Do you have any idea where I can get a copy? Thanks, Zenwino
Dale Joyner (Zenwino@aol.com)

I Shall be released = Novalis "Hymns to the night" (?)
Anonymous

Does Dylan have a chat room? I couldn't find one and I thought he did. Please let me know what it is if there is one. Oh, Your page is pretty good, I'll be back to it I'm sure.
Betsy

How come all of the parts where he talks doesn't show him talk, and how come the y are so short?
EnglandsR

I have been a Dylan fan since my early teens (I'm now 47) and I have always felt that since his breakup with his wife Sarah around 1977 (the year I got married) he still loves her. After listening to several tracks on his latest CD, TOOM, it seems to me that he still misses her as much as ever.
The point is, that after 17 years of marriage, my wife left me recently for another guy. And Dylan's songs about Sarah or relationships in general now hit so close to home that I can't listen to BOTT or TOOM without a major cry.

Anyway, can you recommend any books, articles or reading that may discuss what happened between Bob and his wife, and what he feels about what happened?
I have a catalog from "On The Tracks" and they have many books and periodicals available, but perhaps you know which ones deal with the specific aspect of Bob's life that I can now relate to and am now interested in.
Looking forward to hearing from you or your members. (Feel free to post this).
You have a great website.
Thanx...
Jeff
jeffumla@sprintmail.com (Jeff Umla)

Hi. Cool page. I was wondering if you could help me. I'm doing an extra credit paper in my History of Rock Music class, and I need to find some articles or something about how Bob Dylan's going electric influenced fans as well as other bands. He went electric on my birthday (I don't think I was born yet) :) So, please write back if you can direct me toward the information. Thanks.
a_wilbury@stones.com (Kelly)

This is a great site... I rarely do feedback, but in this case, I wanted to. I read most of the past feedback comments: there was one thing I wanted to add. Somebody posted, wondering who the woman was alongside Dylan on the album slee ve of The Freewheelin'...she is not Albert Grossman's wife Sally, but Suze Rotolo. The picture was taken in February, 1963. Albert Grossman's wife did appear on a Dylan cover, but it was on Bringing It All Back Home. Keep up the good work. Very cool.
Rain

I'd just like to say what a great sight this is, I keep returning to it again and again. It's invaluable for far too many reasons to go into. Keep up the good work.
cp lee

Do you know --
Who is the girl on Dylan's arm on the Freewheelin' Bob Dylan album?
thanks,
Joel Silverman
Atlanta, GA

I am glad to BD have so much support across the generations. I was looking for an address for mail to the man himself. Any new BD info is appreciated.
Meredith Webb

Be curious to know how many Bob fans would want to read a book about his personal life, his relationship with ex-wives, girlfriends, children, sports, etc. and what he does in his free time, even if some of the information might explode the myth, revealing him to sometimes be a self-serving, ego manical person. The book is being written by a long-time girlfriend, who depending on how pissed off he gets, may or may not be sitting next to him at the Kennedy Center Awards this winter.

To answer some of the questions: Renaldo and Clara is impossible to find unless you know him. He keeps it (as best he can, safely locked up in a vault.) He does not read these sites unless there is something particularly interesting one of his friends or employees picks up.
SadieEarp

Why can't I find the bootleg "F**k the Playlist" in your bootleg index. I'd like to see what's contained on the cd.....
Greg

I'm trying to get a letter to Dylan concerning a Woody Guthrie Memorial. Do you have an address (besides Sony/Columbia)where I would have a REASONABLE chance of getting something to him? Thanks.
coltrane@ibm.net

---

yes..just wanting to know if there are any parties before or after Dylan's November 8th concert in Dayton, Ohio at Hara Arena? Also..who will be opening for Dylan that night? thanks a lot...
Dan Taylor (dangohogs@aol.com)

I have an old dylan album called V.D. Blues. Dylan sings songs about V.D.. another songs. If any intrerest give me a call at 760-345-7839 Nites or 760 773-3231. CALIFORNIA
keith

---

waiting in a auwull panic, i resorted to finding all the people involved
anonymous

Dear John,
I just wrote you regarding the Dylan tribute book "If You See Him Say Hello" and realized that I used the word "wonderful" 2 or 3 times in my last email to you!.....so sorry, and so embarrassed....(blushing profusely.)
Trace

---

mrjones
etc
If you want to read The Foot of pride was in a BOOT! or whatever..i see noplapable lull in energy, do you? I hsdto give m all another name, etc jonesy
[*Huh? - JH*]

---

i recently attended boy dylan's concert in mobile. it was very disappointing. no communication at all with crowd (to be expected), played only his new songs (played only a few old ones), and seemed relatively uninspired. few attended and i am beginning to understand why. people come to relive the past in large part because his songs represent signposts along the way of life. no hamonica. no back up vocals. very little acoustic. an electric morass of static with relati vely few lyrics which were inte lligable. is this the norm rather than the exception? your thoughts
Jamie

Recently I've been bothered by the lack of multimedia clips on the net. Do you know of any pages currently boasting vid-clips of Dylan's numerous liveshows taped over the decades? If

not do you and/or other webmasters have p lans in the works?
Take it easy....
Patrick Dietz

Hello, I've been searching for a while now for the guitar tablature and lyrics of the song "you belong to me" from the soundtrack of Natural Born Killers. In the leaflet of this CD, it dates the song as 1952 and was written by pee wee king, red stewart and chilton price, who I don't have a clue who they are. If you can help me find this song, i would appreciate you e-mailing me back some info.
Thank You.
Pierre Gagnon

Great Website. Really enjoyed it. Keep up the good work. Bob Dylan is the greate st songwriter that ever lived. He is the very best. Long live Dylan and God bless him.
Christine

I feel compelled to comment on your site as it is simply brilliant. A very comp rehensive list of highly interesting material. Congratulations!!
(A Baldursson (Iceland))

I'm the editor of a magazine of poetry and reviews, called 'Interchange'. I'm thinking of reviewing 'Time Out of Mind' for the next issue, and I've been using your site to research my article. I'm just in awe at what a coherently-ordered and 'friendly' resource your site is. (I'm a lecturer at the University of Wales - if only our students had similar access to literary journals and articles, etc! Your system of links, whereby everyone shares stuff, is just great. It's how it should be!)
So, thanks for keeping this site going. It gets my vote!
If you're interested in the review, when it appears, let me know ...
Best wishes,
Ric

Want to know if there is any complete catalog about Dylan's bootlegs in CD. Your page is great really!
Bye.
mauricio luja
[*Try* BDBDB *JH*]

I was wondering if I could get the lyrics from the song, "It's All Over Now, Baby Blue." I am writing a paper on the short story that Joyce Carol Oates dedicated to him. Also if you have any another references to that it would help a great deal for my paper. Thank you. I appreciate it.
Sincerely
Krystal of University of California, Irvine

---

i am building a page with links to pages concerning bob dylan, jimmy buffett and the grateful dead may i create a link to your page.
thanks for your time
jeremy

I really would like to have an address to send cards and the occasional fan/than k you note. I have been a loyal fan for thirty years and I really would like to thank him.
Lynn

Hi,
I really enjoyed your web page!
I saw Dylan at the Philadelphia Spectrum in 1979 (large band with violin guy fro m South Philly). I also saw the Greatful Dead with Bob Dylan as the closed JFK s tadium.
Anyway do you know of any well recorded bootlegs from the tour with Mick Taylor? 1984 I believe? The same tour that Real Live came from. I bought a boot of the rehearsals, great sound but no Mick Taylor excpet Maggies farm which was on Real Live.
Any outtakes from Infidels that Taylor plays on? He is very mixed into the backg round on that album.
Also, id there a Bob Dylan Newsgroup?
Thanks,
Skippy
PS. The Rolling Stones have been playing Like A Rolling Ston on their current Br idges To Babylon Tour. The Stones are playing Madision Square Garden on Jan 16th & 17 while Bob Dylan is playing at the Madison Square Garden Theatre in the sam e building. I hope these guys get together for a live jam on Like A Rolling Ston e like they did in 1995!

Do you know anyone who might want to sell an irving plaza ticket. I will reward with rare dylan memorabilia.i
110456.3354@compuserve.com (gary)

---

this is fantastic!best bob site ever stumbled upon... thanks very much... i do h ave a question: do you know where i can find articles/whatever about dylan writt en by christopher ricks...i've looked all thru your site & cant find anything... anywhere else you might know of... again thanks so much for many hours of enjoy ment.
michelle dennis
mdennis@muse.sfusd.k12.ca.us

I thought that you might be interested in http://www.iam.com/people/ jules/dylan.htm, and might even want to create a link to it...
Thanks,
dale

---

hi, was hoping you could help me out
dylan chat gold closed down, but we're meeting at a new place:
http://www2.banned-books.com/chat/freethought#start
hope you can help spread the word, maybe add a link to your page.
thanks
cindy goodman

December 14, 1997
The Metro
Chicago, IL

Surprise Opening!!!
David Bromberg with Bob's Band
Two Chicago Blues Numbers
1) It's Over Baby
2) She Took My Car When She Quit Me
(These are the first lines of the songs, not their titles. Anyone know the correct titles?)
Bob Dylan
1 Maggie's Farm
2 Tonight I'll Be Staying Here With You
3 Cold Irons Bound
4 Simple Twist Of Fate
5 Can't Wait
6 Sylvio
7 Roving Gambler @
8 To Ramona @
9 Tangled Up in Blue @
10 Ragtime Annie @ (instrumental)
(w/David Bromberg acoust. guitar
and Larry on fiddle)
11 Takes A Train to Laugh
(w/David Bromberg electric slide guitar)
12 Joey
13 Till I Fell in Love With You
14 Don't Think Twice @
15 Love Sick
16 Rainy Day Women #12 & 35
Great show, as usual, with wonderful vibes from Bromberg surprise guest appearance. Bromberg's contribution seemed to be a spur of the moment thing (but who knows...). The crew came out to put up a mic and guitar cable at the last minute. Bob and Dave had a great time playing together. One gets the impression lately that Bob has been reaching out to his old friends, which is a real nice thing.
Standouts were all the Bromberg numbers, Simple Twist, and everything from the acoustic set to the end. How refreshing not to hear Highway 61 and Rolling Stone for a change!
The Metro is pretty decrepit and sticky (sorry gang). The sound was too loud for the venue. Bob's voice and guitar were distorted.
Aside to Bob's people: Whoever mixed did not do proper service to Bob's music. I like loud music, but this was just noise overkill. Think about it.
I saw at least two tapers busted, and at least one success story. The Bromberg stuff will make great filler.
Thanks for coming to Chicago, Bob!
Jeff Klepper

---

has bob dylan ever sang or wrote with leonard cohen? if he has done,when and what?
yigit ercevik

Hi! I just wanted to let you know how excited I was to discover your web site and all the other sites dedicated to Bob Dylan. Bob Dylan's work is one of the great joys of my life. I am so thankful for his beautiful translations of human emotions and feelings due to his sensitivity. He really explains things sometimes! I have been reading about him extensively and viewing any

films that he has participated in. I am stumped about one thing (maybe more than one)....how is a person to locate a copy of Renaldo and Clara? I am dying to see this film. If you have any information, please let me know. Once again, thanks so much for you dedication to the art of Bob Dylan.
Sincerely,
Amanda Hannon

Awesome page! I've stumbled upon it many times, most recently from a page about beat influences on music. Great info. Bob rocks!
Kelly

---

big dylan conference @ stanford u jan 17
dogerel@webtv.net

I like the "new look"! It works better underneath my newly revised "Roadmaps for the Soul" toolbar. Best wishes for a super New Year!!!
Joe Cliburn

This may be a totally peculiar request: do you know how i could contact Bob Dylan's managment, booking agent? I am interested in seeing if he would be willing to play at an event i am invovled with in 1999.
any help appreciated
thanks
jgold@umaryland.edu (Jim Gold)

Mr. Howells--
I have been following your site for almost three years now and it does keep getting better and better, both in look and content. What has been the hallmark of your site for me are your own comments and criticisms. They always seem to be right on, even if they differ from most people's. I anticipate reading your page (though I've gone through most of it), and reading your posts on rmd because of them.
Now all you need to do is actually go to a Dylan show. I wouldn't mind hearing what you think of his performances today. I doubt you'd be disappointed.
Brian James

Well, as many of you I've been deeply influenced by Bobby and think his new album is his finest, without any doubt. As for your page, it's great. I live in Slovenia and write since the age of 6, publishing 5 books of poems and one album of songs.
I'd really like to meet Bobby in person, but probably it'll never happen because of my "geografical position".
Wish ya all the best!
Matej

Need to talk more about his personal life.
Anonymous

Thanks for making this Web Site. I knew both Bob and John when they palyed at the "Scholar and the Purple Onion. My girl friends and I used to give them money to buy beer and give them

rides. However, I could never remember if it was 1960 or 1961. That was a long time ago. Now thanks to your page I know. By the way do you know what became of John Keorner? Keep up the good work
Phyllis

This isn't a comment as such, more a query: i'm going thru a real rolling thunder phase at the minute, and trying desperately to track down bootlegs - esp. one that contains the "heavy metal" version of Tangled Up In Blue. Any suggestions?
John Harris
Editor
Select Magazine
London

HI MAN
I have been a Dylan fan since I was 12. I'm 20 now and really want to get into a Dylan fan club and can't find any info on it. Can you help? I really need it. I can't have my mom one up me with her Willie Nelson fan club letters anymore.
Thank you
Dutch Ferral

Pretty awesome! I'm using one of Bob Dylan's pictures for an art project so thanks for being here. What an awesome guy. I wish I had lived in the sixties.
nalini reyes

Out of all the Dylan sites I've found so far yours has the best pictures. I viewed the photos from Blonde on Blonde. I have always assumed the person in the photo of Dylan sitting on a sofa was Allen Ginsberg and the woman in the picture with Dylan was Albert Grossman's wife. But I could be wrong.
Wendy

Looking for any and all outtakes from "Time Out of Mind".
Charles

I'm looking to get a copy of Don't Look Back (a legal copy of course). I don't know if one exists that I could order or pick up at a store if anyone has any info please let me know. Thank you,
Dave Heneise

Mandi dal friuli!!!
Anonymous

Io preferisco Dario Zampa!!!
Astrubale

I remember seeing, years ago, ads in magazines like Rolling Stone for concert ph otos. I thought it would be interesting to try to collect some concert photos of Dylan. I have been doing some digging around on the net a nd have not found anything, and it seems like the ads in Rolling Stone have been replaced by 900 sex businesses. I read that you are not a clearinghouse for tape collectors and merchandise acquirers, and I can't blame you for that,

but if you know of any place I might try for Dyl an concert pics, I would appreciate hearing of it. Finally, I enjoyed your site. Well done. Best, Michael
Michael Mullen

I noticed on the song list of covers, one was missed that I know of. It is "When the Ship Comes In," and it's sung by The Pogues. There version is studio and on their album Pogue Mahone.
Stephen Pace

Great site!!! I like the name alot. Easy to get around, and I will visit often. Been a fan since 1965...(has it been THAT long?) Anyway, i wamted you to know, in case you hadn't seen it that there is a really nice review on MSNBC @www.msnbc.com/news/138198.asp of the Dylan/Van Morrison concert in NYC.I just left that site with a link to yours... (I guess that means you know about it already...) Anyway - great job!
bruce
bwhite49@ix.netcom.com

Does anyone have or know where I can get a transcript of Bob's grammy acceptance speech?
Nv

I have a Bob Dylan yearbook from Hibbing High School, I am thinking of selling. Can you give me some information on how to do this ? Thanks
gfsund@the-bridge.net

ALBUM; Title "BOB DYLAN SEVENTY DOLLAR ROBBERY".If you know anything about t his album e-mail me.
thank you
roy@jane.penn.com

I was speaking with a dylan fanatic and he mentioned that the song hurricane was an account of an actual event and iwas wondering if this was fact or was he full of it?
Anonymous
[*Of course it's based on a true event. - JH*]

In the late seventies, Dylan started what was called 'the never-ending tour'. At the time probably nobody took that literally. Twenty years later, it has beco me clear it was not meant as a joke. I'm a filmmaker trying to find fans who par ticipate in this never-ending tour, people who follow him around. Do you know fans who are (stil) camping?
bigpete@euronet.nl

Enjoyed your site. I've been reading the Mis-heard Lyrics page, which is great fun. Recognized a few of them myself.
One line caught my eye. In "Memphis Blues Again", you have the actual lyric listed as "The (?) preacher looked so baffled". I have always heard this as "The TV preacher looked so baffled." Makes sense to me because TV preachers were a new thing back in '66.
David Malbuff

Hey, heres something I wrote a while ago, 2 mo.s, and I wonder if you might tell me what you think of it?
"I Dreamed I Saw Bob Dylans Wife"
I Dreamed I saw Bob Dylans Wife alive and in the nude
Kvetching about her former life and how she'd been treated rude
she bitched and cried how she'd been used to bear his kids and then
she'd found that more he loved his Muse and liquor in the end
I told her I was sorry and what did her mother think
She said before she could say more she'd have to have a drink
I said OK got out of bed and then crossed to the bar
I made her a dry martini and myself a short Dewars
Not thinking it would matter much I rolled myself a toke
and as I took first drag and sip and turned again she spoke
"My mother" she said fluffing hair "is dead and in the ground,
But, if she knew what I had done why she'd be spinning round
She warned me not to marry him but I said Ma he's a Jew!
She said Anyone can get circumsized today" then She asked "Are you?"
I almost woke up then I was so startled in my sleep
"Well yeah" I said "But arent they all?" I asked, not being too deep
"Or nothing" she snapped quickly "I dont trust what I cant see!"
"Too much" I dreamed I thought I said. I dreamed she smiled at me"
Well anyway what brings you here, and what about his songs?
aren't they what made his career great and who cares about his schlong?"
"But he had to play them over and over all the time
if I'd had to hear 'Hard Rain' once more I would have lost my mind!
And then his groupies oh my god one looked like Mama Ray
another looked like Tracy but much older than today."
"Thats wierd" I said "Hard to believe with money up the ass
that thats the best that he could do." as I took a hit of grass
"But thats just it" she waved, her martini glass in hand
"He believes his Gift is from above and his Muse is some old Black man!"
This time I really did wake up and proved it was a dream
The glass, The joint, The Bitch was gone. I could hear a distant scream
But it felt really spooky sitting in the empty room,
dissappointedly sensing something impending Loom.
copyright 1998 B R Beal
for The EveryDAY CarTOON Prod
all rights reserved
thanks alot for your time
bbeal@hotmail.com (Bruce Beal)

I am a big fan of Bob Dylan. I am very impressed with this site. People shoul not use sick comments when talking about Bob. SHow some respect
John

I love Bob Dylan!!!!
This is a great site!!!!!
Steinar Kristoffersen

Krohn's Boulevard Records has vinyl albums by Bob Dylan for sale at (http://www.kalnet.net/krohn) Rock, Pop, Folk, & Country from the '60s to the '90s; Blues & Jazz from the '50s & before; back issues of music magazines like Goldmine, RS tone, Creem, Musician, Hot Wacks, Spin, & others; Used But Not Abused CDs & Singles. (http://www.kalnet.net/krohn)
krohn@kalnet.net (Bill Krohn)

Love the site! One thing though, on your related artists list, don't you think that the Wallflowers should be included? After all not only is their music grea t, Jakob is as related an artist can get! ~Lolita Grae
PS, you might want to add a link to AJ Webberman's page, I personally have a lot of fun flaming him! (Jakob is sueing AJ !)
Lolita Grae

RE:Ring Them Bells I've thought about this quite a bit in the past what thirteen years since that interview, Dylan has far from endorsed a Jewish standpoint has taken something of what one might consider a detached Christian/theistic standpoint, although references both to the old and new testaments are as frequent in Oh Mercy and Under The Red sky as they were in previous religious albums.
So what about Messianic complex? Well since his conversion of 1978 he's largely written and spoken of his deepest thought and meditations upon his spiritual life in terms that are in many ways (in my limited understanding) non Jewish, in that they are not collective statements of faith, they indicate personal salvation (rather than purely national) they also largely take up the more orthodox Christian view of the falleness of man and the world, the existence of personal evil in the form of the devil and the theology of original sin.
We may want to get down to specifics later
Consider:
Ring Them Bells:
Ring Them Bells, ye heathen, from the city that dreams,
Ring Them Bells,fron the sanctuaries across the valleys and streams,
For they're deep and they're wide,
And The world's on its side,
And time is running backwards,
And so is the bride.
Ring Them Bells, Saint Peter, where the four winds blow,
Ring Them Bells with an iron hand so the people will know.
Oh, its rush hour now
On the wheel and plow,
And the sun is going down on the sacred cow.
Ring Them Bells, Sweet Martha for the poor man's son,
Ring Them Bells so the world will know that God is one.
Oh, the shepherd is asleep
where the willows weep,
And the mountains are filled with lost sheep.
Ring Them Bells for the blind and the deaf
Ring Them bells for all of us who are left.
Ring Them bells,for the chosen few
Who will judge the many when the game is through.

Ring them Bells for the time that flies,
For the child that cries when innocence dies.
Ring Them Bells , Saint Catherine from the top of the room,
Ring them from the fortress for the lilies that bloom.
Oh the lines are long,
and the fighting is strong,
And they're breaking down the distance between right and wrong.
Verse 1 lines 5-6the bride is most likely the church based on Matthew 9:15 and Revelation 19:7-9also Ephesians 5:25. However in the light of Bob's Jewish background and perspective it could also refer to The Marriage of God and Israel Hosea 2:19-20.
Verse 2 line 1 Matthew 14:23-32
Verse 2 line 2 Mindful of Revelation 2:27
Verse 2 line 6 Exodus 32:4
Verse 3 Line 2 Possibly alluding to Dueteronomy 6-4
Verse 3 lines 3-5Ezekiel 34:6 also Matthew 18:12 John 10:11-14
Verse 4 line Matthew 11:2-6
Verse 4 lines 3-4Matthew 22:14 Revelation 17:14
Verse 4 line 1 Corinthians 6:2-3; Matthew 6:8
"Oh, the shepherd is asleep" I do not think is meant to allude to Christ, but to the hireling shepherd or the unfaithful shepherds of Israel perhaps the corrupt "church"..commentators, wrongly I feel , said it cited Dylan's impatience with God for not resolving and judging the wrong in the world; but wouldn't that go against the title Oh Mercy ? Interestingly it may hark back to I Want You with the line "The Saviours are fast asleep they wait for you". Also "The cracked bells and washed out horns..", the cracked bell here is probably The Liberty Bell. Then I think about the new song "Standing In The Doorway"
When the last rays of daylight go down
Buddy you'll roll no more
I can hear the church bells ringing in the yard
I wonder who they're ringing for
I know I can't win
But my heart just won't give in
Last night I danced with a stranger
But she just reminded me you were the one
You left me standing in the doorway, crying
In the dark land of the sun
"And time is running backwards,And so is the bride." the image of time is constant throughout Oh Mercy, remembered love affairs Most of The Time, possibly What Was It You Wanted, reflections on his own mortality in Shooting Star,and What Good Am I.These are links with Time Out Of Mind too. Indeed in an early take he sings the line "Seen a shooting star on the flat land roads, I was a thousand miles away from where the end of time explodes", yes I think your idea about its connection with scientific theories of time/light and space are relevant here. As an aside, I often use the confusion of clockfaces telling no particular time in my own work as I believe art to opperate and interact on another dimension.
Cartwright pointed out, and I agree with him that "The world's on its side" is a picture of the world as some sort of wounded creature crawling back to its hole to die, certainly at least it suggests the world is somehow fatally compromised. However as with all the very best of Bob's work it is the overall mood created by voice piano and spaces between words, the unspoken text, the way in which the images are woven that holds us spellbound. As a song it is very rewarding as it challenges people to feel the sorrow of mankinds' situation to long for some

divine resolution and justice, which after all in a much more crude way the very early songs commented upon as in Song To Woody (The World) "Its sick and its hungry its tired and its torn it looks like its dying and its hardly bin' born" . I must say how great it is to look at Dylan's work over what is now getting on for forty years, like many painters and poets the themes and concerns were thre from the beginning, yet the infinite way he has to expressed his view has the mark of genius.
Martin Beek

---

this is one of the most thorough sites i have ever had the privelege to see. i am looking for any modern beatniks, in ny or calif. i am a pet/singer. lobrien2@hofstra.edu
lobrien2@hofstra.edu (cassidy)

Dylan's Birthday Open Jam/Mike in NYC
On Saturday, May 23, 1998, from 10 PM to 2 AM or so, The Pick-Up Allstars will be hosting an open jam/mike celebrating Dylan's birthday. We will be playing only Dylan and Dylan-related (e.g. The Band, Woody Guthrie, Joan Baez, etc.) songs.
Everyone in the universe is welcome, especially those sporting Leopard-Skin Pill Box Hats, huffin' harmonicats, Saxophone Joe's, dancing children in Chinese suits to play their flutes, Mr. Tambourine Persons and you too Bob. We will have a p.a., drums, amps...etc., just bring your guitars, harps...etc.. If you're considering coming, let us know what you're interested in performing, especially if it has more than three chords, to avoid duplication and allow for preparation. Listeners and Dylanologists of all stripes are also welcome.
We will be convening at Finnegan's Rainbow 60-19 Roosevelt Avenue, Queens NY, USA. Take the 7 Train to 61st Street and Roosevelt. The bar is right under the el.
You can contact us via the Dyl-line -- (718) 729-6019 or via e-mail.
So join us May 23 1998 -- D-DAY -- and get Tangled Up In Bob.
Christopher Caprioglio

I just found your site, and it's great. Thanks
Cathy

Hey John --
Have you heard anything from Olof regarding the 1997 installment of his Chronicles? I sure hope he is planning on doing them. They are incredible!!!
Jeff Gregwan
[*Sadly, no. Olof where are you? - JH*]

It's hard to explain the importance to 16 year olds in the 1960s of Dylan's "tim es they are a changing". They were seminal in the sense that they came from the gramaphone's mouth, not from ours. We now had a legitimate intermediary. My f irst date with my husband of 30-odd years was at the Royal Albert Hall (London). This is a vast and majestic venue that Dylan was able to fill on his own, with guitar, harmonica and his voice. It was an unforgettable evening.
Regards Angela Tappas

Radio station KTCZ, Minneapolis, St. Paul, MN, in the 1997 "Cities Sampler," has Dylan singing backed up by the Tokyo Symphony Orchestra. I forget the song.
Colmbia Record Hour Volume II has Yousf D'Nour singing "Chimes of Freedom" in hi s native African language, with English translation by Bruce Cockburn. Absolutely wonderful!

Doug Johnson

Stunning. A blockbuster. I can't wait for the movie. A lusty, brawling epic. I laughed... I cried... it became a part of me.
george.klotzbaugh@thehartford.com

I find your web pages very well designed in general but I think you should consider adding a scrollbar to the left frame. I run my screen in 640*480 pixels resolution and I can?t view all of the left frame.
Best wishes
Anders J

What drugs did he use.
How did the drugs affect his singing.
How did the singing affect the people.(good and bad)
Anonymous

Lots of Bob Dylan vinyl rock albums & other classic rock artists albums for sale at Krohn's Boulevard Records at http://www.kalnet.net/krohn. Rock, Pop, Folk, & Country from the '60s to the '90s; Blues & Jazz from the '50s and before; back issues of music magazines like Goldmine, RStone, Creem, Crawdaddy, Discoveries, Musician, Hot Wacks, & others; Used But Not Abused CDs & Singles, music movies; http://www.kalnet,net/krohn. Thanks to the owners of this guestbook for letting me have my say and for this service they are doing for music and fans.
krohn@kalnet.net (Bill Krohn)

I recently read Clinton Heylins review of Time out of Mind on this website. Bob Dylan fans are often the most hard him. Whatever this great poet has to say is worth listening to. A lot of people must have disagreed with Heylin, Mr.Dylan won his first Album of the year grammy. That was long overdue. God Bless BOB Dylan And Clinton Heylin learn to have good taste
John Sasser

Your boot lists up to pre-Rolling Thunder 1975 are great, but since my primary boot interest is Rolling Thunder, I'm curious if you are planning to expand the boot information to include 1975 and 1976? I know it's a huge amount of work, so the cutoff is understandable.
Calvin Rice

Great site. Bob Dylan is one of my main guides in life. I think this is a great site and I am going to use it in a project Im doing for a high school class of mine.
Travis Dandy

I noticed subsequent to last date in July through first date in August leaves ample time for travel back to States. Hoping to be surprised in Okemah. Peace
Alan Thummel

A truly excellent site. I visit-and enjoy-it often!
zimmy@ozemail.com.au

During the recent AOL-VH1 chat session with Robbie Robertson, it was mentioned t hat the famous Manchester Free Trade Hall recording was going to be officially r eleased. Do you have any information on this release???
Thanks
Anonymous
[*Columbia announced its release last month and then just as quickly withdrew the announcement from their official website. It's not certain at this time, but look for a possible late September 1998 release - JH*]

Hi,
I'm Israeli poet (26 years old). Bob dylan change my life completely. I explored all his way, by buy Cds (I mean also to artist who influence him) and THE BOOK ("Bound for glory"). In my first Poems-book I dedicate to him, All who love read my poems say to me that it's sounds like Bob dylan. I'm remember very well is last tour in my land, Israel and waiting to see him again. BOB DYLAN, I love you. you one and only for me, and I hope this message arrive to you without fear. I mean after all I'm not CRAZY fan. I'm just fan who GRATEFUL to you. I never forget you and your power.
Oudy

Love the site, and the features. Keep up the great work. I come here often to f ind out when he will be coming the the midwest soon. By the way, if anyone out there has bootleg concert recordings, or if they know where to get them, please contact me.
Evander

I saw Bob Dylan In Jacksonville, Fla in 1966 and I've never seen it listed anywhere. Any ideas ???
Larry Abram

Sorry about the first one,
I have a question. My psych teacher is one of the biggest Dylan Fans and he gave us an extra credit question. The question was, "Name the sixthe studio album of Bob Dylan". If you can help me out I would be much apperciative.
Thanks
Christian
[*Highway 61 Revisited - JH*]

Words truly cannot capture Bob Dylan's influence on my life. I have studied history in school, discussed religion with my father and have discussed philosophy with many, but Dylan's songwriting surpasses all of that. It's truly a shame that he's not given enough recognition for his music, attitude and modesty that makes him BOB DYLAN. Most kids my age (17-18) don't really listen to him since some say they can't "hear" him, others say they don't "understand" him or whatever. T here will never again be another BOB DYLAN & hopefully, before he's through, I'll prove (to all those non-believers) I was right all along. GOOD LUCK BOB!
Jared

I love this site
I think is one of the better sites of Dylan
but Where is the photo of the BOOTLEG SERIES VOL 1-3?

BYE
greetings from MADRID SPAIN
Pablo

Bob Dylan is my God. His music has revolutionised the way I live and I am only 1 3 I love Bob
Cecilia Eleanor

,may god bless and keep you always'. for anyone with irc or access to a webmaste r java board. We have a intime dylan chat: #dylan! It is there for all who wish talk serious dylan/kerouac/the band/related subject s,et al. do not worry if no op is there. talk with whoever is there. the forum is complet ley open.....from the bible to the basement tapes. take care all.
This page inspired the venture. may we meet down the line. and watch the river flow.
john-david lucas

I'm searching for Dylan-mp3 files on the web: rarities etc. Could you help me if you know any? Thanks.
Gabor Bella

Good morning! This web page is fantastic! bob will be studied, listened to, and remembered for centuries to come. he has been a huge influence in my life since the age of 12. i saw him in columbus georgia in late 1997 and he was on top of his game, playfully winking at some southern belle near the stage. keep up the good work. cant wait for the manchester masterpiece to come out. favorite dylan tune is "up to me", although there are so many i can say that about. thanks for the web page.
blessing209@prodigy.net

Howdy:
I have an original program from Bob Dylan's first concert, in NYC, at Carnagie R ecital Hall, in 1961. It was sponsored by the Folklore Center in Greenwich Village, where I got it a c ouple of years later. Apparently, only a few people showed up, and Izzy Young had a stack of them left over. Do you have any idea if people buy and/or trade such items, and how much somethi ng like this would be worth? If you have any info on this, send me a message at mschenker@navpoint.com. Thanks.
mark schenker

Hey- is there any kind of Bob dylan museum in hibbing?
Bryce Christianson

---

never done this before.... maybe its best. i don't have any suggestions or comments, just feel like responding. some how after reading a few words of dylan's my fasination has made me ill..... i want to say i respect him and love how his music effects my life but that sounds crazy weird....... i don't even know the man and he has lived in this world longer than i have been breathing........... i lay awake at night sometimes and think about what he is doing, is he trying to paint a picture that won't seem to understand the mood he is in, is he writing poems that cause a sense of uneasiness and pain, or his he counting out pennies from a little jar just so that he can eat? i guess i wonder if he understands those things most because he lives it......... i feel as if sometimes dreams are impossible to believe in... that everyone is beautiful in their own way

and if we only really knew one another we could see that..... my ming is making no sense, things i have never said or done has left a feeling of emmense regret......... maybe i hoping you will get this.... maybe i hoping somehow he will read my thoughts i don't see him as a famous star... someone who is weighed down from mail and the press, even though i'm sure that has been the case many times........ i see him as an inspiration.... as just a simple man who is trying to get by in a world of confusion........... i'm sure i couldn't think at this moment even if i tried.. i am a young girl, trying to decide if this man, this man who is ages apart from me could have an unspoken connection..... i do not pretend to know what love is or do i understand it.. i just know that somewhere in all my loniness' and dreams... he is there whispering to help me get through one more day... even though i will never look into his eyes..... i feel through his music he has allowed me, even if he didn't realize, understand the true importance of being completely yourself.... no matter how painful that sometimes is......... (i don't have an e-mail address, doesn't really matter...)
Stef H.

Hi. I was looking for song lyrics, but if I had any brains at all I would know that I can find all of them at bobdylan.com, so why am I asking you about it? I guess I'm just real stupid. My mommy is letting me use her computer.
A1SodaPop@aol.com (BlowJob)

If my thought dreams could be seen, They'd probably put my head in a guillotine. This web page is all right ma. I'm only bleedin'
Botticelli's Niece

My eyes collide head on with stuffed
graveyards, false goals, I scuff
At pettiness which plays so rough,
walk upside down inside handcuffs
kick my legs to crash it off,
say OK I've had enough
What else can you show me? - great web page...
Jeanette Zimmerman

---

i am trying to get a hold of dylan bootlegs, i have GD tapes to trade, who do i talk to ?

MNASH41632@AOL.COM

---

correction !!!
sorry, but the exchange between dylan and the the fan from the manchester concert was fan "dylan your a judas,and dylan responses "i don't believe you", the fan yells back "dylan your a f--king judas" and dylan responds "your all f--king liars" then goes right into once upon a time you dress so fine(like a rolling stone).
sorry i got the exchange a little mess up the first time, but this is clearly the exchange on my album....
mnash41632@aol.com

Dear John,
I am a student at the Manchester Metropolitan University in Manchester, England.

I am currently studying the subject of web page design with an emphasis on human - computer interface designing.
Could you please tell me how much research into the topics of designing an interface to suit the needs of all users you carried out before you started to design you wonderful Bob Dylan web site ?
I would appreciate any help you could offer me. Keep up the good work,
David.

---

hello!
just a short note to say thanks for filing the dutch
rockhouse site.. so much appreciated!
best wishes, frances

Your list of Dylan's 1965 US tour with the Hawks still leaves out his Knoxville, TN concert in October 1965. I was there. Great show.
Kent Hendrickson

I'm looking for a recording made back in the 70's. It was rcorded in a "public radio or TV" station studio(I believe it was WVIA in Wilkes Barre PA). The music was all acoustic. I don't even remember what songs were on it but a friend of mine enjoyed it very much and has expressed interest in trying to find the recording
Can you help???
Thank you in advance
Gene
jsys@fast.net

This is a question to anyone out there who cares or may know the answer. I am w ondering what is the best way to get Bob Dylan's autograph. If anyone knows, pl ease respond. Thank you.
Sean
see4@po.cwru.edu

---

i would just like to say that bob dylan is obviously a god of some sort and even if he thinks he is not he is.
Duncan

Thank you so much for the excellent site! It's refreshing to find so much information on the recording of the songs. I do have one question though. Do you know of any recorded version of "Love is Just a Four-Letter Word?" I would prefer to know of one dating close to when it was written ('65?), but any version would be great. I'd hate to live out rest of my life humming the thirty or so seconds of it Joan Baez sings in "Don't Look Back." Thanks again for the amazing site.
Jeremy Pendergast
[*As far as I know, Dylan never recorded a version of this song - JH*]

I want free Dylan-mp3's to download and i want them now cause i don't need them why no free concert from now on
jmj

Cinquanta anni fa l'onu prooclamava ufficialmente la carta dei diritti umani ed in gran parte del mondo si è celebrato l'anniversario. Nel 1963 Bob Dylan ha scritto una celebre canzone "blowing in the wind". Alcuni versi chiedono: "quante strade deve percorrere un uomo prima di essere chiamato uomo Quante orecchie deve avere un solo uomo avere per sentire la gente soffrire? La risposta,amico, soffia nel vento. Questi versi sono ancora attuali? commenta. ROBERTO

Where can I find articles/critiques of Dylan's lyrics by Christopher Ricks, the English Professor from the UK ?
martin.williams.aeq@dial.pipex.com (martin williams)

---

where can i find informations about television appearances of bob dylan (dates,stations,songs performed or interviews)?
please respond
thanx
h.rossacher@doro.com (hannes rossacher)
[*Don't know. I know there's a website somewhere that has this information, but I forget what it is. Anybody know? - JH*]

Bob Dylan is the king! Your site is magnificent, it has helped me to get some us efull information about the man. Keep up the good work!
Dylan Forever!!
Mike from Slovenia (Ex-Yugoslavia)

I noticed that Johnny Cash was missing from your "Friends" links page. Considering the mutual admirations, as well as the collaborations (Nashville '69, Johnny Cash show, etc) I would think that it should be included. http://www.johnnycash.com
dennis
It's there now. Thanks! - JH

I seen bob dylan in carbondal and he sounded like shit you people must like to take it in ass for the money you paid to watch a washed up old bag of bones mutalate every bit of his on music lets burn down this fucker or just give me your 28.50$
some cowardly pathetic anonymous loser

Hi. Great site. I am going to include it in the links to my new Dylan club on Ex cite called Shelter From the Storm. The club is new, but we have some great memb ers. We have a chat room, discussion board, links, etc. I'd appreciate it if you would list our club in your links. The address is http://mycomm.excite.com/mycomm/browse.asp?cid=98154. Thanks a lot.....Marty

---

we saw budda fly across the moon on the fourth of july and the canyon was soliu dad all the children sang the hippys melody but we now fly over the moon so long ago
Anonymous

O.K., I'm a novice and I'm sure it shows. Would anyone out there in cyberspace tell me when Bob Dylan wrote "To Make You Feel My Love" ? I would really like to hear it performed by Dylan. Was it ever commercially produced? This is my son's favorite song and he wants it performed at his wedding. He's not really a big Garth Brooks fan (nor Trisha Yearwood.)

mbullock@levelland.isd.tenet.edu (Marla)

The latest from Dylan:
http://www.conjecture.com/dylan.htm
Anonymous

I love your page it is loaded with information. I have one question about a Dylan song I was hoping you could answer for me. I am a big Bruce fan and was driving home one day when I heard Tweeter and the Monkey Man. You obviously know where this is going but what about the lyrics? Not only is the theme very Bruce i.e. Vietnam, Jersey, Cops, Prison, Factory, but the lyrics are direct titles of his songs.
Jungleland "over the Jersey state line"...Line 7 "across the Jersey line" The titles Stolen Car, Hihgway 99, Mansion of a Hill, Thunder Road, State Trooper, Factory, and Jersey Girl. I think that 7 titles of Bruce songs validate that this was somehow inspired by his writing in addition around the time of the writing of this song a Bside from Bruce came out called Part Man part Monkey hence Monkey Man? Please e mail me with any info if you can. I'll appreciete it greatly
Thank You
Kyoung2@wvu.edu (Kory)

Enjoyed your site...Thanks
Pam Thornton

---

i just got on-line a few day's ago... man this is really sick... now i can totally indulge in my love for dylan's music... people that understand how all of this internet stuff comes together amaze me... I'm lost in the web but enjoying it
she

Hi. I'm the founder of the Shelter From the Storm club on Excite you were good enough to list in your links. I wanted to tell you that the club has been moved to Yahoo and given a new name. Its called Small Talk At the Wall. We had to leave Excite behind because of technical problems. The address is http://clubs.yahoo.com/clubs/smalltalkatthewall . If you could delete Shelter and add Small Talk, it would be most appreciated. Thanks....Marty

---

Do you think that he really understands the impact he has had on folk/rock/blues /etc.? Hell, just on music and/or poetry in general. I've read several intervie ws where he has dismissed his contribution. Hard to tell whether he's just bein g Bob or really humble. Obviously he has seen the results of his work. What do you think? In my opinion our great-great-great-great grandchildren will be quo ting him the way we cite Shakespeare. Is it all just a fad, relevant only to our time?
Raynook@aol.com

Dylan isn't really singing on John Wesley Harding. Nor on Blood on the tracks. H as anyone looked into this?
Anonymous

Bringing it all back home is a collection of songs written and sung by Bob Dylan. This is the last album he recorded. Is this true?
Anonymous

Patrick Humphries and John Bauldie in "Absolutely Dylan" claim that Dylan saw a vision of Christ sitting in some Tucson, Arizona, hotel on November 17, 1978. I was at that concert and was allowed backstage because my brother was hired as l ocal security. I also was invited to the 'after concert' get together with the other members of my local band. Of course, I had never met Dylan before but he seemed very serene and extremely generous. I remember that his Aunt (Mother's sister?), and neice were also in the room. I spoke to him briefly, no doubt sounding as Mr. Jones, but I didn't notice a cross or any other religious artifacts. I imagine that perhaps the authors took some literary license in using Tucson as the venue for his conversion. By the way, the hotel he stayed at was the Plaza International on Speedway Blvd. It's still there and I rarely drive by it without thinking about that night. In any event, for what it's worth. Raynook@aol.com

---

I thought the cat's name on Bringing it back home was puff or smoke. This could have been the name of Edie Sedgwick's cat. I am sure the cat isn't named SARA that is for sure.
Anonymous

Why does Dylan and Paul Simon ask for so much money for their performances? I really think they want TOO MUCH MONEY. Will people start waking-up to this when it cost 1,000 dollars a ticket?
Anonymous

---

sono naturalmente un grande appassionato di Bob Dylan e tutto ci? che lo riguard a mi interessa in maniera particolare. dispiace doverti scrivere in italiano ma il mio inglese fa veramente ridere e no n saprei da dove cominciare per trasmettere un messaggio quantomeno comprensibil e.
ciao e complimenti
gizetaenneti@tiscalinet.it

Hey Bob i'm your biggest fan. I love your music! Mt problem is that i ant to download some of your songs and put them in Winamp. I just cant seeme to find them. I dont know if you dont have them on line or what but if you do then can you tell me where.
AntJamima6@hotmail.com (Kristen)

I have a question concerning a song. I was wondering what the meaning of the song Mr. Tambourine Man is? There is no good explanation why it is refered to as a song about drugs. If you give me any information on it, I would apreciate it.
Thank You
mmorris2@condor.depaul.edu (billy morrissey)

---

dear whosoever might know,
when did Dylan change Sub. Homesick B. to Bringing it all back home??
How rare are albums with the previous title??
If anyone knows please email me It would be most appreciated
Irish BD fan
carson@ireland.com (doug)

Bob, just thought I would let you know what you mean to me and all the people of the world, whether they know it or not or like it or not, thanks & much kudos f or coming down and telling us all how it is, and reminding us just how it's supp sed to be. Thanks again, and know I would like to be standing on the platform a t the station when that slow train comes in.
Rosstaman.

I once had mountains in the palm of my hands and rivers that ran through every d ay - I must have been mad I never Knew what I had until I threw it all away!
Dinny Doberman

Hi, I just came across this site and it's pretty comprehensive. I only had a few comments to make: one, I have spent a lot of time listening to Under the Red Sky and it's really a good record with the exception of just a couple songs. Most reviewers today and many fans comments demonstrate that they aren't in touch with the obvious allusions D is making to blues artists such as Howlin W and Muddy. Also, the lyrics are not just kind of a fairy tale thing: they really depict all aspects of life, spirituality, love, and the situation of society and the world. I was let down so many people trashed the record. "God Knows" has to be one of D's top 100 songs no doubt. Second, I was at the Merriville show the evening after SRVaughn passed away. We stood outside for 90 minutes with Dylan. He was obviously distraught, looked dirty , wore a hat and coat, and basically 'greeted' all the people coming in at the entrance where his bus was parked. Real strange character. but during the show his mood seemed to pick up and he sang friend of the Devil to the aud's delight. During the show he started tallking about "Stevie". Didn't know till later who he was talking about but he introduced the Mercer/Mansini song: This is for Stevie wherever he is. Real nice tribute especially using someone else's song. Finally, I met D once and we were alone for awhile. It was a real, and I suppose rare, treat. He shook hands and was obviously interested in talking abit. Kind of a lonely dirty looking character who seemed real guarded but that's being famous.
Anonymous

---

bob, thank you for the many years of wisdom and words...your work has always touched me in deep spaces, helped me feel the emotions of life, has been that bright light at the end of the dark tunnel. from first seeing you perform in the early 60's in some bleak, village coffee house, me 15, exploring, searching for myself, you only slightly older, with your head so full of ideas. i sometimes wonder what empty spaces i might have if not for your art. continue with your concerts, you're the best live performer in the biz and getting better all the time. best of health i look forward to us both being old men some day. thank you, your friend, frank
frank cianflone

Hey man,
Awesome page, lots of cool stuff indeed. There is one question I have though, is there anybody out there who has or trades Dylan shows like dead fans and phish fans, Bob Dylan plays more live shows than probably both of those band combined and the way i figure there has to be a lot of live recordings out there, but where? Please email me back and give me insight. By the way I have a couple of his albums on my pc in vqf format I'd be willing to give you if you wanted to offer them on you page. There free and I can rip an album for you over night.
hope to hear from you soon
jimbock@hotmail.com (Tapioca)

Hello, About a year ago a friend of mine saw 'Eat the Document' at a theatre in syracuse, NY. He really liked it and told me that should I get a chance to see it to make the effort to go, however I have NEVER seen it since. Is there a way to get a copy of this film or a schedule of when it may be playing in the Chicago area? Any help would be GREATLY appreciated. I can be reached at davebks@aol.com Thank you again, hope to hear some good news, dave
davebks@aol.com (David Marks)

Saw Bob and Paul tonight...
Really dug the show especially Bob's harp! Paul Simon's set was also fun. Question?... A Fatty riding on this question... I say Bob calls Northern California home and others suggest the East Coast... Who Smokes?
the graduate
[*Hah, neither one of you! Bob lives in Southern California, Malibu to be exact. That is, when he's not busy travelling. - JH*]

One of the best sits I have visited! As a fan of the "Band" I learned a lot of many new things about their amazing past and only wish they were still making music. It's going to take more than a couple of hours to explore their great music and colourful past that you have put on your sit. Doug.....

I don;t want to talk to you -
talking to you would just be like talking to me -
BUT...
how do I get a hold of Bob himself -
Now that's EMail worth the time it takes to tap it in!
So,...
do you know Bob's E-Mail Address?
Just a note: I thnik the site is really out of site!
Keep up the good///Great work!
JDV (Host of "The Midnight Hour Broadcast"
Check me out at goldenmlms.com - follow the links!
John D. Velarde (danp@ntwrld.com)

Can we have as much info as possible on Visions of Johanna please as I have to d o degree coursework on the piece! Cheers
Anonymous

From an AP article today, on JFK,JR:
But what really captured his imagination was the history of transportation and folk and blues music. When Brinkley asked him, once, what his own personal anthem would have been, he immediately said it would be Bob Dylan's "Chimes of Freedom"
Anonymous

Hi,
RE: Olof Bjorner's Dylan '98 chronicle:
Is it OK to contact Olof directly with errata? His address is shown on the Chronicles page but is not a live link, so I hesitate...

Among his recommended shows for '98, I was just curious whether "February 2 Newark" meant 2/2 Springfield or 2/1 Newark; and whether "June 6 Stockholm" meant 6/6 Malmo or 6/9 Stockholm.
You may correctly assume I pay pretty close attention to his recommendations; not a lot of people have both (a) heard nearly all the '98 shows and (b) are inclined to communicate their preferences. - Jay
Jay Clark (pj2vaac@concentric.net)

Found a Simon/Dylan tour mp3:
http://Paul.Simon.org/foreveryoung.mp3
Anonymous

---

were can i write to, to get in touch with the greatone himself?
andrew
[*I don't think anyone knows for sure... - JH*]

---

did anyone notice that during jewel's performance at woodstock she sang a song that resembled "just like tom thumb's blues" almost exactly with the additiion of maybe three chords. THIS IS HERESY. THIS CANNOT GO UNPUNISHED. p.s and she didn't have the courtesy to even mention the fact that she was plagerizing (?) that song.
gary

This is John D. Velarde, AKA Issac Stacey, (Feenjon Cafe, circa 1969) and I only have one question, how does someone, like me, contact Bob Dylan?
John D. Velarde
[*You don't - JH*]

Questin #2: How does someone like me, a fan who plays some Dylan songs better than Bob himself, get a chance to play or record with him?
John D. Velarde
[*You can't - JH*]

---

hey john,
the image gallery compendium is great but missing a small yet vista link!
Joaquin's Antiques front door opens at:
http://members.xoom.com/marlesta/pg2.html
all the images you won't find anywhere else!
cheers!
cornelio

Hello! I REALLY like this site!
Stumbled in here in an attempt to locate another Dylan site I forgot to bookmark. It catalogues web sites as "Dylan Resources." I had wanted to submit there f or consideration my E-book, Idiot Wind, which is a small 5-item volume dedicated to The Big One. I have always considered him my "spiritual" mentor, so it seem ed only fitting that my "outing" as a fellow poet be in his honor.
Anyone who knows the name of that site, or its address: Would you please drop m e an email? Sure would appreciate it.

Meanwhile, if anybody here is interested, my book can be accessed at
http://members.xoom.com/SugarpieRabb/IdiotWind.htm
Thanks for this GREAT site!
Sugar
19 August 1999
sugarpierabbit@usa.net (Sugarpie Rabbit)

In the song "Like a Rolling Stone" Bob Dylan sings the following:
Princess on the steeple and all the pretty people,
their out drinkin, thinkin, that they.....got it made,
exchanging all precious gifts, but you better take your
diamond ring....
you better porn it babe!
He does NOT sing:
"They are exchanging precious gifts and things"
or "you'd better lift off your diamond ring"
......what a load of bollocks!!!!!!
THE LYRICS ON THIS WEBSITE ARE INCORRECT, and I don't care what the official lyrics are, its whats on the record that matters, not what some arse has written down.
Kindly correct these mistakes.
Regards.
j.richardson@uclan.ac.uk (THE PIG)
[*You, Sir, are an idiot. First of all, I don't have the lyrics for this song on my site, so I don't know what the hell you're talking about, and neither do you it seems. Secondly, he does not sing "you better* **porn** *it babe!". That's pretty laughable. You know something's happening but you don't know what it is, do you Mr. Pig? - JH*]

Bob Dylan is going to be on DHARMA & GREG!
The 4th episode ...
This is true.
No b.s.
Anonymous

Dylan in Spin 12/85:
Three authors I'd read anything by:
Tacitus
Checkhow
Tolstoy
Anonymous

I just finished reading the story of "Self Portrait", and I'm not sure what to think. I just got into Dylan recently and pretty much only like his first album up to and including Self Portrait so far. I must say, I like "Self Portrait" and "Nashville Skyline" a lot.
A lot of what was said in the story seems to go against what my gut feeling on the album is. Artists go through strange periods, but this period of Dylan's really isn't all that strange. He was always a big fan of Woody Gutherie (not exactly a fringe artist), and the beginning of his career is marked by many performances of traditional folk songs. The description of the improv. nature of the sessions is in line with the way I think versions of traditionals should be. Someone else already "wrote" the song, the person re-doing it is putting their feeling into it,

something which happens more when less planning is involved. The songs an artist chooses to listen to say almost as much about them as their own work.
There may be some weird circumstances surrounding the album's recording and release, but I think it could be explained in a different way. Why would Dylan initially defend the album if it was always a joke? MAYBE he released it, and upon terrible reviews, he changed his tune.
Even if it was a warm-up for his next "real" album, or just an album to have some fun with, it can still tell a lot about Dylan and his flavor of music. People are sometimes at their most vulnerable when their joking. I get a strange mix of emotions ringing through his voice on these tracks which makes more sense now that I've read these things that were said about it.
Is there anything more emotional than a clown with a smile painted on his face?
Possibly for the wrong reasons, I think this album is incredible to listen to. He didn't write the songs, but NO ONE can convince me that he didn't care.
Ethan (ElEspectro@easy-pages.com)

Hi, I am a student at Southern Utah University in Cedar City, Utah. I'm doing an informative speech for my Communications class. The topic I chose to talk on is music of the late 60's and how it affected the music industry. If you have any information thet would be related to this topic, I would appreciate it. Thank you for your time.
Julie (Eber0788@student.suu.edu)

---

excellent site!
"I have dined with kings."
onesickbastard@juno.com

I heard a rumor that Les Crane had actually passed away some time quite recently. Oh, say it ain't so! If so, when did it happen and what happened to him? Thanks!
Rory

I just wanted to say I really like this site. I am twenty years old and I am a huge lover of Dylan. I wish I had more stuff of his I am gradually working on my collection. As of now I have about 19 different albumns, my goal is to have them all at some point. I am a guitar player in my free time and i love to strum Dylans music. how extreamly realaxing and comforting. If you have any information that you think I would like. maybe some other good sites. Or maybe your favorite albums I love the simple acoustic stuff. Live and mellow. Have any suggestions? Thanks so much for making this site. One of my favorite albumns is "good as I been to you". Just to give you an idea of the music I like.
Amanda WHeeler
student at Wisconsin Stevens point.

---

hi John,
I'd like to ask where can I found the lyrics for the song Tweeder and the monkey man
When will Bob come to Europe?
What is on Cooper Station, NY
Lenka,Slovakia

I just found your site. It has some good information on it for us Dylan fans.

I have not been able to find any information about a Dylan album called "The Little White Wonder, Vol. 2". This album is on BUHAY records (BHL 8002). It was made and printed in Milan, Italy.
Here is the track list:
Side 1
Wade In The Water
V.D. Blues
New Orleans Rag
Let Me Follow You Down
Cocaine Blues
Side 2
That's All Right Mama
Stealin'
The Cough Song
Hard Times In New York Town
If I Could Do It All Over
The recording is of poor quality, and the levels are off. I am trying to find any information, including value, for this album.
-Jesse

I have 2 Tickets available for Dylan/Phil Lesh at Continental Airlines Arena on November 13, 1999 which I would like to trade for 2 Tickets to the show in Worcester, Mass. on November 14,1999. If interested please email me at robertrosman@netscape.net

---

Just thought I'd mention that if you don't know, Australian band "The Whitlams" have done a great version of Bob Dylans "Tangled Up In Blue". You can find it on their album "Eternal Nightcap". It isn't planned to be released as a single, but it's really worth having a look at.
Danni

Nice,
And thanks.
Well, as I feel some pain I believe I'll see you again. My life in the last year has been in Germany. Not a big dylan country. But, without a doubt, t he most tolerant country in Europe now (as my Bosnian friends will agree)
Cheers,
Scobie

Don't see a place of audio files here but there is a nice version of Kingsport Town sung by Cat Power as The Winter Wind, at:
http://rafale.worldnet.net/~planetcl/sescat.htm

I just wanted to thank you for making such a great resource for Dylan fans. I am still amazed at the influence Bob has had on me. He has introduced me to literature and music that I would never have found without him. He also made me realize that you have to live life your way.I am a freshman at UK. I love Rimbaud, Guthrie, Beats, Hesse, Leadbelly, Baudelaire, Basho, and tons of other poets and musicians I can't think of right now. Anyone can email me at duncan_jeremy@yahoo.com and my ICQ# is 495996403 feel free to message me. My nickname is Troubadour, tell me your a Dylan fan and I'll authorize you immediately

---

I have never read anything by Greil Marcus, including "Invisible Republic." Now , I never will read it. From reading the excerpt that is reproduced on this page, he seems to have the wrong idea; he has an idea that is contrary to my own about Dylan and how we should view him.
To his credit, Marcus was polite when discussing Kramer's book of photography on Dylan. But, he is critical about the focus that Kramer takes. He disagrees with the effectiveness and validity of shots that do not seem to capture the true essence of Dylan. I know that Marcus is an accompished Dylan researcher and a well respected biographer of Dylan, but he needs to slow down.
Dylan's personal life obviously is of major importance when studying his music. It offers us additional explanations and interpretations of his music. But, we should not forget that Dylan is a calculated man. He was and is very aware of his every public move. Perhaps Marcus should keep this in mind when viewing Kramer's photograph's.
Whether you believe it or not Marcus, Dylan likes to make money too. It may not be wise to overlook the fact that Dylan knew what kind of pictures he was giving Kramer. He was giving Kramer what he wanted him to see -- something that makes the pictures as valuable as any that have been taken. If all they do is capture one true quality of Dylan, even if it is the quality of illusion, as wa captured in the picture of Dlan seeming to talk and hold a cigar when he was really doing neitherr, then the pictures are valid.
The music comes first my friends. To hold his celebrity above his music does not only miss what his celebrity is based on, it does wrong to a man who started out just wanting "to make it." Each picture is a valid representation of Dylan the muscian, whether they agree with Marcus's own interpretation of the man or not.
Kevin Briggs

I enjoy your site very much. I'm also looking forward to reading more about Bob Dylan in the present.
Sincerely
Sharlot-Dylan fan

---

how do I find out about how to play the harmonica like the man him self? this is the bet site other wise.
Forrest Gump

Hello eberybody!
There is a small, new site including two origianl pictures (^t91 & ^t98) on this danish site:
http://home13.inet.tele.dk/pohlmann/hjemmeside
Take a look!
Yours sincerely
Jan P^vhlmann

Hey well done in compiling this superb site. Very impressive. I have a particular interest in the 3 overtly Christian albums which Dylan produced in '79,'80,'8 1 consecutively. Unfortunately I have not been able to access the site relating directly to Dylan and Christianity. I would like to undertake some study on this field which is in some ways a gap in Dylan biography or in another way one just overlooked and naively summed up as a passing phase of Dylan's life and carreer. Have you (i.e. anybody)got any ideas for where, who I could look to in order to develope this study? I would much appreciate your advice and your opinion too if you have one on this subject,

Yours Sincerely,
Graeme Stewart
9647181@lewis.sms.ed.ac.uk

---

can you please tell me what was bob dylans first uk hit single.
col.richards@net.ntl.com (colin)

Hello:
Please send any information on getting Bob Dylan's first album recorded with the group called the GOLDEN CHORDS.
I would appreciate you doing this for me.
Sincerely,
Michael Rumig

---

http://santarosa.net/papers/sonoma/11.05.98/spins-9844.html a '66 picture I've never seen
Anonymous

I really like your site and I was hoping you would check out mine. It's a term paper that I did in High School that I am still very proud of it. Here it is
http://www.geocities.com/SunsetStrip/Arena/1991/
Brother John

Im looking for a photo of Bob dylan in concert between May and June of 1990 play ing at Canadian concerts. I own a stage played guitar and am looking for a photo of Dylan playing it. CAN YOU OR ANYBODY HELP. omgjon@aol.com

---

Well, I'm just glad to be writing to you, a 50 years old she-fan from Italy
annarita

Question
Who was the bloke who shouted "Judas" at the '66 gig?
Doug Milsom
[*To find out the answer to that question, read* Like the Night *by C.P. Lee - JH*]

Dear Mr Dylan
How are you doing today? Fine I hope. I'm writing you to check my system to see if you are receiving. Please e-mail me back if you receive this.
sincerely
charles

I dont have any comments but i do have a question and i do hope you can help me out.I am a 22 year old male and my passions are my guitar and BobDylan and i dont want to settle down with some girl who cant appreciate Dylan.So if you could send me a list of female Dylan fans,single of coarse,I would no longer be the rolling stone I have been...Yours Faithfully DANNY (bootlegbob@bolt.com)

---

just found your site and am writing to thank you,a good and neccesary adjunct to the whole bob thing. thanks. p.s has anyone got an e-mail for \\lily, she gave me it and I lost it,I was Ramon then!
gilpanne@netlineuk.net (jim gilpin)

That's a really great homepage! Congratulations! Well I have a question to you... There's anyway I can talk to Dylan? A E-mail, a adress, anything! I'm despered! Help me PLease!
Julia

What little I have read about rap traces its origins back to hip-hop, and there seems to me to be a strong resemblance between Dylan's early songs and rap. I would enjoy reading about the apparent connection between rap a nd the early Dylan, if indeed there is one. And where, for that matter did Dylan get his "but vandals/stole the the handles" style?In short, a little music hist ory would be appreciated.
Thanks.
Silas Ward

I'm Sick of Love was the last thing you said and the last thing I heard. But th ere's more isn't there. Get on TV again, real soon, please.
The JB
[*Ok, I will! :-)*]

Hey there.. I'm Jim Roemer, creator of "The Book of Bob". I noticed that you have linked my site. Thanks! I'm writing to inform you that I have moved this site to it's final destination: www.slopbucket.com No longer will it be found at: homepage.interaccess.com/~jroemer I thought maybe you'd like to update your link. Regards,

---

Hey there.. I'm Jim Roemer, creator of "The Book of Bob". I noticed that you have linked my site. Thanks! I'm writing to inform you that I have moved this site to it's final destination:
www.slopbucket.com
No longer will it be found at:
homepage.interaccess.com/~jroemer
I thought maybe you'd like to update your link.
Regards,
Jim

To whom it may concern
I am working on an English project about Bob Dylan, and I need to interview a fe w experts on this topic Could you possibly answer a few questions and e-mail the m to me? I'd apprecaite any help you can spare.
1. What impact did Bob Dylan make on rock n'roll?
2. What in your opinion is his best album and why?
3. How do you think Dylan's motorcylce accident in 1968 affect his music there after?
Thanks for your time.
peacelove@hotmail.com (MS)

I would like to tell Bob Dylan that I was sorry to hear about his mother.
tom.bevan@gateway.net

---

memo of a prayr vater unser der du bist im himmel, its notdark yet, you raised u p and say good bye to noone war das in india, puri bitte mein herz ist so schwer. mit liebe gitty zweng, australia
gittyzweng

Here are the musicians playing on the song "Sign language" recorded in March 1976 and released on the Eric Clapton album "NO REASON TO CRY". This is the line-up as given in the box set "CROSSROADS".
Eric Clapton : Lead vocal, guitar.
Bob Dylan : Lead vocal.
Robbie Robertson : Guitar.
Ron Wood : Guitar.
Jesse Ed Davis : Guitar.
George Terry : Guitar.
Dick Sims : Organ.
Carl Radle : Bass.
Jamie Oldaker : Drums.
Sergio Pastora Rodriguez : Percussion.
Hope this addition will help someone.
Sylvain from France.

---

to bob,hope you have recovered from your illness last year.i'm one of your many fans and am the same age,so i've grown up with you.i began singing and playing folk music in app. 1957,and shortly discovered you via 'sing out'i.e hard rains', i nearly fell off the chair.from then on i sang your songs regularly at many sydney folk venues.the people loved it & this was before anyone had heard of you in sydney.your first record was released a year or two later-it was 'the times - changin' which shoows how long it took for the record shops, radio stations etc. to catch on.around that time,i bought a second hand martin 000-18 1958 model no. 165484.they were a couple of americans,and they said it once belonged to a guy called robert zimmerman.could this be true?if you're in australia again,i hope you can spend some time with the local folk crowd,as there are some real people there,who i'm sure you'd like.sincerely kevin.

Hi!
I just wanted to say thanks for adding my Benmont Tench site to your list. I noticed that you have an old URL for the site. The new web address is
http://www.wildbluegator.com/benmont/index.htm.
Take care,
Amy

Is there any possible way to write to Bob Dylan?
Jenny
[*No*]

Hello Serious Bob Dylan Collector!
I just wanted to take a minute of your time to let you know about my auction on eBay! I have for sale an original, first pressing "Freewheeling Bob Dylan" LP!! This album contains four tracks, "Talkin' John Birch Society Blues," "Rocks and Gravel," "Let Me Die In My Footsteps,"

and "Gamblin' Willie's Dead Man's Hand. These tracks were deleted and replaced by 4 others before the album was distributed. To my knowledge, there are only 4 other copies in the world! Complete details about the album can be found in the book Goldmine's Price Guide To Collectable Record Albums (fourth edition) ,pages 49 & 50, under the article titled "The World's Most Valuable Album." A copy of this album has not been available for sale to the public since 1992 and at that time it sold for over $10,000 (US)
Needless to say, it is extremely rare!! If you have any interest in adding this valuable collector's piece to your collection, please check out the auction on eBay.
Just click:
http://cgi.ebay.com/aw-cgi/eBayISAPI.dll?MfcISAPICommand=ViewItem&item=293286036
(AOL users may have to go strait to eBay then to Item #293286036.)

Thank you and Good Luck!!!

What an Awesome show last night in Rochester, Minnesota Lots of songs he played I had not sean him perform before (the other 4 times I saw him). Bob Dylan forever. Like a really great verson of country pie.
John Witzke

Where can I find bob dylan video's from. I think bob can do no wrong apart from not coming to the south island of new zealand to put on a concert and meating with me.I live in a little hick town called alexandra, central- otago.Give my regards to the king of FOLK.
reece-j.gregory@xtra.co.nz (Reece.)

---

hey
only one question.
O.K., the front cover of "Bringing it All Back Home"
yes, stupid trivia bio question-
who's the chick ?
Please Reply else I'm gonna do something stupid like read Robert Davies again.
n-zyme
[*Too bad you didn't leave a valid email address, or else I would have replied to you directly. Oh well. The "chick" in question is Sally Grossman, wife of Dylan's then manager Albert Grossman. - JH*]

ONLY A LETTER TO
BOB DYLAN
it`s night here, in zurich. seventeen years old, calls schalch.
(codain)
i want to thank you master, for all these amazing melodys, lyrics, dreams and ways to the sky. passsion`s artist. i`m playing the (base-)& guitar and i write my words, a freak of me.
i`ve heard your sound often, when i was in a mountain-pseudo-school (youth prison), my young way through the storm, of rage and bloody tears. You gaved me the courage, to be resist. ever i heared you in all this time, now i believe. in my eyes

GOD IS ONE DEVIL IS ONE
IT`S THE SAME
ONE
LIKE A CARD
TWO SIDES
TWO FACES

in the astrology way i`m a fish, 23.2.1983. i want to go to your concert in the city, but i`ve got damned no money. i came to the prison because i was on a runaway train. alone in the street, like mud clown. with the mask of a punk, colours in the dark city smoke. so many faces, names and ??
now i`m outside, free to shit, smoke, and just try to find yourself. sorry, for my fucking english, but i`ve learned from your book lyrics 1962-1985. i see you as a master, you know the world. you`re one of the greatest poets and songwriter in this world, maybe the greatest. rebel.
i`m a child of a precius son. and myself`s a losing son.
thank you really for just nothing, in the way of death.
like the universe in one breath, you live forever in my head. with god on your side
DESIRE
i can`t stand still
i`m hard like rain
i`ve got a mask
of hair, mud & bones
the deaths face
but they won it
yeah,
they wont buy it
yeah,
but no money can buy
your peace in sleep
desire like fire
money, money, money.....get your rocks off
i can`t stand still
then we see
what nothing be
worlds hungry mouth
the ashtray of bad desire
fucking kings
with money for thenthousand mouths
we can nothing see
we`re too young they said
soon they`ll see....
it`s night, so beautiful, i don`t see the moon, but i feel it. i wish you, maybe see you again in dreams
goodnight
philip schalch

Not sure who I'm talkin' to but I bet It ain't Bob. But anyway, I'm leo from Liv erpool. I'm an old arsed sudent at the mo'. I'm well into His BObness. Think he' s a brilliant poet. I'm in a poetry society at the moment but I'm a crap poet . I'll talk again soon gotta go.
See you soon Leo the scouser

I WAS WONDERING IF YOU'VE THOUGHT OF ADDING AN ORIGINAL COMPOSITIONS PAGE TO YOU R SITE.HERE'S ONE TO GET THE BALL ROLLING:"THE FACELESS MEN IN GREY SUIT'S/ARE MEETING LATE TONIGHT/YOU CAN SEE THEM SITTING ROUND THE

WAR TABLES/BENEATH THE PALE MOONLIGHT/AND WHILE THERE COUNTING OUT THERE DOLLAR'S/AND FIGURING UP THEIR TAKE/OUR NATION'S BEING WASHED UP/ BURNT OUT ON DEBTOR'S LAKE/....FOR THE WORLD IS OUT THERE BURNING IN A FIERY RAIN/THAT'S RAGING IN THE SHADOW'S/LIKE A WHIPPING HURRICANE/THAT'S MOVING NOW SO FAST/AS THE JUDGEMENT BELL'S BLAST/THAT ALL ACROSS THE SKIES/MY FRIEND..THE HISTORY DICE ARE CAST/".....''BUT NOTHING LAST'S FOREVER BABY EVEN TIME MUST PASS/AND THOSE WHO SUFFER NOW MY FRIEND/WILL ONE DAY RUN FAST/OUT ACROSS THE SPARKLING NIGHT/WERE A JEWELLED AND DANCING HAND/CAN BE SEEN HEALING EVERY WOUNDED RHYTHM /HEAR THE MUSIC OF THE BLUESMAN"... "FOR NOW FREEDOM'S CHASING HISTORY/OUT ON A DESERT PLAIN/THAT'S FILLING UP WITH MERCY AS THE HEAVENLY FALLING RAIN/POUR'S AN OCEAN OF LIGHT/TO GIVE THE BLINDMAN BACK HIS SIGHT/AS HE TAKE'S THEM FOR A RIDE/ACROSS THE WATER'S OF THE NIGHT /..ON WHICH WE ALL FACE UNSEEN DANGER'S EACH AND EVERYDAY/AND THOUGH WE TRAVEL WITH UNKNOWN STRANGER'S/WE'RE ALL LOOKING FOR THE WAY/FOR WE'LL NEVER STOP TRYING /THROUGH THE PAIN AND THE DYING/TO LET OUR SPIRIT'S SOAR MY FRIEND/TO WERE THE MAN OF PEACE IS FLYING/.................."BECAUSE NOTHING LAST'S FOREVER BABY EVEN TIME MUST PASS/AND THOSE WHO SUFFER NOW MY FRIEND/WILL ONE DAY RUN FAST/OUT ACROSS THE SPARKLING NIGHT/WERE A JEWELLED AND DANCING HAND/CAN BE SEEN HEALING EVERY WOUNDED RHYTHM/..HEAR THE MUSIC OF THE BLUESMAN"...THIS SONG IS TITLED "THE BLUESMAN"
ANTHONY BARLOW

It's hard for an Italian boy to be a Dylan fan, for two reasons :1st we are one in a million and I have been forced to buy (pay) the ticket to my girlfriend to have her on my side the 28th (Dylan live in Milan);2nd, and I think this a world wide problem of young fans, we can only meet Rocklegends when, after 30 years of signing autographs, they 're totally fed up of it! I have heard strange stories of his behaviour with fans. I only hope I will be lucky enough to shake his hand at the airport (that's where I'm working) by the way...this site is great!
YoungItalianBDFan

Hey.....I jumped on to your Dylan site via a study of the beat poets.Terrific site here.I see Bob's shows annually.Here's my/Hip Waiters web page......some original music etc. Doug

---

cool page
Anonymous

---

i believe in two guys , first one is god the other is bob dylan . i just wanna thank people like u who does stuff like this as great as this to ke ep the new generations aware of the presence of a man on earth who speaks truly what he wants too: bob dylan. if u can say hi to him do not hesitate please , maybe an authograph could do it , thanks man. good luck and keep up the spirit , what u r doin is really awesome. bye
patrick bejjani

Just wanted to say that I was very lucky to witness two phantastic Dylan concerts here in Germany! Ever since I cannot help but being a desperate fan and I need to collect anything...

Well, if you can get a bootleg of that concert in Cologne from May 2ooo - don^tt think twice and grab it! ;)
one question that is really important to me: WHERE can I get that video "RENALDO AND CLARA"??? it seems hard to get in Germany. Is there anyone who can help me? Even a copy would be great!
kind greetings to all of you and thanks in advance, Jess

HEARD YOU SING IN IRELAND 90'S FULL MARKS FOR SHOW
BIG GROUPIE KATE KEEP ON ROCKING IN THE FREE WORLD
AND IF YOU EVER GET A BIG BRASS BED CONTACT ME
LOVE AND PEACE
KATIE

Hello!
May somebody tell me where the following songs come from? They are all songs I've heard on concerts, but don't know where come from.
1) The All New Minglewood Blues
2) White Dove
3) Duncan & Brady
4) Rovin' Gambler
- Marius

I wonder what ever happened between Joan Baez and Dylan? Were they ever an item ? Do they talk now?
Thanks
Erin

Nice site! :)
Anna

Hi, I enjoyed your site very much. Thanks. I saw the concert in San Diego Satu rday night. It was wonderful. I was eight in line and there were about 15,000 people there! Do you happen to know where I can learn more about Larry Campbell and his music? Thanks again.
Barbara
[*You might want to try the* Larry Campbell site *- JH*]

EXCELLENT SITE! Incredible amount of info. Love the new home page look.
I'm not sure if I have emailed you my compliments before, so I am doing so now.
WOW!
Take care,
Lisa

---

a very fine dylan site. i must commend you. there's a lot out there and you distinguish yrself.
sincerely,
N
http://www.geocities.com/temptations_page

I have just recently discovered Bob Dylan, my journey into his music has been a remarcable experience. Although I still have only seen a glimse of what this man has done I am sure I w ill never meet another like him. Ya i know this may sound horrible cliche but for the sake of history I will say never have I meet a man whom strummed the courds of heart like him. He reaches deep creates a storm and then passes through. I am younge 19 to be specific, I sould be listening to garbage, no? Shit the door he opened. I saw him play once 2 years ago. I went for the opening act (Ani Difranco)and d id not stay for his set. I had no idea what the man in front of me had done. I knew the hits and well but never did i concive of the wisdom he has. The purpose of this dose not fit the purposed intention for this box... it is ju st so I can physically see the words. They are not adequate but they'll do for now. My email address is enclosed do what you will with it.
That is a cyber invitation.
tonya
Columbia_Show@hotmail.com

Hi
I'm a great fan of Bob Dylan. I'm only 15 years old bnut I think he is the best, not this rave bullshit, and all this other modern music! I have one question. What song is it where bob has banners with words on it (i saw the video but ican't remember the song)
bye
Bob15

I have just found your site. I am not even close to reading the whole thing, but want you to know that you have relayed your Dylan-ness very well. I can relate.....and that's really something for me!! OK....gonna go read more......that's all Iwanted to say......for now....... maybe later......donno now....

There is no maybe about it, the disk jockey who introduced Dylan at Forest Hills on Aug. 28, 1965 was Murray The K. He put his right foot forward, took his right hand and shoved his hat over his forehead, and said "Bob Dylan is what's happening baby." As the boos poured down, he beat a quick retreat.
As an aside ... despite reports (AP each year lists this event on this date in music history as the day Dylan was booed off the stage ... he wasn't) that things were thrown at Bob ... the concert was at the Forest Hills Tennis Center ... and during the second set 2 tennis balls were tossed towards the stage (I don't think either one made it, I remember one rolling across the law.)
Tom Lubart

So what's an eighteen year old girl doing on a Bob Dylan fan page? Shouldn't I be listening to Brittney Spears, or some other empty, predictable musician of my own generation? No, I've been a fan of Bob's since I learned to read. He is t he most amazing phenomenon to come out of the 60's and political protest era. W ords can't even do justice for this one man.
Katey Schubert

---

thanks for doing a homepage of Bobby Dylan, I believe in him ...here 's a bit of a poem I wrote, and sing it too , in hopes to put a smile on your face or anyone.
Music of the wilbury where playing in the night.
Midnight special of the Roy Orbison flight
We are not alone stone people

Hardtimes come again no more.
violet from afar.

I love the page it's great fun, more to listen to would make the site even lovelier
Jules

My mother Nancy is one of Dylan's BIGGEST fans. I grew up listening to Dylan, and I am glad to see such a good site about him and his music/poetry! We had the fortune to have 3rd row seats @ Shoreline at his August show in the Bay Area and he still ROCKS! Blew this hard rocker away! Rock on and keep it up! ~A True Dylan Fan in California~

Hi!
Just wanted to thank you... you've probably saved my grade in English! I've got to do this oral presentation of an American artist... And where did I get the information?
See you later, dude
/Björn

Do you know where the Bob Dylan 1961-2000 39 years of great concert performances cd being released by sony japan is going to be available. How can we get a copy of it.
Ian
[*Don't know. Maybe it will be available from Amazon.com or cdnow.com - JH*]

Outlaw Blues is influenced by the MUDDY WATERS version of Nine Below Zero
Obviously 5 Believers is probably influenced by Sonny Boy Williamson's Help Me or Good Morning Little School Girl
Lawrence Davies

I just felt that i had to say keep up with the good work on the site. Dylan is my all time hero, i am 25years old, and still the sounds of Dylan can get me through the good times and the bad. I'd love to just shake his hand and let him know how powerful his words actually are.Good luck Dylan and god bless.

BOB DYLAN IS THE GREATEST ARTIST, OF ANY SORT, OF THE 20TH CENTURY.
frankie lee

Hello there. I just took a look at your site, and I have to say that it is a wonderful site for Dylan fans!! I'm a 23 year old Bob Dylan fan. I discovered his music almost 9 months ago. I haven't seen all of the site yet, I just wanted to compliment you on your work. Your site is very accessible for the blind. I was born two months premature which left me sightless, so I have to use voice software to navigate on the web, chatting, email, letters, and just about everything else to do with computers. This may be an impossible request, but if you do post pictures on your site, could you give a description of them? That would help me see what one looks like instead of my family having to lean over the screen and tell me. I loved the interviews on the site. I've read all of them! Keep up the good work!
Sad-eyed-lady

---

this is more of a question about Dylan than a comment about your great site.

Do you know of anywhere i can get footage or Audio of Dylan playing at Greenwood in 1963 (except for "dont look back) or of him playing "only a pawn in their ga me" live anywhere. Ive searched the internet and cant find it any where, any response would be much apprieciated.
Regards
Natha Kosmina
[*E-mail bounced. The answer is no, the footage in Dont Look Back is all that's in circulation. - JH*]

Bob has always been a good artist and produces some amazing artwork. There is a sketch he made in the 60's that shows a person outside of a door, straining under a load of presents that he is trying to deliver to a group of people on the other side of the door. No one seems to be answering the door so he looks like he is about to kick it in. A great sketch! Does anyone know how I can get a look at what he is doing now.
Thanks, Tom

I was wondering if Dylan had any plans of making a new studio album. And if not , what new albums might be coming out?
Dan

Well Freinds,
Regaurding the commentary on Self Portrait I can only say that I'm sorry. Every one seems so quick to judge the genius of a man, to label his subtltes, placing imaginative motives behind his soulful expressions.
It occured to me the first time I ever heard this incredible album what it was that drew me to Dylan's music. The synthesis of aeons of timeless music, placed in the hands of the roughest most poetic being I have ever experienced. The title of the album was such a simple gesture of thanks to all the artist he'd covered_SELF PORTRAIT_"This music is what made me what I am!"
I reaize that I too am quick to label the music of Bobby, but he himself answer inqueries into his music with the question of "I don't Know; What does it mean to you? I just wrote it." And there it is, the real motive of behind the album: mind your own business! And if you dont like it, Let it Be.
Sincerely,
A huge fan.

BLIND BOY GRUNT IS DOING A TRIBUTE TOUR TO BOB DYLAN BEGINNING ON BOBS SIXTIETH BIRTHDAY MAY 8TH OPENING IN HELENA MT AND PROCEEDING A 16 CITY 29 SHOW TOUR. BLI ND BOY GRUNT IS A 5 PIECE BAND DOING PLUGGED AND UNPLUGGED TRIBUTES TO BOB DYLA N, NEIL, BRUCE,TOM, ENDING WITH THEIR NEW CD 'WHAT IT MEANS' ON COBRA RECORDS DI STRIBUTED BY ALLIGATOR RECORDS. INTERESTED E MAIL US.
chrisj@montana.com (BLIND BOY GRUNT)

Dear Sir !
I am a musical and personally tween to you.
24 th of May I am 60 years old.
I am living here in Norway and my wife want to go to the festival june in Trondheim unfortenately I cannot be there.
I feel some much the same as you. IT IS THE TIM NOW THAT WE MEET 11

Yours
sincerely
Knut-Gunnar Knudsen
Scheel gt 3m 2315 HAMAR NORWAY
knut.gunnar.knudsen@tine.no
Please meet me in PARIS,FRANCE on our birthday, next time there will be nothing,

---

Hey! our Bobby D site rocks! Dylan is the best artist ever, and this site really is cool. :)
-Chelsey

I know that something is happening here, but I just don't know what it is.
Mr. Jones

Hey this is the only place I've been able to find lyrics to "Positevely Van Gogh " from the Denver hotel 1966.
thanks very much.
Here is an addition to those lyrics:
(last verse)
camilla's house stood on the outskirts
how strange to see the chandeliers destroyed
I'll send more clarifications as they occur to me
adam

I'm just writing to say that I enjoy your site and have found it very useful. I detected an error on this page:
http://www.bjorner.com/955-7.htm
It states: October 18, 1995 - Birmingham, Tennessee. It should say Birmingham, Alabama.
I just thought that you might want to know.
Best wishes,
Skip
http://hometown.aol.com/Sship72902/Index.html

I think that Bob Dylan is the pinnacal of music perfection. I am only thirteen years old and I can look at Dylan and see this mans phenomenal talent beyond compare. So why can't the rest of the world? Young teens today are so busy filling their minds with this pathetic mind rotting noise that they miss one of the most talented men alive. He is truly an amazing and inspirational man from his benign humility to his stricking sense of humor-this man is a role model for aspiring artists and poets worldwide. He should therefore be recognizedas just what he is-a genius with a pen.
Harmony(yes,that really is my name)

---

bob dylan is a fucking crazy shit and i live him because he is my god...i wish more people could relize that they should be more like him and forget about themselves and their fucking sorry lives.....
anonymous

Hello. I am new here, but an old fan of Bob's from South Texas, around Austin and SanAnto.I went on the road in 70s, left the 33rpms behind. Hope somebody's playin em.Never got back

into collecting discs, except having a cassette in my bag to play in a car I had thumbed down. I've listened to Bob's songs so much that I don't need recordings, the words are written on my soul. I even bang out some on two guitars I have, one a Mexican with nylon strings and a thick neck, the other a pretty nice Hohner. I think of Bob often, wonderin' how he is. I am 63. and Bob's words will always ring true.
Runnin out of space here, so I'll just say, "Good Luck!"
Julius Payne

Hello,
Since I am searching for years for a certain Dylan song, and never managed to get it I saw this opertunity to ask about it on this site. I don't know the title of that song since there are no lyrics on it.
It's a ballade, and Bob's voice sounds very high with high notes in it. He only use 'La la la' to the notes.
I think the song dates from the early 70's.....
Can somebody help me by telling the title of that song?
Please?
Many greetings from: Lin
[*You didn't leave an email address, so I couldn't respond personally. The song is almost certainly "Wigwam" from the Self Portrait album. - JH*]

I would like to know if Mr Dylan made the song every one nust get stoned. I am in my 50's and always liked hom and I love that song it was from my time. Did you sing it and if you did where can I get it. I had one but can't get one now Thank you
Margaret

---

i read a book about the children of god and the women said the bob dylan was a member. is that fact or fiction. i have read books that say he was going to a harikrishna temple. just curious about his religious beleives...
sue

Just trying to get the word out that there will be a special screening of: "Don't Look Back" on Friday, August 3, 2001 8:00 PM Ford Amphitheater in Hollywood, CA This is being presented by the International Documentary Association, here is the link to our web page about the event.
http://www.documentary.org/test/events/fordevent2001.html
This is an outdoor screening, preceded by a live concert celebrating Dylan's musical influence, along with presentation of the IDA 2001 Mentor Award to concert film legend Pennebaker. We hope that you can come! Thank you.

Hey, I know it's a bit cheeky, but I was wondering if you could possibly find time to link to my Dylan page. It's called Buckets Of Dylan - The Complete Guide To Bob Dylan, (the title is supposed to be tongue-in-cheek). You'll find it at www.geocities.com/paul_82_allen. You will also find a link to your page at www.geocities.com/paul_82_allen/links.html.
Thanks

I'm Olivia
I'm thirteen

I spend my time on a farm in Wisconsin
I can't believe my first concert has to be yours
(usually my mom really loves me)
I looked at this web site to see who you are.
see you in telluride - (my uncle lives there)
p.s. caribbean wind is alright. I love it there.

---

amazing that all the matter in the universe has come to this tho found in the labyrinth of the eclectic and floundered in the mouth of the wail joined thru measures in the bearpit and glued in the soup of the eternal,picked up and stranded in the moments of the blink,fattened and blessed with the eye of denial.
david

The new disk is out, unfortunately it coincides with a very sad day in history. Lives lost at the Trade Center, the Pentagon, among others. Those Masters of War guys are a pitiful lot. Mr. Dylan told us that long ago.
-mjs

I just purchased Love and Theft. I am a 52-year old female. I have always loved your music/lyrics/messages/the way you have the ability to revise your music and it is always great. If I had to choose just one artist since the 60s until present, it would by you. I have most of your albums, Highway 60 Revisited, Blonde on Blonde, Blood on the Tracks, Skyline, Time Out of Mind, etc., however, my FAVORITE one and I know from the bio book I have that it was not well received is the Budokan album. I have listened to that album (first the tape and then CD) at least a thousand times! (My most treasured T-shirt is from one of your concerts). Whenever my husband asks what I would like for a gift, my reply is "anything Dylan". I wish you happiness, health and peace. Please never stop making music. How else could I feel sad, happy, depressed, politically oriented, emotionally dyfunctional, introverted, extroverted; you say it all. It's incredible how some of your recordings from a very long time ago, unfortunately, relate to the tragic recent events in our country.
You truly are special.
Linda Orsini

---

i love bob dylan with all me heart and soul. i first started listening to him when i heard the song "the hurricane". the way he spoke so eloquently and peacefully about the story of rueben carter absolutely moved me and made me realize what an absolutely brillant artist bob dylan is. i since then have bought numerous tapes and cds by bob dylan. he inspired me to start playing the guitar and sing. i think he is one of the greatest songwriters of our time and will forever remain my favorite artist.
katie o'brien

To my cousin, Bobby Dylan,
I have never met you.
I know you through your music.
I hope one day our roads will cross.
I am emailing you from your former home:
The Hillel Foundation
University of Minnesota-Twin Cities
1521 University Avenue SE#102

Minneapolis, MN 55414
(612) 379-4026
May the world finally realize that Bobby Zimmerman is a true TZADDIK!!!
Be Well,
Jeff Elliot Kaner
Grandson of Rose and Hymen Kaner
Home Duluth, MN
Place of Residence
600 10th Avenue SE #102
Minneapolis, MN 55414
(612) 378-4795
jekaner@hotmail.com
P.S. if you do not respond, I will understand.

Where do I begin?
There are so many things I would like to say that I don't know where to begin... ......
I would like to say something special, but I'm afraid I won't.........
It's so hard to say something about you really original, everybody tried to do it for almost forty years long, and nobody did.
I think the only thing could do is explaining my feelings in the most simple way I can.
You are great.
You are the greatest poet of the 20th century.
You changed my life.
No, this is is wrong, you don't changed my life, you chenged my way of thinking, you opened my mind.
You have written some of the best poems I've ever read (and I've read a lot of poems....)
EVERY TIME I FEEL EMPTY YOUR SONGS FILL ME.
THANK YOU.
Bye, Pelo

(Upon further listening)
This song is obviously an unfinished work in progress. The various comments made during the course of it have been included because they may offer insight into the way Dylan writes a song. On the other hand, they may not ;-)
(D=Dylan's comments)
[U=Unknown Person's comments]
POSITIVELY VAN GOGH
(False start here, with indecipherable conversation between D and U, with the exception of D- "Terrible")
When I'd ask why the painting was deadly
Nobody could pick up my sign
'Cept for the cook, she was always friendly
But she'd only ask, "What's on your mind?"
She'd say that especially when it was raining
I'd say "Oh, I don't know"
But then she'd press and I'd say, "You see that painting?
Do you think it's been done by Van Gogh?"
The cook she said call her Maria
She'd always point for the same boy to come forth

Saying, "He trades cattle, it's his own idea
And he also makes trips to the North
Have you ever seen his naked calf bleed?"
I'd say, "Oh no, why does it show?"
And she'd whisper in my ear that he's a half-breed
And I'd say, "Fine, but can he paint like Van Gogh?"
[U-laughter]
(D-"Wait, the tune is gonna come, man. It's on the right tune.")
I can't remember his name he never gave it
But I always figured he could go home
Til when he'd gave me his card and said, "Save it"
I could see by his eyes he was alone
But it was sad how his four leaf clover
Drawn on his calling card showed
That it was given back to him a-many times over
And it most definitely was not done by Van Gogh.
It was either she or the maid just to please me
Though I sensed she could not understand
And she made a thing out of it by saying, "Go easy
He's a straight, but he's a very crooked straight man."
And I'd say, "Does the girl in the calendar doubt it?
And by the way is it Marilyn Monroe?"
But she'd just speak softly and say, "Why you wanna know about it?"
And I'd say, "I was just wondering if she ever sat for Van Gogh."
It was either her or the straight man who introduced me...
[Many false starts and comments here]
(D-"Alright. That's the wrong beat. I'm playing the wrong thing. Oh. I... Here's the lead guitar part. Play it here. Here's the lead guitar part. Play it here. No, no, I'm sorry. I'm sorry. Okay. Oh. Oh, gosh. Oh, there it is. Only, only very funky...or if not very funky, very sweet.")
It was either her or the straight man who introduced me
To Jeanette, Camilla's friend
Who later on falsely accused me of stealing her locket and pen
When I said "I don't have the locket"
She said "You steal pictures of everybody's mother I know"
And I said "There's no locket
No picture of any mother I would pocket
Unless it's been done by Van Gogh."
(D-"What was it {?} now...Oh, this is a great, great part here. Oh. Oh yes, yes. Oh. Here's a...you know, I could take it further, but I'd have to look through all of them. This is the part about Camilla. This is all about Camilla.")
Camilla's house stood on the outskirts
How strange to see the chandeliers destroyed
While (???) beneath the velvet carpet
of fox hunts and (love far before?)
(D-"Oh, I was getting it. Oh yeah. You just hold still, Bob. We'll be getting to that thing in a minute. We have locked the last fucking reporters up, man, with a...")
(U-indecipherable)
(D-"Oh yeah, say something.")
Robin Jatko

---

hi everybody!
Does anybody know about artwork(painting,sculptures, whatever)that shows or is directly inspired Bob Dylan? I'm looking for any relation between Bob Dylans music and other artforms. If anybody knows something please contact me!!!
thank you!
coronkl@aol.com

---

hoi,I dont know who Im talking to.But if its about Dylan,it must be ok.I dont know mutch about the internet.I would like to find more information about Bob Dylan on the web.and about his songs albums,well about anything that involves him. Can you give me some advice? Wailet.

To whom...,
I'd like to get a copy of Gaslight Cafe on CD...Know where this can be done? I have it on tape but the quality isn't too good.
Colby McCarren
cjmmccarren@hotmail.com

Just found your site. Excellent compilation of articles. I look forward to reading more. Did you hear that Bob is going to be writing his autobiography? I wonder if he is going to do it solo or will he work with someone? I would think working with someone would be helpful to help shape the piece, kind of like an editor does for a novelist. Somone who stays out of way but could help with details etc. Any thoughts on who that person could be? Greil Marcus has written some good books on contemp. music but I thought his last review of Bob's new album in the NY Times was self-indulgent and egocentric. It read like Mr. Marcus was trying to outwrite Bob himself. What did you think? By the way, I saw the LA show recently at Staples Ctr. Great show! Bob opened with Song To Woody, with the poignant lyric about he earth "dyin' before it's even been born"...one couldn't help but think about Afghanistan. Show included Masters of War (who are the masters now?) Baby Blue (all your seasick sailors they are rowing home) Rainy Day Women (stoning women now? not getting stoned on pot!?) Bob is amazing! 40 years on the scene and still relevant as he ever was. I've been listening to Bringing It All Back Home and Live '66. Those records keep the concert alive and loud ("play it fuckin' loud") on the freeways at 6 am. Good job. Terry.

To: The Poet
I am compelled by your words as they are echoed throught my car. I am comforted by your guitar as it strums me to sleep. I fall in love while listening to your harmonica. I want to thank you for what you have given me; music is a large part of my life. I don't know you, but I know how you make me feel. Listening to your song like "Forever Young," makes me stop and think to live my life to the best of my ablilty and not to waste a minute.
I joke to my friends about how I am going to marry you when I grow up. Honestly though, I am going to have your songs sung at my wedding. And played on my CD player everyday from now till then.
Long Live The Legend,
Keziah Keller

Hello,

We have a recent review of Bob's 10/28/01 Milwaukee performance on our music +magazine site, ConcertLivewire.com. If you'd like to place a link to it on your site our link address is: http://www.concertlivewire.com
If you plan on using the link, I'd greatly appreciate it if you could let me +know by shooting me an email.
Thanks much,
Tony Bonyata
ConcertLivewire.com - Editor
P.O. Box 5
Lake Geneva, WI 53147
http://www.concertlivewire.com
p.s. We also have CD reviews of "Love and Theft" and "Time Out of Mind," as well +as two previous concert reviews (Milwaukee '97 and East Troy, WI '00)

Just found your site. Excellent compilation of articles. I look forward to reading more. Did you hear that Bob is going to be writing his autobiography? I wonder if he is going to do it solo or will he work with someone? I would think working with someone would be helpful to help shape the piece, kind of like an editor does for a novelist. Somone who stays out of way but could help with details etc. Any thoughts on who that person could be? Greil Marcus has written some good books on contemp. music but I thought his last review of Bob's new album in the NY Times was self-indulgent and egocentric. It read like Mr. Marcus was trying to outwrite Bob himself. What did you think? By the way, I saw the LA show recently at Staples Ctr. Great show!
Bob opened with Song To Woody, with the poignant lyric about he earth "dyin' before it's even been born"...one couldn't help but think about Afghanistan. Show included Masters of War (who are the masters now?) Baby Blue (all your seasick sailors they are rowing home) Rainy Day Women (stoning women now? not getting stoned on pot!?) Bob is amazing! 40 years on the scene and still relevant as he ever was. I've been listening to Bringing It All Back Home and Live '66. Those records keep the concert alive and loud ("play it fuckin' loud") on the freeways at 6 am. Good job. Terry.

Mr. Dylan,
Many many years ago, you found Woody Gutherie in New Jersey at a house of a women who brought him home from the hospital.That women, Sidcel Gleason is my grandmother. She now lives in southern California She recently told my son about meeting you along with stories about Woody. But I think he doesn't believe her. Can you please verify her story? My son and I would love to take her to see you in concert if your playing in southern Ca. this year if your scheduled. Thank you for your time. Treva-Karene

---

There are many types of freedom.Religious,material,social,artistic,and the list goes on and on.But the only freedom that has any real or lasting value is spiritul freedom.Anything else is only a false sense of freedom which continually keeps the soul bound into the illusion with its many fasseted seperate compartments and only promotes compartmental thinking.This is explainded in detail by Meher Baba in Discourses
anonymous

This is my first time looking up information on dylan on the net I am exstremely pleased with the effort you all have taken to put information out on my favorite artist. I also am very pleased with your no nonsense policies I cannot wait to to get the tons of informaion from the

net that you dylan lovers have made available to others, I have been a dylan fan for a long time I really thought I knew a lot about him untilI I started pulling up information from the different sites Thank you thank you. Last but not least I don't think dylan was in a bad state or at his worse when re made self portraitI agree with dylan listen to it again, I think what it is people got use to dylan's style and could not except something different maybe as a result of the criticism we may have stopped him from delivering other good stuff in a different style sometimes I can pretty much take dylan as he come at this point I feel like I know him as a person, also as most of us we do and say things according to what's going on in our life. again thanks
stephanie

HALLO,
i am a singer songwriter in the style of bob dylan , based in belgium , where very little interest is shown for this type of music ...
i am looking for help with cd distribution and promotion of my material . here are two websites to explain more , with music on mp3 .
http:/clik.to/daveadrian
http:/zap.to/dave-adrian
these sites are constantly being upgraded with new material .
i hope you like some of this eclectic material , and that you might be able to help in any way .
e mail :
patrick.roberts@planetinternet.be

Hey Man,
Kick Ass Site
Click On All The Time
Thank You.
I'm Not One For Correction It's Not My Thing.
However It Seems That Your Into Accuracy.
11-9-90
There Is No Fox Theatre In Chicago
Mr. Bob Played The Chicago Theatre That Night
Once Again Not A Correction.
Just Some General Useless Information.
THANX
Have A Good 2002
Steve
[*You're probably referring to something in Olof's Chronicles, which is not on my site, therefore nothing I can do about it. Thanks anyway, though. - JH*]

About 25 years ago I read a science fiction novel with Dylan as the main figure.I read it in german,but it was an american writer.I've forgotten nearly everything about it.So what I would like to know is, does anyone know anything about such a book?
thanks anyway
Hans Christian Jacobi

Hi
Great site.
I have three versions of Idiot Wind (Hard Rain,BOTT,& Bootleg Vol 2. Are there any other

versions?
Your comments about the basement tapes are interesting.
I do recall reading a Robbie Robertson interview where he said these sessions helped both parties avoid insanity.
Best wishes
PG Scully

John,
Love this site. It's a well of good info. I program a station called Deep Tracks on XM Satellite Radio (xmradio.com). Coming from a few decades of playing classic rock on FM stations, it's a pleasure to have the freedom to roll out any and all of Bob's library for Dylan fans everywhere. We are probably the only station in the country that leaned heavily on "Love And Theft" ... and loved every minute of it.
Thought I'd let you know you're work is appreciated.
GTM

---

all i have to say is that i loved bob dylan untill 11-13-01. i ahve seen hima a few times and liked what i saw. after that concert i will see that jewish bastard again. the surcuity and everything about that concert sucked. dylan is now just an old has been who doenst do anything now but stand around like an itiot. write back i want to here your comment.
mailto:jrod1423@yahoo.com
mailto:jrod1423@yahoo.com

---

great site,plenty of interesting stuff about the mighty Zim! i am presently awaiting manchester (9:5:02)Dylan seems to be interested in being a performer again as opposed to a 'legend coasting on reputation alone'.Speaking as a fan who has attended some truly average performances from the bard, this obviously can only be a good thing!
terry

ISO- The location of the watchtower spoken of in Dylan's song "All ALong the +Watchtower"
If anyone can help me out, it would be much appreciated!

mailto:jrod1423@yahoo.comdiddy@sovereignsociety.com

I was wonddering what why you can not fine the traveling wilbury cds anywhere does bob have any plans to work on that kind of band any time soon
Ricky
[*The Wilburys albums are owned by the estate of George Harrison, who took them off the market when he left his last record company. He had plans on reissuing them before his death, but now it's unknown what the plans may be. Dylan has nothing to do with them. As for Dylan participating in another group effort, who knows? There was talk of a Wilburys reunion before George's death, but now those plans are off. - JH*]

Thanks for the Web page. I am a big fan of Bob Dylan. His art and philosophy have both entertained me and enriched my life? Does he ever read messages on this page?
Gail Hagen

[*Probably not - JMH*]

You r really cool
moonkay

Hello,
my name is Lucas Bols and I'm studying communications in Belgium at the Artevelde Hogeschool Ghent. I'm doing a thesis concerning Bob Dylan that is titled "Bob Dylan, still alive and kicking?" But I can't find a lot of information about Dylan fanclubs. I would be very grateful if you could give me this information (e-mailadresses, adresses, phonenumbers, internetsites,...) I'm very satisfied with your fansite! The lay-out is great, the images are just fine and you can find a lot of useful information on the subject. I would like to thank you already for your help and I hope for an early reply
Lucas Bols

I have a Zippo lighter still in the box. It is silver with a picture of Bob singing into a mic on the bottom half and his autograph on the top half. the etching is in black. It has the year 2000 on the bottom and the roman numeral XVI. It is not in any of his catalogs handed out at concerts. It was in his dressing room after a concert. I would like to know its value and any special significance it might have. This is not my computer but I can be reached at 563-505-0466. please, I could use help. I would like to sell it and I know nothing about it. Casey

---

Observation:
I'm pretty sure that at this year's Grammys that Bob Dylan played the melody and guitar riffs to "Lonesome Day Blues" (TRACK 5) but sang the lyrics to "Cry A-While" (2nd to last track). This is no doubt a trick he often uses, but probably savored playing it on the Grammy onlookers. Too bad that for most (99% of them) the joke was lost on them.
Please advise as necessary
Signed,
You heard it hear first
Florida Swamps

---

who are responding to the billions of fans groups, is one bOb out there?
susan,aka snark

Hey John,
thanks very much for putting up the comic which I'd never come across before. Most entertaining (and rather better than Don Delillo's Dylan story from the same era)
best
Dave

Great site, a top quality database of Dylan! I'm 16 and saw Dylan last night at the London Arena, England (11/5/02). He was incredible, what a first time to see the great man live! One question - do you know what the boards said in Subterranean Homesick Blues? I used to have the video on my Highway 61 Revisted CD-ROM, but it won't re-install for me to view it. If you do know, I would be extremely grateful if you could e-mail them to gleneckett@deadparrot.co.uk. Thanks very much, and keep up the good work on the site!
Glen Eckett

---

dear bob
my name is hannah and i absolutly love your music i'm only 12 and i sometimes get made fun of at school for liking you but i'll never stop liking you. I've been looking every where for a concert but I can't find one and by the time i'm 20 you probably won't be singing any more(i'm not saying your old or anything) but one thing i want to do before i die is to see you and mark knopfler.
all the best with your songs and cocerts.
tons and tons of love
hannah whittaker.

I am from Oxford, AL. I'm 59 years old and absolutely love two musicians, one of which is Bob Dylan (the other is Eric Clapton). Otis Redding is also a favorite. Wish he had lived to add more of his talent to the music world.
I liked Bob from the very befinning of his career. He reminds me of my youngest brother, Jeff Wlliams, a very talented musician and sings along the lines of Bob.
It really upsets me when the media (TV, etc.) sometimes make fun of his singing saying they cannot understand him. Fortunately, I have never had a problem understanding him and admire him greatly. I don't believe those people really understand his outstanding talent and imagination.
I wish there was a way to e-mail him personally to let him know of his popularity in Alabama. I don't care how popular a person is, they need to hear from the "common" people who remain faithful to him and his music. Anytime he is going to appear on TV, I would really like to know. One of my favorite CDs of Bob is the "Unplugged" CD. "I Saw a Shooting Star Tonight" and "Desolation Row" are two of my very favorite songs. Another of his albums ("Love and Theft") is slightly different, but great in my opinion. I'm sure I have made my position on Bob Dylan very clear!
I pray he maintains good health and can give us much more of his wonderful music in the future.
Brenda Hill

Do you know me?
Sam Silva
[*No - JMH*]

In the documentary film "dont look back" does anybody know the original title or artist of the song that he sings in the room with joan baez "I was just a lad nearly twenty two need a good lord band not a kid like you(?).............a goin down that lost highway. please help I couldnt catch all the words and i cant figure out for the life of me what song their singing!!!
ryan
[*The song is called "Lost Highway" by Hank Williams - JMH*]

Yo,Mr.Tambourine Man!How are you?If Woody G. could choose Someone to continue his work here on Earth,he would choose you man.Hey,say hello to Ms.Baez if you see her!Peace on Earth......
Ana Zlatanovic

I was looking under your pictures in the category of Hibbing, and i read the article from the wisconsin Journal. There were a few things not quite right with the article. Now Hibbing has a sign which mentions having the World's Largest open pit mine, it also has a birthplace of Greyhound museum. I grew up in Northern Minnesota and for two years i lived in Hibbing.And for three years after that I lived thirteen miles from Hibbing. Hibbing has always tried to respect the privacy of their "favorite sons". I remember when I was in Highschool in the early 1990's, when Dylan's boyhood home was up for sale, the hibbing paper had an interview with one of his cousins, who said that Bob comes home more than people realize. He just keeps a low profile.
Sonja

BOB DYLAN IS THE BEST, FOREVER YOUNG.
Antonio

Good friend of mine is ill with Hep C and has an extensive Dylan collection of audio/video he must let go of in order to survive, please help David out by contacting him at
daveyboyz2002@yahoo.com
- Dawn

---

hi bob! i'm from spain, and i don't know very good how to write in english, but i'm trying it. I only want to tell you, that i'm 16, and my father loves you, he has all your records, and since I was 2, i'm listening your songs, and now I love your music too. We want that you record more records and that you will how you are now. Never change, and come to spain, here the people loves you, I think I'm gonna work with you, I'm dreaming. You are the best. kisses from spain. muak

---

give me a 3 page report on yourself please??
Dall
[*Get it yourself - JH*]

Very good work for all Dylan's fan !!
J have added a link to this site in my web page
http://www.al-diesan.it
Thank a lot
Al Diesan
ITALY

BOB,i have had the greatest respect for you since i could walk. I would really like to jam with you sometime. i am 32 and new guy
tony

Hello
is there someone who can tell me more about a tape, called/dated:
1/77 Leonard Cohen session, Los Angeles Studios, Los Angeles, CA
Rob

Shaking Through.net has posted a review of Live 1975:
http://www.shakingthrough.net/music/reviews/2002/bob_dylan_live_1975_2002.html

Erik Kasem

I've been listening to Dylan since my HS English texher intoduced us to him back in 1964.
I want to warn other Dylan fans of the rip-off tape of Dylan's world tour of 1966. His drummer on the tour (Mickey Jones) shot some home movie crap that he tries to pass off as some sort of documentary. Actually, it is more about him than Dylan. I bought this tape for my brother (another die-hard fan)on his birthday and boy, we were both hurt.
Please don't waste your money !!!
I wish Dylan would get involved in stopping the continued sale of this mess.
Rich

I have just started an unofficial Bob Dylan message board.
www.LunasBackPages.com
Won't you come join us?
Luna

Hi folks! the italian dylan meeting is on the way...at the end of may.for more informations visit us at Http://digilander.libero.it/dylanmeeting2003/ and...spread the voice around!!!!
Doriano

Me and my husband (50) as well as my kids (24-22) are big fans. We wonder why the big man did not already wrote a song to make the people aware that War Is Never A Sollution! I think if, now that John Lennon is dead, Bob Dylan is the only man who could achieve this!
Love From Holland

Mr Dylan: Greenwich Village 1963/1964, have been following you for some time, have just about all your music. However having to be a Viet Nam Vet 1968, why did you name that album after the bombing "ROLLING THUNDER" or was this a hindsight? Have you ever been to Cherry Valley,New York and what year.
THANKS
bill dixon

Dear folks, I live in New haven CT and am part of a group here working feverishly to help the homeless. One of our biggest shelters is being forced to close on April 30th and we are faced with having to raise $40,000 before then to avert what will be a tragedy for so many men. Our idea other than writing mad proposals to church groups and such is to organise a concert. We have been given a church, an enormous church situated on our city green with a large capacity to this end and it is my personal goal to invite Mr. Dylan to play for one night for free for those who have nothing. Should that happen now during the terrible propaganda and campaigns of our government would be such a message for those who are working for the good. Do you have anyway to get him my message? I can be reached at 203 785-9254 here in town or by email at whitedogandharriet@inorbit.com. Time is of the essence. I will try thorough Columbia, but am trying everyway I can think of. All love, elizabeth

---

Hi, I was first introduced to Dylan when I was 12, and he's been my favourite muscian since. I have only question about the man; I heard through the grapevine that Bob Dylan is/was vegetarian, is this true?
Keri

[*That's what I've heard as well - JH*]

I am so grateful I stumbled on this, it's awesome. Now I know what to do on those rare nights when I must must must discuss Bob. A friend and I once disgusted a third party when we got off on Bob during a road trip and went seven hours w/o stopping. But that's LIVE talk. Amazing how much there is to say/hear. Thanks for gathering so much in one place. I have one eternal question that no one ever answers: on what thing did "I'm not there" appear? it is soooo elusive. maybe someday answer will appear. See you guys in a chat room soon, habit must be fed.
Many thanks for a great site, you guys!
bucky

I'm writing this in May 2003. A Bob show at a 36,000 seat arena was cancelled recently because fewer than 2,000 tickets were sold. When I saw him at the Washington D.C. MCI Center several years ago, the auditorium was about half-full. I've been a fan for 35 years (yea, I'm really old, but lots younger than Bob) and I've got a message to everybody reading. Whether you are just discovering him at age 16 or you are a long-time fan since the 60's who has seen "several" shows: I have seen 40+ concerts. All you people who are so into him but will not hassle for tickets or drive to a town an hour away to see him should be ashamed. Bob is NOT going to tour forever. If you really love Bob, pull yourself together and go to the next nearest concert and the one after that. With millions of fans and being America's greatest living artist, what do you think it is like for him, still touring and writing truly great songs NOW when his show is cancelled for no ticket sales or he is playing to a half empty hall? If you really love Bob, go in person so he can SEE you. I feel sure he is affected by having a good, enthusiastic crowd and this is the best way to show your appreciation of him, go be in his audience. As to the people compiling the book of stories about how you asked him for an autograph or followed the tour bus, I say this: the other thing you will do if you really love Bob is: if you encounter him somewhere (as happened to me when I lived just below Macdougal street for several years and could have dogged him all over), LEAVE HIM ALONE. Go to the concerts and he will know you are there. He should not be playing to half-full houses. And don't hassle him personally. His life does belong to HIM you know, and to encourage people to send in stories about following him or bothering him when he's out in public is horrible. Don't you know that is the LAST THING he wants, to be followed and bugged and spied on and stopped by everybody in the world who is into him? If we all did it, he would have no life at all. If you want personal experience, go to the concert. Anything else is harrassment that belies any real love or concern for him. Think about how you would like to have to deal with a million devoted stalkers! He's touring so you can see him in person. Better that than making yourself a nuisance to him in his private life. GO BUY A TICKET! PLEASE! It is the best way to thank him and show your appreciation.
Miss MaryJane

Just visited the site for the first time. Really enjoyed my stay. Read the cartoon. Kind of reminded me of the Disney movie "The Kid" but looks like it predates that movie. I have an all-Dylan radio show that airs once a month in Cincinnati, Ohio on community radio station WAIF-FM (88.3). I call it "Chimes of Freedom" and it's on every 4th Wednesday of the month from 10pm to midnight. I've been doing a show on Hendrix when there's a fifth Wednesday in the same time slot for four years, but when the monthly slot opened I suggested a Dylan show which the station accepted eagerly. I've just presented my second Chimes of Freedom, and most of my insight material has come from the Howard Sowndes book "Down the Highway."

What I try to do in my show is to enlighten my listeners to points about an artist that they might not ever hear elsewhere. I really like to present these personal facets in the artists own words whenever possible. Dylan is a very private man, and information on him seems to be rather scarce. I've always been able to find a lot of interviews with Hendrix, but I'm finding it very difficult to find any recorded interviews with Dylan, or any in print for that matter. Can anyone point me in the right direction?---Ron Liggett

---

Accusing Bob Dylan of plagiarism is like busting a homeless man for shoplifting because he picked up a cigarette butt from a department store's showroom floor. Still in the name of justice--Shove and bet:
he's got a head start but he won't get far,
watch out now, he's about to sing, have you got your rolex,
have you got your rings?
don't be thinking about your PIN or what you keep your secrets in make sure while your listening you ain't got nothing missing why, he could steal the water from your stream while your're standing there pissing.
so check your bankroll, check your soul, check your doughnut for its hole, check your wallet, check your pockets, better call com edison to check the light sockets, check anything for easy lifting or for anything shaking loose, better check for your golden tooth pick, better check your golden tooth, better check around the corner for that public telephone booth, better check the plumbing, better check the garden, better count your cousins, better look in on the children, better make sure your refrigerator's still running and chilling, better check your cotton, better check your flannels, don't be watching tv with him 'cause he'll steall all your channels.
he'll lift your finger prints in a wink, he already took the kitchen sink, he'll be breaking and entering your mind next to steal what you will think. there's nothing up his sleeve you can believe or gives you relief, you can't trust him, you can't bust him, but God almighty you got to love him, the hipster-joker they call the Minnesota thief.
i cried over the dozen diamond roses you sent me, as i watched each petal fall to shatter like store-bought glass, so i know it doesn't matter, but i still want to ask, like dancing with a dozen of them new york show girls with a double dozen of them long distance stalking legs, did you work me around the salle de mort again just to hear me beg?
is this another charade, another incognito raid like all the rest?
i know you'll never confess, but did you steal from a yakuza doctor-author a dozen lines--more or less- on a CD Sony titled, 'love and theft'?
Passing Through

Have you heard the Wilco song "Bob Dylan's Beard"? I like it. I'm a little unclear though how Bob Dylan specifically wore his beard. Is Tweedy talking about when Dylan shaved except under his chin/jaw? Is there a picture on the web that sort of defines the beard the song refers to?
Thanks for any help.
Lee

Hi John -
You may remember that I started the rec.music.dylan group way back when (while I was still at Penn State). You even sent me a couple of MTV Unplugged cassette outtakes (much appreciated).

Anyway, just wanted to tell you that I love your web site (first time I've seen it) - ESPECIALLY the creative headings on the home page. Brilliant!
I hope you're well, and I'll try to stop by often.
Take care, John -
Tom

I WANNA THANK GOD ALMIGHTY FOR BOB allen DYLAN
annemarie

Howdy Howdy sir,
i haven't heard of ya untill recently, and what i hear is perty dang positive. i haven't heard your stuff as yet, but, judging from tha folk that speak of You, tha look in their i's till more than one would care to believe. any ah how, i am contacting U cause im in need of help. i am a 38 year old feller, looking for help in tha music field. my band name is last of the cowboys and so far, i am thee only member. i have bout 200 + songs, and some of them are up on my mp3 web site. mirage, my love, cheap thrills, world's gone crazy (im currently working on this one). i have a mini rv with a generater and play here in san diego. i plug my stuff into it and take tha music to the people. they are very hungry n thirsty for sound, song, and being-ness. if ya would, please listen to ma sound of song and if ya would care to...join in. i am married with 5 kids, my wife is an envirornmental scientist, and i am a bookkeeper (i really say a flunky accountant). ma youngins all have an ear for music, we just need help. the real catch is, i haven't been into music before. untill recently. for 1 year now. i have come along ways, but help is needed. if you think you can help, and, the music if you care to listen, please pitch in. if your after money, there will be alot of that, but, it'll destroy ya, make ya lose family and friends, and it'll also create a fucked, more fucked discontentment than you already have, any ah how, you probably realize this. my stuff is at mp3.com. then you'll search for last of the cowboys. if this is all stupid, then please forget i mentioned this, i will tell you, your fans hold you in high regards!
cowboy
last of the cowboys

---

nice..
worldmusic/babukishan
www.babukishan.com

Dear Mr. Robert Zimmerman,
we like you since we're 13 years old. Now we're much older. Love and kisses. The hempeltempel from Franfurt/Main in Germany. My grandpa was jewish. I have a lot of history things from him. You look like him when he was young. Please excuse my broken english.
Sarah from the hempeltempel

Bringing it all back home...Dylan is still doing that..a musical journey, worldwide, mindwide, and music gifted.
The guy's got visions of poetry rhyming in his head...and then...here comes the song.
Lost love, what coulda been...prophetic, what's on the horizon, (he hasn't been wrong yet), and putting emotions into words and crystalizing truth.
Only one other guy came close at one time, John Prine.
These are the true outlaws living honest outside the law.
I hope Dylan stays with his roots and brings it all back home. I'm confident he will.
Lifelong fan since '62,

John

---

i have been a bob dylan fan since i was born. first without choice then forever by choice. i was named after his wife and have seen him in concert more times then i can count and i am only 21. through tough times it seems strange but i would turn to bobby.his music has always had such a way about to me.i got a tattoo of the eye symbol on my back but for the past year all of my searching for what it means has turned up empty.any clue?
sarah

---

hi i am a greAT FAN OF U
jack

---

hello
i live in morroco,i like bob dylan music,the problem here is that we can't have all the albums of bob,may be it's a problem of distribution,specially the early albums,for a long time i've a so sweet dream,to be able to listen all the products of all the artists that i love,but here we don't have always money to do all that we dream of
abdenssar kadat
morroco

Hi bob,can i just say your music is fantastic and lyrics are genius
from scott In Scotland

---

jncftrd tbxs bf,7 4
68fcvgb q't-bqz $*ùkl$
12
432
kibiuf,tn
[*Your words are not clear. You better spit out your gum - JM*]

---

just heard his bobness live in 64 is set to be released in march this truly is the lords doing for was it not fortold that one day our ears wold at last bathed in nasel tones of what it was like to ,if you will'be there'and hear its alright ma , mr tam,and talkin WWWIII,alive and how it should be and how dont look back promised it would be.for if not fortold then it surly was an over sight on big mans behalf.MY EARS HAVE SEEN THE COMING OF THE GLORY.....and so forth ...that is all ...though surly enough
allan

---

hey, Bub--
been meaning to tell you how much i love your site -- it's a fine thing and i've learned much in these pages over the years-- the article on the Genuine Basements led me to something called "A Tree with Roots", which, if you can get your hands on it, yeah it's pretty good.
however, i saw some massage here about Renaldo & Clara, and wanted to alert any who might be interested that there's a thing out there called The Unofficial Bob Dylan Free Tape Library-- if you were to check it out with a little search, you would find it a wonderful resource....
-- "with a blowtorch"
gypsy davy

Just to say thanks for the information.
Best wishes
Bridie

Hi im 16 years old and i love Bob Dylan... does anyone think thats strange????
Jimbob

So Bobby, the eternal iconoclast, just where were you during the "Concert For George" huh? Noticeably absent were we? I am sure you could have put aside any of your "petty" differences with the Wilbury's etc. fo a song or two for George, buddy. George.! This gentle and beautiful soul should have been honored by you. I have been a fan of yours since '62...seen ya alot, some great shows, some, well, I won't go there you are only human, remind yourself of that and be not so full of yourself You are lucky most folks worship you, I am disgusted. There is no good excuse for you to have missed this once in a lifetime opportunity to honor such a great human being. I hope you are sorry and regret this foolish "non" action for the rest of your days...fare ye well,
PER.

---

hi i love the site it is great!!
stacey

---

hi,
I attended a Bob Dylan concert in toronto, canada on march 20th/04. i am a big dylan fan and have seen him in concert before. it was however, a huge disappointment. he wore a cowboy hat and suit, and played the keyboards all night. he never once played the guitar. wondering if anyone else has had a similar experience at one of his concerts recently. it was tres weird.
thanks
sandra

This is more of a comment, and a question. I don't know if you keep up with Bob's manager or should I say old manager, or if you know of any way I can get closer to Bob himself. My sister is the reason Victor got fired if you know the story. So my mission is to get a hold of Bob if I can and tell him what really happened. Don't think I am crazy, if you need to research the supposed reason Victor got fired. Thank you - Shellie

---

Hey Now!! Have a quick question for you. Dylan played with a young girl in, I believe, the mid to late 60's. She had an incredible blues voice and I remember it saying he either played on the album or on the album it said he played with her somewhere. I think I remember her having died way back then. Do you know her name? Would appreciate any answers @ azdead@yahoo.com . Thanks.
May the four winds blow you safely home.
Sam

I love this website and I have been a Bob Dylan fan for many year. I would love to hear from all of you Bob Dylan fans out there. He is such a great artist and poet.
Nancy

For any of you interested in Bob's recent appearances, he's gone and done a commerical for Victoria's Secret. He's the man who once wrote the lines:
Advertising signs that con you
Into thinking you're the one
That can do what's never been done
That can win what's never been won
Meantime life outside goes on
All around you.
What the F is going on here? If anyone has any rational explanation, please indulge.
some anonymous person

I'm looking for the "recent interview" (?) in which I've been told Bob Dylan discusses Hamish Henderson's bagpipe playing as an influence on "The Times They are A'Changin'." Who knows, it was a put-on, since Bob hates the press. But it was in the context of his fairly recent (2003?) visit to Edinburgh, if that's of any use. If you want to email me offline, fine. If it's worth talking about online, fine too. I'll get out of your way, with thanks - John

---

Bob Dylan is the greatest lyricist of all time and I have followed his career since 1965. That said, "Masked and Anonymous" is the worst movie of all time. They must have paid Dylan a fortune to get him to trash his whole legacy.
Robert

The Oklahoma Gazette is raising funds for the purchase of Charles Banks Wilson's painting "Woody Guthrie - This Land is Made for You and Me" which will be displayed in the Oklahoma State Capitol Building. The Gazette is matching donors contributions to raise $25,000 to fund this project. Contributions of $100 will be accepted from the first 125 readers. For more information, go to www.okgazette.com and click on "HangWoody". Please tell Bob Dylan about this project. Thanks
Linda Meoli

Hey Bob,
I think your the biggest legend, your music is awesome!!!
I'm writting you an e-mail to ask if you could come an do some gigs in london some time soon!!!!!!!!!!!!!
I'm 14 and all my friends at my boarding school, King's Canterbury, love you!!!!!!!!!!!!!!
I live in london so you will usually find me on the kings road!!!!!!!!!!
In the mean time, keep making your oh so awesome music!!!
Because you are my biggest legend!!!!!
Thank you for inspiring me so much, there is now never a dull moment i my life.
Write Back,
All My Love,
Lucy xxxxxxxxxxxxxxx

I see Bob Dylan in Concert Bonn(Germany)29.06.2004 . Fantastic!!!
peter

Bob Dylan, I have most of you CD's, but I'm not writing about that. What happened Bob, you used to be a protest singer. I haven't heard any protest songs about an illegal war in Iraq?

Doesn't it matter anymore to you or the other folk singers from the Viet Nam era? Don't you write anymore? I have a son serving in Baghdad right now and it matters to me and all the other families. Where are the protest songs???????? Where are the artists? I know Phil Ochs is dead, but if he were still alive...........
john zimmerman

Hey What's up I just wanted to drop a line and tell you I received my middle name from you and my first name from Graham Nash.
Nash Dylan

I heard that Dylan comes to Little Rock sometimes to perform down by the River. I don't know if that would "officially" be listed on "Tour" information. Am I a fan? Well, I can honestly say that since I found out he opened a Hamburger/grill place in Minnesota, I will definatley let you know if it's a four star! Who knows, he might choose that very day to come in,...by some simple twist of fate.
Aly F.
p.s. Your wallpaper is great!

Dear Lanlord, As I went out one morning, I saw a hundred birds sitting all along the watchtower and thought I heard them singing the ballad of frankie-lee and judas priest and was saying to myself,"How can I pity the poor immigrant" when I am a lonesome hobo walking down along the cove they call 'Drifter's Escape' just waiting for the wicked messenger to hit me like a rolling stone. Here I am all ragged and dirty with blood in my eyes, when all I really want to do is be tangled up in blue. But like a slow train , the times they are a-changin' and my back pages are blowin' in the wind, going, going, gone. That hurricane under the red sky has past and now I am watching the river flow with dignity! So when on a night like this your looking for the man of peace, just stop and pick up the buckets of rain that have been whispering that ballad in plain d and drink up 'cuz chimes of freedom are just down the highway. Swallow your foot of pride because your simple twist of fate has arrived, so things have changed and you ain't going nowhere. so wake up, 'cuz it's all over now baby blue! Sincerely, Lily, Rosemary and The Jack of Hearts P.S. "what was it you wanted?" Thanks for reading. Love this site!!!
SHELLY dylanfan51803@earthlink.net (just needed 2 vent, please vent back!)

Hi!! I'm a 12 year old Dylan fan. Younger fans are hard to find these days, but I love and appreciate him just as much as anyone older than I. I've grown up with Dylan, and only really got interested in him last August, he's my favorite artist, and poet likewise, I love his poetry. Great great site, whenever I'm in the mood to read a good Dylan article I drop on by, I've got it in my favorites. I love Dylan, I saw him and Willie last week in Altoona, Dylan was greater than great, and it was my first concert.
I'm going to seventh grade, so far I'm the only Bob Dylan fan in my grade, but I'm hoping to change that.
It's upsetting sometimes to think that I missed Dylan when he revolutionizing music, just because I'm 12 and not 57. Aw well.
Dylan is great, awesome, and I hope he lives a real real long time.
Wonderful site on a wonderful guy...
Well, bye bye...

Bob Dylan is one of the greatest songwriters/artist of all time with few equals who defined the 60's even though he's a mediocre singer. I first became of him when I was about 11/12

years old way back in 75/76 while it's too bad he never wrote any songs with the late, great John Lennon.
Wayne L.

---

describe dylan in one word.
timothy
[*indescribable - JH*]

How did you physickly run your whole career?
Johan van den Hil

Congradulations! From a Napolean in Rags. This is an amazing site! Thank you for helping all Dylan fans decipher the Nightingale's Code...
chris nightbird

HE HAS TOUCHED OUR HEARTS WITH LYRICS MADE OF SOUL AND LIFE. DYLAN AMEN!!!!!!!!!!
carol

Hello Bob Dylan,
I have Listened to your music, read your work and captured thee escence of each piece. I have been a big fan of your work,which actually, inspired me to be a writer. I have read Edgar Poe. I am a big fan of his work too. I wanted let you know that. I live in Indiana. Most of the kids don't know who you are in my town. Well that will change when I introduce your excellent work to my friends. My favorite is last thoughts on Woody Guthry. I am out of time.
Bye.
Andrea Townsend

---

i love dylan, but these damn assholes that try to decode his records for some secret message need to be locked up some where, Dylan one of the best song writers ever(olny equal to Woodie Guthrie, Robert Jhonson and possibly Neil Young) HE HAS NO HIDDEN MESSAGES IN HIS SONGS!!!!!!!!!!!!
Nick

I have a song that was typed by Bob which he did in school and gave to his Grandmother who in turn gave to my Aunt who resided in Hibbing Minnesota.She was a friend of my Aunt.On it he typed his name as Bobby Dylan.Are you interested?
[*Yes*]

My uncle was a music teacher in Hibbing Minnesota, and he was one of Rober Zimmermans teachers. I remember as a young man in Minneapolis, there was a Coffee house on the West Bank of the U.of M. The West Bank was the hangout for all the beatnick and developed into the psychodleic area.. This coffee house was called the "Schollar" it was painted industrial red with black trim on the ouside,, I remember hearing Bob Dylan when he first came to Minneapolis from Hibbing there. i Beleve the years were around 1958 or 1960,, This mans influence has been a major force of contemplation and change in my life,, I knew it then when i was a young man and i know it now.. Thankyou Steve S.

I was born 1950, makes me a member of your generation, yes or no? You inspired me during the 60'ties through 3 continents, where fortune wanted me to live. I am now 54 years of age (still female).
Looking back and listenting to your songs of those super years I can't help but feeling cheated by you personally.
To my opinion YOUR SONG "it ain't me babe" could have been sung by a male voice IF ONLY YOU had become a trifle self critcal in your male role. In other words, the text of that particular song has become entirely outdated. In other words rewrite it..... make those words sexless.
After more than 25 years in the real world, outnumberd by men, our common ground being computers, physics and medicine I can only conclude that men are just as emotionally "instable" as women are. Assuming that you are still the man originating from the '60s (integer) I would appreciate an honest answer with respect to the fact that "it ain't babe) could also apply to a man.
Looking forward to an honest answer. When answering, please be remindend of the fact that my country is still really media independant, nationally and globally so.
regards
AMZ

---

what is it about one man that has reached 2 generations and who will probably never be forgotten? I know for a fact that our 2 kids will know him well and they are only 9 and 5!!
karen

Question please.
Thank you for providing such wonderful historical information.
I am looking at the photo on your John Bucklen tape page. The photo is titled dylan_54.
Do you have any information on the source of this photo? Where was dylan when the photo was taken?
I have a hunch it could be dylan as a camper at camp herzl.
Thank you for your time
Scott

Hello, I doubt that this will get to the Bob, my heroe, I heard him say on sixty minutes or a similar show, that he no longer has that partuclar miracle that used to help him write songs. I do not believe it. Bob, u will always have it. Please keep sharing.
Wallflowers rock too !
Jenny

---

i am 50 yrs old. i feel young. my mother is 75, and she says she doesnt feel old, she only feels that other people are younger. your music is part of my life. how do you feel about age ?
ronnie

BEAT'S ME WHAT I SAID SO WRONG? FACE IT, THIS SOCIETY OR PHYSICAL ENVIRONMENT ALONE DEALS OUT REALITY EVEN IF PEOPLE HAD DIRECT CONTROL IN IT'S STEERING! I MENTIONED THE FELLOW MUSICIAN DAVEY GRAHAM WHO'S WRITING OF THE SONG "ANJI" IN THE 60's PROMPTED PAUL SIMON (SIMON & GARFUNCKEL) TO PLAY THE SAME SONG RECORDING HIS (SIMON'S) OWN VERSION (PAUL HAD GONE TO ENGLAND IN THE 60's)! I ALSO MENTIONED CARLY SIMON'S STUFF SAYING SHE HAD A UNIQUE GIFT. THE DILLARD's, GRASS ROOTS, HAWAIIAN

SLACK KEY, LIGHTNIN' HOPKIN'S (AS GOOD ON ELECTRIC AS ERIC CLAPTON), BERT JANSCH & JOHN RENBOURN (THE JR SITE IS THE ONLY ONE AIN'T KICKED ME OUT YET).....A COUPLE DAYS BACK I WAS JUST KICKED OUT OF LED ZEPPELIN'S SITE. WHY? I DON'T KNOW.......AS I'VE BOUGHT (7) OF THEIR RECORDS!.........AND I HAD MENTIONED BOB DYLAN'S 'NEW MORNING' RECORD I GOT. ANOTHERWORDS NOTHIN' NEW!--sun-dot (r.m.r.).
[*Huh? - JH*]

Hi!
I really like those pictures you got on the index-page, and the rest of the site too. The one picture with Bob and the two cow-girls had me laughin' for days. He really got it a-made...
From: "I happen to be a swede myself"

Dear Mr. Bob Dylan,
thanks for your music. I was growing up with you.
Greetings from a very big fan from Frankfurt/Main in Germany.
GO ON!
A fan from Frankfurt/Main in Germany

This is an excellent site.I am a dylanphite,let all the fans of Dylan be united under the red sky.
minko dasgupta

---

hey friends i am a dylanfreak from india.iam a 22 years old boy and have been a dylanphite since 15.i wanna make friends with other dylan fans,please mail me at minkodg@rediffmail.com.No one can take away our love for dylan and his songs,even our girlfriends wont be able to manage that.
LOVE
MINKO

I recently made a ragged 24-minute movie of people talking about Dylan's Self Portrait.
Anyone interested in seeing it can download it here:
http://www.palacefamilysteakhouse.com/2005/03/self-portrait.html
Thanks.
Trott

This spoof/play on Serve Somebody might amuse some Dylan fans
http://www.oliverbaker.com/node/28
Anonymous

I love this place!!! I've been working on an essay about Dylan's influence on popular culture in general and music in particular. This website is a treasure trove of reference material.
Only one single complaint: I've read Clinton Heylin's marvelous "Bootleg-A secret History . . ." but the link you've provided for his webpage calls up an ERROR screen.
Thought you'd wanna know. There are more than obviously five believers . . .
Derek W. Brown

A little note I saw, about "A Fool Such As I". You have noted it was made popular, by Elvis Presley. I learned that song from Hank Snow who had a hit with it years before. I don't even remember the year........N/J

I think this web page is very informative. I am curretly working on an oral interpretation of Bob Dylan's song"Who Killed Davey Moore?" I was hoping to find a quote or any piece of mind that Bob said about this piece. I have the Live Halloween Concert 1964 cd's which feature a small book with information on the song, but I was hoping to find more. Your page was a blast to read through. Thanks!
Eme VanDeWiel

Im 16 and would just like to say that bob dylan was a really good artist x x x

---

To Dylan fans: I'm not sure if you can tell me anything but seeing that you are apparently a huge Dylan fan I am thinking you could have some kind of relation or clue to what I am looking for. Let me just say that I am not a huge Dylan fan but I truly love the album Desire. I have listened to it many times before but today something exceptional happened. While listening to "Hey, Sister" I was suddenly taken into the song and had an incredible mystical experience. My soul felt the energy of the song as if I had suddenly become the song and could feel every emotion that Dylan would have had while writing it. My heart started beating faster, my breathing got deeper, I got tears in my eyes and could feel my whole body and soul vibrating to the spirit of the song. Now this may seem very strange to you but I can assure you that this happened and I am still in shock. I know that music has certain effects on people but I definately think that it could have something to do with the genius of Bob Dylan, his ability to transmit his own emotions and desires into music. I guess what I want to know is that since you are such a huge fan and I am sure you have a very close connection with his music, his beliefs and his history, maybe you could have some information that could pertain to this experience of mine. I hope I don't disturb you with such a personal request. At the least, if you have nothing to tell me, can you recommend me a couple of your favorite Dylan songs so I can listen to them? Thank you for your time!
Sincerely,
Amy

I was looking at the lyrics page and saw a song titled "Gypsy Lou", but couldn't find what album, bootleg, etc. it is featured on. Is there anyone who knows?
Dana

There are just 2 things I would like to know:
1. The Subterranean cards sequence was filmed (according to Pennebaker) in an alley behind the Savoy Hotel, where they stayed. I have looked there, but there is no alley. Has anyone found it, and if so, where is it?
2. Andy Kershaw discovered and recorded the true perpetrator of 'Judas'. It wasn't Keith Butler, as asserted by CP Lee. Who was it, and where does he live now?
Thankyou
ROB REEVES

Hi,

As a Bob Dylan fan you might be interested in this months offer to new subscribers which is a Bob Dylan T-Shirt and a free album of new and established singer songwriters. The Song Makers Project Vol 1 is probably the best roots and acoustic compilation released in recent times. It includes greats like Bert Jansch, Billy Bragg, Eric Bibb and interesting new stars like Sam Genders and Emily Slade who was voted Best New Comer in The BBC Folk Awards 2002.
I started rootsmusic.co.uk to bring some attention to new and not so new roots and acoustic acts that are making great music but maybe being ignored by the main stream media. To subscribe for a whole year and receive the free gifts is only $9.00 a year.
The subscription fee goes into running the site and making another compilation album of great acoustic talent which will also be free to subscribers. Although most of the site is free to access subscribers have their own password protected section with many more interviews features and competitions etc. Subscribe now at www.rootsmusic.co.uk.
Best regards
Ayo Bamidele
P.S Can you pass this on to anyone who might be interested and if you know in good roots and acoustic artists we should cover please let me know.

Hey, this is such an amazing site! I have loved Dylan for a while now and this site has opened up so many new doors! The Basement Tapes section is particulary brilliant, John Howells is a fantastic writer. I especially loved his article called "Discovering Bob Dylan...", I will buy that Blood, Sweat And Tears album right away! So...thanks for making such a great site!
Bobby

Dear Mr. Dylan,
I wish to thank you for your contribution to our society as a wonderful songwriter.
Sincerely,
David Bruce Ouellette
Orlando, Florida

Correction for
http://www.punkhart.com/dylan/tapes/63-apr.html
The Oscar Brand Show is on WNYC-AM Saturday nights from 10pm to 11 pm Saturday nights, (I'm listening right now :) and has been on every week on the same station since 1945! WNYC-AM and FM were owned by New York City, thus the professional recording. Dylan was very likely in the studio, you could mail Oscar and ask him.
http://www.oscarbrand.com
BobCat

Your site is realy very interesting. http://www.bignews.com
Mery

---

michael jackson (a british radio host, not the gloved one) had a radio show playing folk music in the early 60's that i would listen to sitting in my parents car while they shopped. it would have been saturday or sunday. he played dylan. i remember thinking his voice was atrocious. then in 1965 i a precocious 15 year old watched dylan through the gap in the stage door of the santa monica civic auditorium. the first half of the performance was just him and his accoustic works, we must have looked odd, a pile of teens lineing a crack in the door. at the intermission we banged on the door and michael bloomfield came to the door behind the security guard, we

asked mike to let us in, he smiled and he would but indicated the security with a freindly shrug.and the door was closed. we went to the front entrance where older people(probably younger than us now) were leaveing to avoid the new electrical stuff and were giveing away there ticket stubs to those quick enough to have there hands out. i wasn't quick enough. the lobby was all glass with many doors, all with pushbars on the inside, unlocked. the lobby filled with ebb and flow of bodies, an arm comes out of the mass and opens a door, disappearing in the masses. we gained entrance, breached the lobby, to the seats!, found stubs on the floor(still have mine). and watched and listened, and were awed. forever changed, forever young.
AL KOOPER was on keyboards as i have learned later mike was on guitar, as you know "the band" went to england on the 1966 tour and this concert was in december of 1965 as it says on the stub. i think KOOPER has played with him since but don't think mike played with him again.
funny life coincidence:
years later, in my twenties a girlfreind of mine took me to marin to stay at her best freinds house. turned out her freinds husband was in mike bloomfields band at the time. i think his name was BOB JONES, i think his wifes nickname was MA. didn't meet mike again though. a year or two before that in 1967 or 68 i went with another freind visiting a lady. it turned out it was mikes lady staying at his place, the place on fulton , i believe. she played reel to reel tapes of mikes blues and gospel collection, i remember the lighting, funny how memory is.
i saw dylan twice since 65.once at the forum in l.a. with "the band" in the 70's i guess. the last time was when he toured with paul simon and the venue was the hollywood bowl. i was able to afford the " inexpensive" rows just below the "cheap" seats. these seats are reserved in the steep heights of the bowl for miscreants (sp) that the romans would never allow in the coloseum on a slow day. they've spent there ticket saveings on imbibing agents and find the need to swing coolers into the back of peoples heads to enjoy paul simon singing still crazy after all these years, i am not a violent man, but my wife was ill with cancer at the time and this fellow near hit her after clubing me with it mumbleing about people stealing there seats. security is at my ear in a flash as i was explaining to the twenty something gentleman who's face was an inch or so from mine that perhaps he had made a mistake and would he please refrain from bludgeoning us further. security calmly explained that they had mtsread there tickets and were sitting in the wrong end of a row somewere that put us between them and the bar or restrooms. they circumnavigated the bowl to avoid even bothering to to cross anywhere near us, they were so embarrased. i'm sure paul heard the yelling. it was brief but so poignant.
i hope you are as entertained by my ramble as i am by your webpage, thanks, good work. i was doing a search for the next dylan tour near me when i ran accross it.
steve

You just have to get out of Hibbing, Minn.
And get on the Road
www.wildernessroad.net

Discovering Bob Dylan
I don't know anything about Bob Dylan. I used to consider his music "old person" music from a bygone era. I watched the Martin Scorsese directed documentary American Masters No Direction Home: Bob Dylan recently and the film offered some insight on Dylan's life and music during his critical peak in the early to mid sixties. The footage captured in the film was extraordinary fully encapsulating the emotions Dylan was going through at the time with his reluctance to take the helm as a generation's unofficial spokesman.

I've always heard about the influence Dylan had on contemporary music. Many credit him as the individual who brought folk music out of the coffee shops and into the mainstream. Others call Dylan a forerunner to the genres folk rock and country rock. I'm not going to analyze the man and go off on some Greil Marcus-like rant since I'm oblivious too much of his music and don't look at him as god like or anything. I've heard the big hits and have no favouritism to any Dylan era having really first encountered the singer in the late eighties when he was a member of The Travelling Willburys. Even then I paid no attention to him thinking Roy Orbison was the stand out performer of the bunch.
I just want to understand why everyone thinks he's so great. Why is his appeal so lasting? Why is someone who plays pop music the subject of countless debate, analysis and reference? I want to cut through the bullshit and discover Dylan on my own terms without any outside influence from any popular music publication, Internet forum or Scorsese movie.
With the exception of a few great artists, I never had the chance to make my own realization based upon my own pure, original thoughts. I wasn't alive when The Beatles played Sullivan, or when Hendrix played Monterey or when The Ramones were a CBGBs fixture. The only modern day act that made waves on an international scale where the media didn't corrupt my outlook was Nirvana. I'm not saying I was in Seattle at some dive watching them before they were famous. But they literally came out of nowhere and the media was clueless at first. For a brief few months they were really unclassifiable. When I first heard Nirvana in late 91' I never said 'that's a grunge band.' There was no such word at the time. But I knew at the time that a revolution, maybe not on a cultural scale like hip-hop, but on a musical level was unfolding before my eyes.
Maybe it's inevitable. Maybe if you love music you're destined to discover Bob Dylan sometime or another. I'm at the age now and frame of mind where I can truly appreciate good music of all varieties regardless of popularity. My previous attempts to comprehend Dylan and his music failed miserably in the past. I passed his music over numerous times for the contemporary music acts of the day. I settled for whatever someone else told me was good.
Nothing really manipulates my tastes now even if coincidently the new Bob Dylan documentary aired on PBS around the same time as my interest perked up in singer. Maybe the film's release inadvertently influenced my subconscious in some way but I've wanted to discover Dylan long before the documentary was even a glimmer in Scorsese's eye.
Now the question is where to begin? Should I start with a hits album or such classics as The Free Wheelin' Bob Dylan or Highway 61 Revisited? Those would be logical introductions to Dylan's discography especially since I'm impartial to any Dylan era. But I don't really want to focus on his most well known material at first. I'm going to start off with something a little less known but not any less deserving of praise such as Dylan's 1969 country album Nashville Skyline, which I discovered buried in my parent's record collection alongside Kenney Rogers' The Gambler and Neil Diamond's Jonathon Livingston Seagull. The follow up to the rustic classic John Wesley Harding and Dylan's first full-blown country record (featuring Johnny Cash on one track), I figure it's as good as any place to start.
Trent McMartin
[*Best place to start is **Highway 61 Revisited**. That's the one that did it for me. - JH*]

Well I'm from Hibbing and I didn't like it there as a young musician child growing up. My views as a young teen was different from the rest. Now my son wants to be a drummer and I'm not afraid of letting him go with it because he's not held back from a lot of crap that I'd seen in Hibbing. And we're not talking about the 50s we'er talking about the 70s when I went to school there. It's the 05 and 06 and I'm so glad I'm not in Hibbing MN. Sorry, But it's the truth.

....and I can sing with you about the range anytime........
Lori

I awoke one recent morning morning from yet another wonderful dream about Bob Dylan. I've had many of them over the years and they always make me wake up happy. A while back I started thinking that there must be many people who've dreamed of Bob, recurrently or sporadically, who might like to share their dreams. So I've decided to write a book about dreaming about Bob and would love to hear any dreams any of you have had. Any dreamers who prefer to remain anonymous can do so. Yes, this is Mary Lee of Mary Lee's Corvette, the Blood On The Tracks girl.
Mary Lee Kortez
magdalane2@aol.com

Thank you for bringing your words and music to my life. Your work and the person you are remains a part of who I was growing up in the 1960's and who I strive to be in mid-life. I am privileged to know you through your music.
Sheri Dornhecker

Bob: Your good 'ol CD 'Slow Train Comin' continues to bless! Yesterday my 3-6 yr olds @ OKC's Kehilat Rosh Pinah (Messianic Jewish Congregation) enjoyed dancing to "Man Gave Names to All the Animals...In the Beginning...Long Time Ago" (Beresheet = In the Beginning/Genesis). This was the day all Jewish Congregations study the Torah portion Genesis 1:1-6:8. Just wanting to let you know, and to invite you to OKC NEXT WEEKEND (11/4-11/6/05) for MJAA's Heartland Regional Conference "Go Through the Gates." Great Yeshiva, Dance Workshops, Youth Program, Children's Program, Anointed Concerts(!), Praise & Worship for all. Concerts: Kol Sincha, Ted Pierce & others. Contact MJAA's website for more info: http://messianicconferences.org. Yeshiva info: (Isaiah: The Prophet of the Cleansed Lips (Friday) by Jeff Adler, info: yeshiva @IAMCS.org
... Bob I sure hope you get this message. I was prayin for you long long before Slow Train Comin...and am lately LOTS, again for some reason. You are a precious vessel...Shalom. Connie D. =^.^=

Story on Bob Dylan's earliest writings for sale....
http://tinyurl.com/bgbob
Anonymous

Hey, man...
...Umm... I know that I'm no more to you then the last guy who sent you a letter; prolly' askin' for Bob's phone number or somethin' outta' this world like that... but... you see... I just started writing songs about a month ago... or maybe it was two... (who knows how long it's been... I loose track of time... on and off) and I live in this little "peanut-in-a-shit" town and no one here knows where I'm comin' from! There's not a single person (pupil wise) who likes Bob Dylan and does anything but listen to emo music that sings about finding safety in kitchen knives and mutilating themselves. I just think if you're gonna' live... LIVE! You only get one life, man. Live it to the fullest.
...It's like these kids just walk around the halls with all their pasted smiles (super glued on by the mega-media corporations and all the shit they throw in modern day society's direction) and think whatever MTV wants them to think. It's like the self-mutilating emo stars, and the gangsta' hip-hop artists, and all the big businessmen with their golden suits and ties {that have

anything to do with the programs teens listen to and watch these days} nail a vacuum tube down the youth body's throats and suck all the individualism right the fuck out of their souls! It's like media cooperations are creating a vast, zombified culture... a pile of youth waste that will grow up to amount to nothing [creatively]. Sure, mommy and daddy will pay they're way through law school and they'll come out on top with pockets full of cash... but they'll all be the same person over and over again... like a vast field of carrots; just a bunch of the same closed minds buried up to their necks in the same patch of topsoil with only their vacant heads exposed. The thought of the brainwashed masses makes me sick! Seriously, man.
...And not to mention the fact that the school systems have the whole entire student body bent over their desks with their pants pulled down with their dicks up their asses with massive grins across their faces and money signs in their eyes. Greedy bastards. They're so egomaniacal that they think they've got it made. I go to one of the poorest schools that I know of... in debt up to their tallest strains of hair 'cause they think they got it all figured out. We know better than they do... how to live... how to maintain. It's like a bunch of Pop Warner peewee preschool football players coaching the NFL.
...Hey, man... I'm sorry for goin' off on such a tangent like that but I just need someone with relevant intelligence to open my mind too! It's like I'm holding all these thoughts and ideas inside and there's no one I know my age with enough brainpower to comprehend the things I'm saying. So in a way... I should be thanking you very much for listening to me... If you do infact read this.
...Anyways... after all this... alls I want is Bob Dylan's mailing address. I know you can't trust anyone these days you don't know {or anyone for that matter}... but I want to send him some of my work and get some insightful input that actually means something... not coming from the minds of my girlfriend or my parents that filter out all the bad, you know. But yeah... Bob's everything in my life and quite possibly my best friend (for I spend more time a day with him than anybody else).
...Thanks, for if nothing anything more than reading what was on my mind at this very moment in time (there's much more but I'm still learning how to go abouts writing them all down in an orderly fashion).
Thank you oh so much,
Colin Drayer
P.S. Keep on keepin' on, man!

Where did you get that incredible picture of George Bush flipping the bird? Is it real? That picture needs to be on the front page of every newspaper in this country.
I don't care who said what to the man, the President of the United States of America should NOT be flipping the bird to anyone - unless of course, it was to Dick Cheney - in which case I would make an exception. Dick Cheney is the REAL Master of War.
carla

I think your cartoon making fun of Bob Dylan is bullshit. He is the greatest musician of all time and if you think people are gonna laugh at that crap, you got another thing comin. If I were you, Id find somebody else, like brittany mears or whatever the fuck her name is, and leave the legends alone.
no

Umm....I'm not sure if you have a biography here, and if you do...then its REALLY FUCKING HARD TO FIND!! And if you don't then, you should add one!
[*Everybody already knows who Bob Dylan is. Go buy a book - JH*]

Dear Mr. Dylan,
I'am your biggest fan!
I'am 13 yers old and love playing the guitar.
Please answer me!
Alex

Geez. Do you know how long it takes to read 4,000 reader comments scrolling down one at a time a gazillion lines???
Mr. Dylan is good person and brilliant talent.
Could you at least organize the fucking letters so they're easier to read??? Like by YEAR or something? Man.
Isis
[*No - JH*]

Hey John,
I find what you find interesting about Dylan to be real interesting too. I can't believe that your presence on the net even predated bobdylan.com that's amazing. I have a homemade site called RanchoBozo.com that is built on the premise of what a site would look like if you taught an aging hippy a little html . . .
this is the first time I've included a Dylan link . . . I like your independence and your choice of materials . . . I was enthusiastic about the National Lampoon in the seventies and remember those original comic parodies. KEEP UP THE GOOD WORK . . . WAYNE

I am 8. I Love Your Music So Much. My All Time favorte Songs Are MAGGIES Farm And Huriccane
Ryan

Bob, i know first by your cd greatist hits, and i don't understand some lyric, its from subtereanean homesickblues, you sing there about 11dollarbills but i only have ten......as an Filipino from the filipinijns i've heard you don't have 11dollarbills in America, you only have ten....so i wonder. please let me know, iam traveling soon to america...greetings
Psjariel Gootnasch.

Dear John Howells,
I'm a Bob Dylan fan, poet and a singer. Recently my poetry collections book titled "Bob Dylan The Man With A Vision" is going to be released. I've about 15 poems on Mr. Bob Dylan. Hope this book will be interesting to the great Dylan fans.
Thanks,
Sincerely,
Khalid

Just a comment on the Radio Unnameable January 1966 WBAI "interview" by Bob Fass of Bob Dylan and friends.
I haven't heard this since the night it was broadcast, but I do remember the experience - I was home (in Flushing) from college in Boston, a confirmed member of the "Hallucination Generation". No headphones, just a tiny radio under the pillow. Of course I listened to Jean Shepherd on AM until 11:15, then switched over to Bob Fass. At first I thought it was Ed

Sanders, for some reason, but I caught on that it was Dylan and just lay there chuckling to myself until they left the studio.
Fass was so hip to the scene - that's what made this show unique. I think I remember someone calling in and asking Dylan if he'd taken "the A train" to get there, and that the somewhat nervous answer was to the effect that, no, they'd come the other way. At least I think I remember that!
I'd love to hear that thing again - but maybe it's even better this way!
Len Smiley

I'm a French, so I will make this comment in english and in french english : I think that "Self Portrait" is probably the best Dylan album since Blonde on Blonde, even if Blonde on Blonde IS the best ever. A seriously underrated lp.
Fran?ais : je pense que Self Portrait est probablement le meilleur de Dylan depuis +Blonde on Blonde, m?me si Blonde on Blonde EST le meilleur absolu. Un album gravement sous-estim?.
Copper Kettle

Hey Bob Dylan, how are you doing, it is a pleasure to be writting to you. man guess what today i just found out you were on tour and that you came here to my state NM yesterday, i am so fucking pissed off, i never heard about you being on tour or anything, fuck, that sucks. but you are awesome and i love listening to your music, i am like a way younger generation thatn you are, im graduating high school this year, i love your music. take care,
peace
claire

Thank you for this web site. I find myself coming back here often. Somehow I feel closer to Mr. Dylan here. I've always been a fan, but especially after the Martin Scorsese documentary, I have completely flipped out over Bob Dylan. He's my new hero. Heroes are in short supply these days. I know Mr. Dylan doesn't like adoration or deification. I know he isn't a deity. But he is cool, he's a father, he's honest, he's a story teller.
I feel like he's my brother. I feel like he won't be around forever. I feel like we should let him know, we should say "Thanks" for putting up with incredible BS to keep following his art. We're all better for it.
At least you know.
Now, could you please at least put dates on the letters?
Many thanks,
judy

[*Judy, just for you I'll do it - (posted April 18, 2006) - JH*]

PRESS RELEASE
For Immediate Release
April 17, 2006

SIXTEENTH ANNUAL BOB DYLAN FEST
featuring ANDY HILL & RENEE SAFER plus many special guests
At CHEVRON PARK, EL SEGUNDO, CA
MAY 7, 2006, from Noon til 8:00

Award winning Los Angeles singer/songwriters Andy Hill and Renee Safier will be hosting their

16th annual Bob Dylan Festival at Chevron Park in El Segundo on May 7, 2006. What started out as a small once-a-year backyard party where a loose conglomerate of close friends would take turns performing Dylan classics all day and well into the night (or until the cops came), has evolved into a full-blown music festival attended by hundreds of fans and featuring many of L.A.'s top musicians. Besides Andy Hill and Renee Safier, artists who will be playing this year include top L.A. session guitarist Marty Rifkin (currently on tour with Bruce Springsteen), indie singer/songwriter/pianist Bob Malone (who has toured as the Neville Brothers support act) and the premier Bob Dylan tribute band in the world, Highway 61 Revisited.
As many as 50 special musical guests are expected to perform interpretations of Bob Dylan material that cover a broad spectrum of musical styles. And what goes on in the audience has become almost as much of a spectacle as what happens on stage - as many crowd members come elaborately dressed as characters or scenes from various Bob Dylan songs.
Andy & Renee, along with their band Hard Rain, have taken their unique sound and multi-instrumental skills (as well as being riveting vocalists, they both play guitars and keyboards) to venues large and small all over the world. Local Southern California highlights include House of Blues and the El Rey Theatre in Hollywood, and the Hermosa Beach Civic Center. They have also played at Kerrville Folk Festival, Napa Valley Folk Festival, Sierra Songwriter's Festival, and were headliners at the Bob Dylan 60th Birthday Festival in Italy.
Their seven independent CD releases have won them countless awards, including: Best Duo/Group at the 2005 International Acoustic Music Awards, Qweevak.com "Top-40 CDs of the year (for their latest: "A River is Gone"), runner-up for best folk act at the 1999 Crossroads Music Awards, and a two year run in the Musician Magazine "Best Unsigned Band" Semifinals. In 2005, Renee Safier, showcasing her prodigious blues and jazz vocal chops, won the Telluride Blues Festival Acoustic Blues Competition, receiving a rousing response from the 8,000-plus festival crowd.
Chevron Park is located just west of Sepulveda Blvd on El Segundo Blvd, in El Segundo. $15 donation (adults). Patrons should bring a picnic and a blanket or lawn chair. For more information visit www.andyandrenee.com or call 310-324-3663.

Sanity, Humor, Vision...Thanks :)
James A. Mutz

Hello i purchased and organ from a man that work in frisko area that state the a band had left an organ there after the 67 festival and it has maggies farm painted on the organ in two places the organ was in storage for over 30 years when i had purchased it and seviced it inside it was like brand new very little playing to it, the question that i have is could this organ have been with dylan in the 60s if so what an incredible piece of history that i have man this thing gives me shivers when i play it you can feel the history in it, well thanks for reading if you find any info on it let me know it is a gibson g-101 organ.
Monty
[I tried emailing this, but it bounced back.
Intriguing thought, but I doubt the organ was used by Dylan or anyone in his band in the '60s for a several reasons:
1. Only two keyboard players played with Dylan on stage in the '60s: Al Kooper and Garth Hudson. Although Al Kooper is most closely associated with Hammond organ, he did play some sort of portable non-Hammond organ at two out of the three gigs he did with Dylan before quitting to join the Blues Project (he played a Hammond at Newport '65). It's remotely possible that he used a Gibson g-101, but much more likely that he used either a Vox or a Farfisa, both of which were very popular at the time. Garth Hudson, on the other hand, played

a Lowrey organ exclusively. I don't think he ever played anything else. I would suggest emailing Al Kooper (go to alkooper.com) and ask him what type of organ he played with Dylan at Forest Hills and Hollywood Bowl in 1965. He answers his mail, but don't be surprised if you get a very terse response.
2. It seems unlikely that Al Kooper would write "Maggie's Farm" on the organ, but I suppose anything is possible. If you mention that in your email to him, it might spur a memory.
3. You say that the organ was left after a 1967 festival. What festival? Dylan didn't play anywhere in 1967. His last live show before going into semi-retirement was in May 1966. He didn't return to the stage until 1969 at the Isle of Wight festival in England and didn't resume full touring until 1974. Whoever played this organ at a 1967 festival was certainly not Dylan's band. Now Al Kooper did play the 1967 Monterey Pop Festival, so the remote possibility that it was his organ still exists. I'd like to hear his answer on this. Still, I can't see him writing "Maggie's Farm" on the organ. It seems more likely to me that the organ belonged to a keyboard player in a group that called itself Maggie's Farm, although I have never heard of such a band - and I live in the SF bay area, and was around here in 1967. Could be a local band that played few gigs. Or it could just be that the keyboard player for whatever band he was in just liked the name and wrote it on his equipment for laughs.
I wouldn't hold out much hope, but your only chance is that the organ belonged to Al Kooper. I would like to believe that myself, so I encourage you to drop him a line and ask him. - JH]

---

theres a smell of fish do something real like walk a dog go to the park get away from this monster idol syndrome what the fuck
cloud

Hello all fellow lovers of Bob,
Bluerailroad is up - Paul Zollo's new webzine. As most of you know, Paul interviewed Bob in 1993 - the only interview Bob has ever done that focusses solely on music and songwriting. That interview is in the Bluerailroad archives - available at all times - no charge!
There's also "SHOES FOR EVERYONE" ("I've made shoes for everyone, even you, and I still go barefoot..") - a regular column each issue in which questions to and answers from Bob are featured. This months question and answer is from 1966 - about why Bob first "went electric."
Bluerailroad also features great interviews with Rickie Lee Jones, Lou Reed, Merle Haggard, Leonard Cohen and others.
Check it out. It's free to get on - and it's a great ride.
Yr pal, Henry Crinkle,
Publisher,
bluerailroad.
www.bluerailroad.com
henrycrinkle@bluerailroad.com

---

gbfw actxm pagxnk qorjum kcpy clefwrd qxhr
oizblwuj@mail.com (ecgzqs knaioytx)
[*That's easy for YOU to say! -- JH*]

---

comment about Bringing It All Back Homepage: --- Hello, I think it was in 1964... the first time I ever heard, and even saw Robert... he was on TV... I have followed his work, studied, and sang his songs ever since! (small-town hotel singer in Northern Ontario mining tows, and then out west... even got fired a few times in the

60's for refusing to exclude his songs!). I am trying to find out how I could obtain a copy of that first sighting!
He was singing if front of a sort of shanty or log cabin, and was being introduced incorrectly as Bob Dilon... Anybody know what I am referring to? Can this tape be obtained anywhere? (Just finished a great cottage and lake jam last weekend... my musician friends loved the Dylan stuff!)
Robert

Bob, my family has alot of history with you, I have two daughters named Isis and Sara , The lyrics fit them perfectly. Didnt realise that at the time they were born, they are now 23 and 18. Love you Vicki

---

I have tried many times to find out some information. In the 1960's, when I was a very young girl, I met a nice man on a train to California. He played cards with me numerous times over several days. Before I left the train, I asked him for his autograph. Just because he had been so nice and was a great memory. He signed it "Bob Dylan". I had a guitar with him. I have always wondered if it was the same Bob Dylan. Does anyone know how I can get this question answered?
Marcia Withers

---

hello. i'm trying to find out exactly which model of altec tube mixers and uher tape recorder were used to record the basement tapes...? any information would be greatly appreciated! thanks for a fantastic site!!!
cheers,
josh

Was I the only one who woke up at 5AM to tune into the live broadcast of the announcement of the Noble Prize for literature, only to be doubly disappointed that our favorite writer didn't win, having reached people of all abilities to read, write or understand great writing and ideas, and then to have the webcast interupted just before the announcement? Shame on the Swedish Academy and the Nobel Prize organization, but then we don't need them to tell us who is the best living writer. I'm still hoping to live long enough to see Mr. Dylan in his morning coat and to hear him say something about how "does it feel" to have been overlooked for so long and finally be rewarded with what he has so justly deserved for so many years.
Anonymous

Some of your readers were looking for copies of Dylan Vs Weberman...it's on Youtube under taht name siince December 28th as is the full version of I'm Not There. Enjoy!
Anonymous

---

can u put up some in information for research for school projects
Anonymous
[*No -- JH*]

A suggested (temporary) Sixth Verse:
Our economy has faltered but we can't let her fail,
And in the wars that Bush started we still must prevail.
We ain't out of the woods but we're back on the trail,

And Obama will be leading us onward.
And Bush, Cheney, and Rumsfeld ought to end up in jail (!),
For the times they still are a-changing.
(Thank you, Bob, for a lifetime of passionate inspiration.)
-just some old guy, out in California... (Buy American folks)
Tks.
Bill Schuler

FINAL REVISION: the fraud and forger known as 'lowgen'
On 22 August 2015, I received a copy of a forged undated letter, ca. 1978, purportedly written by my akhi/brother Dalton Delan (an honoured film maker) to 'Jacques von Son' in Holland, accusing me of stealing (freely available) materials (from individuals I have never heard of, did not know then, or now), of creating for Dalton a 'hoax' tape), and not being honest with my close friend Robert Shelton in London. None of this transpired, and is not true. I discuss this below. This forgery has been perpetrated by a cyberian prankster named 'lowgen', who is not a genuine student of the Yehu'dit paradigms of Shabtai Zisel/'Bob Dylan'. 'lowgen' attempted 22 August 2015 to distort the complex, sensitive, and important post-Auschwitz historical record of scholarship on Shabtai Zisel/'Bob Dylan''s poetics, by concocting a 'letter' from Dalton Delan (my close friend and film maker) to Jacques van Son -- which is an outright forgery by Jacques van Son. (For a clumsy, obvious forgery, it is hardly on the level of the metafictions of 'Araki Yasusada'.) I forwarded this to Dalton, who on 25 August 2015, refuted lowgen's lies on the record. 'lowgen' said I was fabricating the letter from Dalton Delan. It can be empirically verified that Stephan Pickering and Dalton Delan are actual hominids, and not animatronic similitudes.
In the past, 'lowgen' has questioned, e.g., if the Barry Feinstein photograph of 3 January 1974 of Bob/Shabtai and I is real; if Bill Graham and I knew each other (cf. Scott Marshall's Restless Pilgrim for discussions of my relationship with Bill and his production assistant, Peter Barsotti, or my own 1975 Bob Dylan Approximately...one of my closest friends is Bill's orphanage survivor intimate Yitzhak Amato); if my information about Bob/Shabtai's ba'al teshuvah public appearance 20 September 1983 in Yerusalaim, at haKotel is genuine. I have (and shall be publishing) 2 wonderful colour photos of him taken by the Yisra'eli photographer/artist Tzavi Kohen, along with a statement from the photographer, and comments given to me, in private, by the CHaBaD-Lubavitcher shluchim who were present on behalf of the Rebbe. I also quote statements from Reb Allen Ginsberg on Bob/Shabtai's wonderful re/turn. As Reb Allen told me years ago, 'Bob's questions overcome our loneliness'. In attendance was Sara Dylan (which 'lowgen' does not believe), who took numerous colour film cartridges, 2 of her Yerusalaim photographs used forInfidel's cover and inner sleeve; Bob/Shabtai's mother (I have a not-entirely-reliable statement from her), other family members. His son had a belated bar mitzvah during the public repentance for the 1979 apostasy and its chate'u/'sins'. Bob/Shabtai was wearing (which he still has) his own tefillin and tallis gadol. He had with him the silver-covered Mikra originally belonging to Mike Bloomfield's grandmother (which Mr Bloomfield gave to him 14 November 1980).
As Shabtai Zisel/'Bob Dylan' stated in 1985: 'I'm not a believer in that "born-again" type thing'.
In Chapter 2 of my monograph-in-progress, I devote over 20 pages to the entire sequence of his repentance (which began 1981, when he finally gives a repudiation of natz'rut in 'Caribbean Wind' of 7 April 1981), the three documented steps involved, which the Rebbe and his assistants were quite aware of. Not being a scholar, but a lying fraud, 'lowgen' is not a party to my research. The entire chapter segment opens with a colour photograph of the Rebbe and

Shabtai/Bob studying Torah together in Crown Heights. To be sure, all of this is ignored by the 'born again' natz'rut TypeWriter in the UK, who derisively speaks of 'an ultra-Orthodox [sic] Hasidic sect [sic] called the Lubavitchers'.
On 9 September 2015, 'lowgen' continues the masquerade by claiming it was Stephan Pickering himself who forged Dalton Delan's 25 August 2015 letter to Stephan Pickering (which refuted lowgen's revealing the 22 August 2015 Jacques van Son forgery).
This is an attempt to smear both Stephan Pickering and Dalton Delan with a rather flimsy paradigm of victim pathography. Through his actions of fraudulent lying, and perpetrating a criminal forgery, 'lowgen' is, like other Cyberian pranksters, claiming to be a (pseudo-) victim. In the process, 'lowgen' has permanently destroyed any pretense of credibility as a so-called 'Dylan collector', and volitionally places his actions among a proliferating body of similarly destructive, fraudulent work in Cyberia.
For those interested, my refutation of 'lowgen' is an appendix to my Chapter 2. (It was printed at a Denmark 'Bob Dylan' website briefly, but they have a problem with post-Shoah 'Jews', and it was removed, along with my scholarly contributions.)
FOR THE RECORD:
1) the undated 'Dalton Delan' letter to 'Jacques van Son' was not written by Dalton Delan, but is a forgery from Jacques van Son distributed gleefully by 'lowgen';
2) Dalton Delan is the author of the 25 August 2015 letter to Stephan Pickering, completely repudiating the 'Dalton Delan' forgery being perpetrated by 'lowgen', after it was immediately brought to Dalton Delan's attention by Stephan Pickering.
Dalton wrote to me: 'Of course that "letter" in broken English is not from my typewriter! The grammar reminds me of one of those "wallet stolen" email solicitations one gets from Nigeria and the Ukraine...I am happy to completely deny authorship to anyone you need. L'Chaim, Dalton' ;
3) Stephan Pickering has carefully elucidated the forgery: 'lowgen''s obfuscating statements are constructed on a series of lies and phantasies, mentioning individuals I do not know (I do not know 'lowgen'), events which never took place, and saying, as mentioned above, I forged Dalton's 25 August 2015 letter to me!;
4) this morning, 10 September 2015, Dalton read the above, approves it, and I am disseminating this warning.
'lowgen' is a liar, a forger, a fraud, a bigot, who hides behind an alias, refusing to provide complete honest data of who/where he is.
Stephan Pickering has never heard of various individuals 'lowgen' claims I had contact with over 40 years ago...with the exception of the late Robert Shelton, to whose 1986 biography No Direction Home Stephan Pickering made numerous contributions gratefully acknowledged by Mr Shelton in print. Robert Shelton was an individual whose memory and friendship and kindness with me I cherish... zekher tzaddik livrahkazek.
As a Torah chassidish Yehu'di, I am presenting this as a WARNING to individuals in the 'Bob Dylan world' for whom I have profound respect. I do not want any of you victimised by this fabricating hate monger.

~~~~~~

STEPHAN PICKERING / אברהם בן מ"ח חפץ
Torah אלילה Yehu'di Apikores / Philologia Kabbalistica Speculativa Researcher
ולשגשג רב זמן לחיות
THE KABBALAH FRACTALS PROJECT
801 Brookhaven Drive # A
Brookings, Oregon 97415-8134
stephanpickering47@gmail.com
~~~~~~

Just trying to thank you for the BS&T/Dylan/Al piece you wrote. I enjoyed it very much
@l k%per
[*Thanks, Al. It's an honor to have you stop by!*]

I did not realise I had misheard this line from Just Like Tom Thumb's Blues until I happened to see the lyrics posted in a group...
It never occurred to me to look them up, even though I have had The Complete Lyrics Aporoximately since 1970
"Inside the museums insanity goes up on trial"
It made perfect sense to me...
-- Hilda Fernhour

It's All Over Now, Baby Don
You must leave now, take what you need, you think will last
But whatever you wish to keep, you better grab it fast
Yonder stands the NRA with their guns
The Founding Fathers lament at what they've done
Look out, Bob Mueller's comin' on
And it's all over now, Baby Don
The highway's for Samaritans, better use your sense
Take what Comey's gathered from coincidence
The empty-handed people from the streets
Cannot post their words below your tweets
This witch hunt, it just keeps goin' on
And it's all over now, Baby Don
All your White House spinners, they are going home
All your overfunded armies, where will they roam?
The Russians who just walked out your door
Have taken intel secrets from the floor
The chessboard, too, is moving the white pawn
And it's all over now, Baby Don
Leave your electoral polls behind, someone calls for you
Forget that Flynn has left, he will not follow you
A son of man who's knocking at your door
Is standing in the clothes you never wore
Read the subway walls, before they're gone
And it's all over now, Baby Don
-- Oreopagus

Acknowledgments

There are a number of people I would like to thank. Some of them know me and some do not. Regardless, my interest in the works of Bob Dylan has been greatly enhanced by the following people:

In no particular order…

Paul Williams, Olof Bjorner, George Rothe, Peter Stone Brown, C.P. Lee, John Bauldie, Seth Kulik, Al Kooper, Michael Krogsgaard, Karl Erik Andersen, Ed Ricardo, Bill Pagel, Stephen Scobie, Steve Michel, Glen Dundas, Ben Taylor, Levi Asher, Adam Powers, Steve Farowich, Richard Shapiro, Tom Buckley, Steven Pickering, Roger Ford, Bob Meyer, Dan Levy, David Wolf, Joe Cliburn, Alan Fraser, Bob Stacy, Andrew Muir, Ron Mura, Ron Chester, Bryan Styble, Larry Yudelson, John Lattanzio, Giulio Molfese, Paul Cable, and of course Bob Dylan himself.

Some websites worth checking out:

- Boblinks (*Bill Pagel*)
- Expecting Rain (*Karl Erik Andersen*)
- I Happen To Be a Swede Myself (*Olof's Chronicles*)
- Breadcrumb Sins (*Giulio Molfese*)
- EDLIS Dylan Bibliography (*Ron Chester*)
- Electric Dylan (*Roger Ford*)
- Searching for a Gem - Official Rarities (*Alan Fraser*)
- Tangled Up In Jews (*Larry Yudelson*)
- Sights and Sounds (*Joe Cliburn*)
- Roots of Bob (*Seth Kulick*)
- EDLIS Centrale
- ISIS Magazine Homepage

About the Author

John Howells has been a Bob Dylan fan since at least 1970 when he first listened really hard, for the first time, to *Highway 61 Revisited* and suddenly GOT IT. His years of collecting and listening to Dylan tapes began and really got off to a start when he connected with other Dylan collectors on the nascent Internet back in the mid 1980s. Prior to that, he had to be content with buying all the vinyl bootlegs he could find at the local head shops in the town he grew up in: San Jose, California.

In 1994, he noticed that although there was a lot of information about Bob Dylan scattered throughout the Internet, there was no official Bob Dylan page or a truly comprehensive fan website, so he set out to create one that would pull together all the disparate sites into one massive resource. That website was called *Bringing It All Back Homepage*. It still exists as of this writing, but who knows for how much longer?

John is still a huge Dylan fan, but he spends most of his time these days tending to the official Graham Parker website, which can be found at http://www.grahamparker.net.

Lightning Source UK Ltd.
Milton Keynes UK
UKHW040851021222
413231UK00013B/224/J